Speech, Language, and Hearing Disorders

SECOND EDITION

SPEECH, LANGUAGE, and HEARING DISORDERS

A Guide for the Teacher

Herbert J. Oyer
The Ohio State University

Barbara J. Hall
Metropolitan School District of Warren County, Indiana

William H. Haas
Florida State University

Allyn and Bacon
Boston • London • Toronto • Sydney • Tokyo • Singapore

Copyright © 1994, 1987 by Allyn and Bacon
A Division of Simon & Schuster, Inc.
160 Gould Street
Needham Heights, Massachusetts 02194

Library of Congress Cataloging-in-Publication Data

Oyer, Herbert J.
    Speech, language, and hearing disorders : a guide for the teacher /
Herbert J. Oyer, Barbara J. Hall, William H. Haas. — 2nd ed.
        p.   cm.
    Includes bibliographical references (p.   ) and index.
    ISBN 0-205-14908-1
    1. Speech disorders in children—United States. 2. Language
disorders in children—United States. 3. Hearing disorders in
children—United States. I. Hall, Barbara J. II. Haas, William H.
III. Title.
LB3454.094 1993
371.91'4—dc20   93-22943
                                                                          CIP

Printed in the United States of America

10 9 8 7 6 5 4 3   97 96 95

Dedicated to Jane, Bob, and Ann

ABOUT THE AUTHORS

Dr. Herbert J. Oyer has worked professionally in various settings, including public schools, hospitals, and university clinics. Early in his career he taught in public schools and after completing a masters degree at Bowling Green State University became a Speech and Hearing Clinician in public schools. Dr. Oyer completed his Ph.D. degree at The Ohio State University and continued clinical, teaching, research, and administrative assignments at Michigan State University and The Ohio State University. He was President of the Michigan Speech and Hearing Association and was awarded the Honors of the Association. He is a Fellow of the American Speech-Language-Hearing Association and received its highest award, the Honors of the Association. He is presently a vice president of the world-wide speech-language-hearing association, the International Association of Logopedics and Phoniatrics. Dr. Oyer has authored, co-authored, and edited ten books and over 60 journal articles in the field.

Dr. Barbara J. (Crowe) Hall earned both her bachelors and masters degrees from Purdue University and earned her doctorate from The Ohio State University. She has worked with both children and adults, with a variety of communication disorders and has worked in various settings, including schools, hospitals, and university clinics. She has also taught college—one of her favorite courses being the one for which this book is written. She has presented workshops and papers at state and national meetings. Recently, she returned to the public school system where she works primarily with preschoolers and elementary students. Dr. Hall is especially concerned with the effect communication problems have on how children are perceived by other children and adults. How negative are the perceptions? when do they emerge? and how can they be modified or improved?

Dr. William H. Haas received his Ph.D. degree from Michigan State University in 1970. He presently serves as a professor of communication disorders in the College of Communication at Florida State University. Previously, he also chaired the Department of Communication Disorders. He holds a Certificate of Clincal Competence in both audiology and speech-language pathology from the American Speech-Language-Hearing Association, is a Fellow with the American Academy of Audiology and the International Collegium of Rehabilitative Audiology, and was awarded Dinstinguished Alumni status by the College of Communication Arts and Sciences at Michigan State in 1988. Dr. Haas's major teaching and research interest is aural rehabilitation. He began his professional career as a public school speech-language pathologist and later directed programs, with special emphasis on hearing-impaired children.

CONTENTS

Preface   xiii

1   **Introduction to Speech, Language, and Hearing Problems in the Schools**   **1**
Who Is the Speech-Language Pathologist?   2
Are There Speech-Language Pathology Aides (as There are Teacher Aides)?   3
Does Every School Have a Speech-Language Pathologist?   3
What Does Federal Law Have to Do with Speech-Language Pathology and Audiology?   3
Are There Differences in the Terms Communication, Language, *and* Speech?   6
What Kinds of Communicative Disorders Should the Teacher Look for in the Classroom?   7
What Causes Speech and Language Problems?   8
What are the Responsibilities of the Speech-Language Pathologist?   8
Summary   21
Self-Test   22
References   23

2   **Articulation and Phonological Disorders**   **25**
What Is a Speech Sound?   25
What Types of Speech Sound Problems Do Children Exhibit?   29
Articulation   31
Phonology   35
What Causes Articulatory or Phonological Errors to Occur?   36
Assessment   38
Treatment   40
When Should Children Be Dismissed from Therapy?   45
Are There Children Who Should Not Be in Therapy?   45
How Can a Teacher Help?   45
Is There a Relationship Between Speech Sound Errors and Academic Subjects, such as Reading and Spelling?   46
Articulation, Phonology, Dialects, and English as a Second Language   47
Case Histories   48
Summary   49
Self-Test   51
References   52

3   Language Disabilities   54
Just What Is the Relationship Between Learning Disabilities and Language Disabilities?   56
How Many Children Have Difficulty with Language?   56
What Causes Language Disabilities?   57
What Is Language?   57
Assessment   61
What Are the Characteristics of a Language Disability?   64
What Effects Do Language Disabilities Have on Academic Performance?   71
Do Language Disabilities Affect Psychological and Sociological Adjustment?   72
What About Remediation?   72
What Does the Future Hold for Language-Disabled Children and Youth?   74
Case History   75
Summary   75
Self-Test   77
Suggested Readings   78
References   79

4   Stuttering   82
What Is Fluent Speech?   83
What Is Stuttering?   84
Causes of Stuttering   84
Multi-cultural Considerations   86
Can Those Who Stutter Be Helped?   87
Case Histories   90
Summary   92
Self-Test   94
References   95

5   Voice Disorders   96
Do Many Children Exhibit Voice Disorders?   97
If Voice Problems Are Undetected, Can They Really Be All That Serious?   98
What Kinds of Voice Disorders Are There?   99
What Causes Voice Disorders?   100
What Do Voice Assessment and Therapy Entail?   105
When Should a Teacher Refer a Child to a Speech-Language Pathologist?   107
What Is Cleft Palate?   107

Case Histories   109
Summary   111
Self-Test   112
References   113

6   Hearing and Hearing Loss   116
What Is Sound?   116
What Is Normal Hearing?   117
How Do We Hear?   119
How Do We Understand What We Hear?   120
How Is Hearing Measured?   121
What Are the Types and Common Causes of Hearing Loss in Children?   123
What Are the Classifications of Hearing?   125
What Is the Prevalence of Hearing Loss in Children?   126
Case History   126
Summary   127
Self-Test   128
References   130

7   Hearing Impaired School Children   131
How Are Hearing Losses Detected?   131
Can a Teacher Identify Hearing Loss in Students?   133
What Types of Speech and Language Problems Do Hearing Impaired Children Have?   133
How Do Hearing Impaired Children Learn Language and Speech?   133
What Special Programs Are Provided for Hearing Impaired Children?   144
What Is the Role of the Classroom Teacher?   144
Case Histories   146
Summary   148
Self-Test   150
References   150

8   Other Populations with Potential Communicative Problems   152
Cerebral Palsy   153
Case Histories   154
Developmental Delay   156
Syndromes   161

Drug Abuse   163
AIDS-HIV Positive   165
Lead Poisoning   165
Head Injuries   165
Emotional Disturbance   166
Case History   169
Dialect Differences and Bilingualism   169
Alternative-Augmentative Modes of Communication   171
Summary   172
Self-Test   178
References   179

9   General Responsibilities of Teachers to Students with Communicative Problems   182
General Responsibilities of a Teacher   182
Summary   189
Questions to Ask Yourself   190
Suggested Readings on Peer Tutoring   190
References   191

Appendix A   Books Useful to Teachers   193

Appendix B   Answers to Self-Test Questions   207

Index   211

PREFACE

The revision of this book still holds to the original purpose of the text, namely, that of providing for two special groups of people. These two groups are those preparing to become teachers in regular or special classrooms, and those who are teachers in those settings. This book will also serve as a helpful resource to anyone who wishes to achieve a better understanding of the communication process, as well as the communication disorders observed frequently in school children.

As in the first edition, we discuss articulation, language, voice, and hearing, and the problems frequently associated with these functions in children. Stuttering receives special attention, as a disorder.

The discussion of special populations of children with potential communicative problems has been expanded to include causes such as motivation, overprotection, sibling rivalry, poverty, genetic syndromes, child abuse, drug abuse, head injuries, and AIDS. Those special populations discussed in the first edition—cerebral palsy, developmental delay, dialectical differences, and emotional disturbances—have been updated and expanded.

Approximately 250 teachers and teachers-in-training contributed to the development of this book. Their responses to our inquiries about their questions concerning speech and language problems in children, guided us and assured greater relevance of the material to teachers.

Our primary objective is to present information teachers need to be effective in meeting the special educational and emotional needs of children with speech, language, or hearing problems, and also to suggest ways to promote speech and language development of all children in their classrooms.

The authors's personal experiences with children have contributed significantly to the development of the book. The experiences of others who have contributed to the literature have also been very helpful. In order to highlight many of the discussions, we have presented additional case histories.

We have drawn special attention to Public Laws 94-142 and 99-457 because they are of paramount importance to both teachers and speech-language pathologists who work with children with communicative disorders. We hope that the discussion of these public laws will provide greater understanding in support of programs for speech-language and hearing impaired children.

A self-testing section is located at the end of each chapter to provide readers with an opportunity to evaluate their understanding of the materials presented. The summary of each chapter provides a rapid review of the chapter. Appendix A at the end of the book presents a listing and brief description of children's books that should be helpful to teachers and children, in supporting individual programs of therapy.

We sincerely hope that those preparing to become teachers and those who are teachers in regular classrooms or in special eduation programs will, as they read this book, gain a greater understanding and appreciation of communicatively impaired children.

ACKNOWLEDGMENTS

The authors wish to express their gratitude to Professor Leo V. Deal of Michigan State University, to Professor Norman Lass of the University of West Virginia and to Colleen Noe, graduate student in Audiology at The Ohio State University for the many suggestions made in their reviews of this revised edition of our book.

We also wish to acknowledge, with deep affection, the hundreds of children and parents whom we have served through the years, and the many classroom teachers with whom we have worked. The learning and insights accrued from these interactions are inestimable.

Speech, Language, and Hearing Disorders

1

INTRODUCTION TO SPEECH, LANGUAGE, AND HEARING PROBLEMS IN THE SCHOOLS

The purpose of this book is to provide you, the teacher, with information that will enable you to promote the speech and language development of all children in your classroom and, more particularly, to help children with specific speech, language, or hearing difficulties. Figures regarding the numbers of children with speech, language, or hearing disorders vary considerably and are not precisely known (Matthews, 1986; Neidecker, 1987; Van Riper & Emerick, 1984); however, it is generally accepted that the number is large and is growing larger (Neidecker, 1987). In fact, as was noted by Garbee (1985), the largest segment of handicapped children in the schools is those with speech, language, or hearing disorders. Therefore, *all* teachers, but especially elementary and special education teachers, can fully expect to have children with significant communicative disorders in their classrooms. Needless to say, communication is vital to educational achievement, social and psychological development and vocational success. Van Hattum (1985) said it well when he wrote, "Emotional and social adjustment and educational achievement are intimately related to each individual's communication behavior. Persons with communication skills commensurate with their total abilities are better adjusted, possess better social skills, and are more likely to perform to their potentials in school environments and in later occupational pursuits than those who do not develop these skills to their ultimate potential" (p.1).

The specialists who are trained to help these children and to work with other school personnel in their efforts to help these children are the

1

speech-language pathologist and the audiologist. The audiologist, who studies hearing and hearing impairments, will be discussed further in Chapters 5 and 7.

WHO IS THE SPEECH-LANGUAGE PATHOLOGIST?

Over the years this professional has been referred to by many names, including *speech teacher, speech correctionist, speech therapist, speech and hearing therapist, speech clinician, speech and language clinician, communication disorders specialist,* and *speech-language pathologist.* Taylor (1980) found that various state departments of education used 19 different titles to refer to this professional, whereas other state departments of education never referred to the professional directly but to the profession itself, calling it by 14 different names, including *speech correction, basic speech and language, standard speech and language, speech pathology, speech and language pathology, and speech and communication disorders.* The American Speech-Language-Hearing Association (ASHA), the professional organization for those working in the field of speech-language pathology and audiology, currently recognizes *speech-language pathologist* as the term of choice. However, Van Hattum (1985) expressed a favorable attitude to the use of the term *speech-language specialist* in schools. The authors found that the terms *speech clinician* and *speech-language clinician* are also frequently used in public schools.

The goal of the speech-language pathologist is to help people with communicative problems to correct their problems or to achieve their maximum communicative potential, which may involve compensatory techniques and/or augmentative equipment. In schools, the speech-language pathologist is not only involved in helping speech-language impaired children but also may serve hearing impaired children, if educational audiologists are not employed by the school districts. If educational audiologists are employed, they will be the ones likely to serve the hearing impaired.

The speech-language pathologist also works in other environments, including hospitals, universities, community clinics, rehabilitation centers, and in private practice. Occasionally, the public school speech-language pathologist will refer children with communicative disorders to colleagues in one of these settings (because a second opinion is sometimes desirable), and expensive equipment that may be useful in assessment is often not available to the public school speech-language pathologist.

The speech-language pathologist in the public schools must hold at least a bachelor's degree and teacher certification in speech-language pathology. However, in most states, additional training is becoming the educational minimum. Many public school speech-language pathologists with a master's degree will also hold a certificate of clinical competence (CCC) in speech-language pathology from ASHA, as well as state licensure in speech-language pathology (licensure is required in the majority of states for work settings other than schools). ASHA members are required to abide by the ASHA Code of Ethics and are encouraged to participate in continuing education.

ARE THERE SPEECH-LANGUAGE PATHOLOGY AIDES (AS THERE ARE TEACHER AIDES)?

Yes. Referred to as *aides, paraprofessionals,* or *supportive personnel,* these people are allowed in some states to work in the schools under the supervision of speech-language pathologists. Bilingual paraprofessionals work with children who speak English as a second language (ESL); they are also invaluable in communicating with parents and the community of foreign speakers at-large. The same is true of bidialectical paraprofessionals. In the future, paraprofessionals may become more widely employed in public schools.

DOES EVERY SCHOOL HAVE A SPEECH-LANGUAGE PATHOLOGIST?

One of the first, public school speech correction programs began in Chicago, in 1910, with several of the larger, urban school districts following in the next decade (Moore & Kester, 1953). The number of children served, especially in the smaller and rural districts, expanded tremendously during the 1950s and 1960s. Obviously then, speech-language pathologists are relatively new in many schools. However, the answer to the above question is now a definite "yes." To comply with federal laws, all public schools must have a trained speech-language pathologist available to serve the needs of communicatively handicapped children.

WHAT DOES FEDERAL LAW HAVE TO DO WITH SPEECH-LANGUAGE PATHOLOGY AND AUDIOLOGY?

Several federal laws are relevant to the children that speech-language pathologists and audiologists work with in schools. Two of the most important ones are PL 94-142 and PL 99-457. PL refers to Public Law. The number preceding the hyphen represents the session of Congress during which the law was passed, and the number following the hyphen represents the number of the law passed in that session. Therefore, PL 94-142 was the 142nd law passed by the 94th session of Congress. All laws are printed in volumes entitled the *United States Statutes at Large,* and the regulations relating to the laws can be found in the *Federal Register.*

PL 94-142, entitled the Education for All Handicapped Children Act of 1975, mandated that all disabled children receive a free education that is appropriate to their needs. Although some disabled children were receiving an education before the enactment of PL 94-142, over one million were not. Of those being served, it was estimated that over one-half were not receiving an appropriate education. Before Congress acted, state and local educational agencies had the option of providing or not providing education to the disabled. PL 94-142 addressed the needs of disabled children, regardless of the degree of severity, between the ages of three and 21. Exceptions to age inclusions were granted in states where state laws, regulations, or court orders were in conflict with PL 94-142, and then children below age five and above age 18 were excluded. Each state had to enact its own legislation, rules, and regulations to comply with PL 94-142.

PL 99-457, Education of the Handicapped Act Amendments of 1986, no longer gave the states a choice regarding children from age three to kindergarten enrollment and mandated that services begin at age three. It also provided incentives to states to serve newborns to three-year olds.

In 1990, the title of the Education of the Handicapped Act (EHA), which included PL 94-142 and PL 99-457, was changed to Individuals with Disabilities Education Act (IDEA). Teachers will encounter these laws many times in their educational studies and careers and will need to examine them in far more depth than is presented here.

PL 94-142 specified that an *individualized educational program* (IEP) must be completed for each disabled child and that the education must be provided in the *least restrictive environment* (LRE). Although each school district may develop its own IEP form, the IEP must include a statement specifying:

1. the child's present level of performance
2. the special educational or related services to be provided
3. the long-term (annual) goals and short-term objectives
4. the date that services are to be initiated
5. an estimate regarding how long the services will be necessary
6. the educational setting(s) that the child will be placed within for such services (The setting(s) must meet the least restrictive environment requirement)
7. the evaluation procedures and criteria that will be used to de-

termine whether or not the goals and objectives have been met, and

8. at age 16, or earlier if appropriate, a statement of any necessary transition services.

The IEP is developed by a team of appropriate school personnel, the parents, and sometimes the child (when the team members deem it appropriate); is signed by the team members, including the parents; and is reviewed and updated at least annually. Parents have the right to disagree with the IEP that the school suggests and to exercise their due process rights by appealing. If they refuse services that the school has recommended for their child, the school can ask for an impartial hearing.

Least restrictive environment refers to the most "regular" or "normal" setting in which the child can function for the school day or for a portion of the school day. The word *mainstreaming* is commonly used to describe the process of children being placed with their normal peers for as much of the day as possible, although the word mainstreaming does not appear in the law itself.

What does PL 94-142 have to do with speech-language pathology and audiology? Communicative disorders are one of the most prevalent disabling conditions in the United States today. Every school-aged child who is identified as having a communicative disorder (speech, language, or hearing) that adversely affects educational achievement falls under the jurisdiction of this law. An IEP must be completed and appropriate services rendered.

If the child qualifies for another special educational program, speech and language services are regarded as related services. If the child qualifies only for speech or language services, then those services are considered special education. This distinction is important for federal funding. Knowing how the terminology is defined and derived allows one to help parents understand why their child is categorized as requiring special education, especially if their child's problem is relatively minor, such as a "w" substitution for an "r."

PL 99-457 calls for participation of multiple agencies in providing special education and related kinds of services to handicapped preschoolers. As a community agency, the schools play a major role. Teachers and others will see these children and their families coming to school for services. PL 99-457 focuses on the family, with assessment and remediation being directed at both the child and the family. Instead of an IEP, an *individualized family service plan* (IFSP) is developed specifying:

1. the child's present level of development
2. the family's strengths and needs relating to the development of the child

3. the major goals to be achieved for both the child and the family
4. the services to be provided to the child and the family
5. the criteria and timelines to be used in evaluating progress
6. the estimated date that services are to be initiated
7. an estimate regarding how long the services will be needed, and
8. the transitional steps necessary when the child reaches school-age.

ARE THERE DIFFERENCES IN THE TERMS *COMMUNICATION, LANGUAGE,* AND *SPEECH*?

Communication. Language. Speech. These three terms are interchangeable for many people. However, for the purposes of this book, distinctions will need to be made among them.

Communication, the most general of the terms, implies a transfer of knowledge, ideas, opinions, and feelings. Most often this transfer is via language. However, there are other means. For example, body language can be a powerful tool of communication although most linguists would not be willing to classify body language as an example, of a formal language because it is nonlinguistic in nature, involving body movements, such as pointing, waving, fidgeting, and facial expressions rather than the signs and symbols of a language. Communication between an infant and its caregiver is present at birth although the infant has not yet learned to use language or speech (Matthews, 1986).

Language, a more specific term, can be defined simply as a formalized method of communication consisting of (1) the signs and symbols by which ideas can be represented, and (2) the rules governing these signs and symbols (e.g., how the symbols can be combined). Language occurs among a community of language users, which means that the person expressing the linguistic message and the person or persons receiving it must have shared meanings attached to the message content. Language is unique to humans because only human beings are able to use language to communicate about the past and the future as well as the present (Bolton, 1981). There are several modes by which humans may communicate their language, including reading, writing, speaking, and listening. These modes can be classified either as receptive or expressive language. Reading and listening are examples of receptive language (i.e., the message is received and decoded or interpreted). Writing and speaking are forms of expressive language whereby the message is encoded or produced.

Speech, the narrowest of the terms, is the vocal or spoken production of language and, as such, is the fastest and most efficient means of communicating. It may be defined as the motor production of speech sounds (i.e., the individual consonant and vowel sounds). Speech sounds have rules governing their use and combination. Motor production involves the movements made by the various parts of the body in order to produce sound waves that travel through the air, eventually impinging upon the listener's ears. Motor production of speech sounds will be referred to as articulation.

WHAT KINDS OF COMMUNICATIVE DISORDERS SHOULD THE TEACHER LOOK FOR IN THE CLASSROOM?

This question might be divided into two questions, one dealing with speech and one with language (hearing impairments are dealt with in Chapter 7). One could first ask what kinds of speech problems are there, or how can the teacher determine when a child might have a speech problem and when should a child be referred to the speech-language pathologist?

For years the standard definition in the field of speech-language pathology has been that speech is abnormal when it is conspicuous, unintelligible, unpleasant, interferes with communication, or causes the speaker to be maladjusted (Van Riper & Emerick, 1984). In other words, the listener is so intrigued with *how* the message is being communicated that attention is drawn away from *what* is being communicated. However, the definition makes it clear that individual circumstances, such as the speaker's age, cultural norms, and environment, also must be considered. For example, a three-year-old child is not expected to articulate (produce speech sounds) as well as a ten-year-old child or an adult. We would not tend to be distracted from the content of the message "I'm goin' to dreth up like a thkeleton for Halloween" if we were talking to a three year old, but we might be if we were talking to a ten year old. In some localities, words such as "runnin' " for "running," "warsh" for "wash," and even "dese" and "dem" for "these" and "them" are quite acceptable and are unnoticed in that environment, but they would certainly be noticed on the six o'clock news.

Problems that are labeled as abnormal speech are typically placed in one or more of the following categories:

- Speech Sound Disorders: These problems involve both articulatory disorders and phonological disorders. *Articulation* refers to the motor ability to produce speech sounds while *phonology* involves acquisition of the abstract linguistic rules that govern speech sounds. More detail will be presented in Chapters 2 and 7.
- Fluency Disorders: Fluency problems are characterized by repetitions, prolongations, or blocks that interrupt the flow or rhythm

of speech to an abnormal degree and are further discussed in Chapter 4.
- Voice Disorders: Deviations in pitch, pitch patterns, range of pitch, vocal quality (words such as *hoarse, nasal,* and *breathy* help describe disorders of vocal quality), loudness, or loudness patterns constitute voice disorders. Sometimes such deviations are not pleasant to listen to and often are not appropriate for the age or sex of the speaker. These are covered in Chapters 5 and 7.

What kinds of language impairments are there? Briefly, they involve problems (in relation to the child's cognitive status) in one or more of the dimensions or components of language: (1) syntax, (2) semantics, (3) morphology, (4) pragmatics, and (5) phonology. The first four are discussed in Chapter 3, whereas phonology is examined in Chapter 2.

WHAT CAUSES SPEECH AND LANGUAGE PROBLEMS?

Causes vary and are not always known. Attempts are made to determine the cause(s) of any particular disorder so that if the source of the problem is still present, it can be eliminated or corrected. If the cause cannot be rectified, it may be possible to improve speech by teaching compensatory techniques. On the other hand, if the cause cannot be determined, it may still be possible for speech therapy to be successful. Causes will be dealt with for each specific disorder in the following chapters. Speech and language are complicated processes. To communicate vocally the speaker must possess certain physical prerequisites, including neurological integrity.

WHAT ARE THE RESPONSIBILITIES OF THE SPEECH-LANGUAGE PATHOLOGIST?

In this introductory chapter, each responsibility will be discussed in a general fashion. More specific details relating to various disorders will be presented in appropriate chapters.

Assessment

Assessment involves the appraisal of the communicative status of an individual in terms of speech or language abilities. There are two aspects to assessment: initial assessment involves identification and diagnosis; ongoing assessment continues during therapy, in order to monitor or evaluate a child's progress, and after dismissal from therapy, when the child is checked for possible regression (or back-sliding). Ongoing assessment during therapy may result in a continuation or a modification of therapeutic techniques or programs.

This discussion will focus on initial assessment, which in school is at least a two-stage process involving screening and individual diagnosis. In some school districts the process may be divided into three steps: (1) rapid screening, (2) extensive screening of those identified during the rapid screening as possibly demonstrating problems, and (3) complete diagnostic assessment of those identified during the extensive screening as potential candidates for remediation. It should be noted that federal law mandates that (1) assessments be performed in the child's native language as well as English, if English is a second language, and (2) written notifications to parents be in their native language.

Screening

Screening is a rapid assessment done in order to identify those children who need further assessment or diagnosis. Who is screened will vary from school district to school district and within some districts will vary from school building to school building. In some school districts, all kindergartners, all other children new to the school district (e.g., children who have moved into the district), teacher referrals, and parent referrals may be screened. In other school districts, children may not be screened until they enter the second or third grade, on the assumption that maturity for speech is not complete until age seven or eight. Another plan involves screening all children in certain grade levels every year, much the way vision testing is implemented. In yet other districts, no general screening may take place and speech-language pathologists rely solely on referrals from teachers, parents, and other school personnel. Self-referrals, particularly at the secondary level, may also be encouraged.

The practice of relying solely on referrals allows for those in the individual's environment to decide whether a communicative disorder is present (McDermott, 1985). It has been argued that accountability in terms of time and money expended can best be achieved when speech-language pathologists do not screen all students, since most of the children will not exhibit communicative problems (Gantwerk, 1985). This procedure may work very well in school systems where teachers, other school personnel, and even parents have received training in recognizing and referring children with suspected problems.

However, if the prerequisite training is not provided, some problems, particularly voice problems, will not be identified (Sommers & Hatton, 1985). One-time training, such as a college course or an inservice education program, although helpful, may not be sufficient. Phillips (1976, p. 148) reported that there was a relationship between the grade taught and awareness of speech disorders in children; the "lower the grade taught, the more aware [teachers were] of speech disorders." Yet referrals are often relied on as a measure of identification at the secondary level, even when the speech-language pathologist does the screening at the elementary level (Neal, 1976). Therefore, the secondary teacher should be especially cognizant of students with possible speech and language problems.

Screening of non-referrals takes place throughout the school year, although many speech-language pathologists try to complete as much as possible at the beginning of the school year. The speech-language pathologist assigned to a school building may do all of the screening, or a team of speech-language pathologists in the district may work together to screen an entire school within a day, helping to minimize disruptions. When a child is identified as having no problem, this information is recorded and, depending on screening procedures, the child might not be automatically screened again. This is a time-efficient procedure; however, there are two problems. First, the screenings are rapid, and subtle problems may be missed. Second, some problems, especially fluency and voice problems, may develop later. Therefore, teachers should never be reluctant to refer a child for testing; even when they know that the child previously passed a screening. It should be noted that referrals must be assessed within the time stipulated by law.

According to ASHA, the average screening takes approximately five minutes per child (Task Force Report on School Speech, Hearing, and Language Screening Procedures, 1973). Assessment of a child immediately identified as needing further assessment may not require five minutes if a more extensive screening is to be conducted, while assessment of a child who has no problems may require more than five minutes.

The speech-language pathologist may set up the rapid screening in a variety of ways. Frequently, a small group of children is taken into a quiet hallway or to a therapy room. Each child may be asked to give his or her name, read, describe a picture, name pictures of objects, count, repeat sentences, and answer open-ended questions to elicit a speech and language sample from which the speech-language pathologist will judge intelligibility, articulation, voice, fluency, and language. As the speech-language pathologist finishes with each child, that child may be sent back to the classroom so that another child may leave the room and join the group or all of the children may return together while a new group joins the speech-language pathologist. There is a time-saving advantage to this procedure since each child (except the first in a group) has an opportunity to observe several other children being tested. The speech-language pathologist may not need to give as many directions and the children may be more relaxed (Task Force Report on School Speech, Hearing, and Language Screening Procedures, 1973). Extensive screening is more often conducted in a therapy room with only one child present. Parental permission is not required for screening. However, many school systems, out of courtesy and an interest in good school-parent relationships and in order to comply with state or local policy, will notify parents of upcoming screenings. This notification may provide an impetus to parents who have questioned their child's communicative abilities to contact the speech-language pathologist. (Hearing screenings are dealt with in Chapter 7.)

Individual Diagnosis
Written parental permission is required by law for individual diagnosis. The diagnostic procedure may take up to two hours or more and involves a careful assessment that should result in a diagnosis of speech and language status. It should also provide information pertaining to the goals and objectives that should be set for a child and an idea of the kinds of therapeutic techniques that are most apt to be successful with that child. A variety of procedures is involved and, depending on individual circumstances, may include:

1. an oral peripheral examination (a visual determination of whether the oral structures appear to be capable of producing normal speech)
2. an articulation test (an evaluation of the child's ability to produce speech sounds in isolation, words, sentences, and spontaneous speech)
3. a measure of auditory discrimination ability (can the child hear the difference between a correct speech sound and the sound that he or she substitutes for the correct one)
4. a measure of stimulability (can the child produce the sound he or she is asked to produce with or without specific directions; if so, the child is stimulable)
5. tests of expressive and receptive language skills (using standardized tests as well as an analysis of spontaneous speech)
6. an evaluation of fluency
7. an evaluation of voice
8. a hearing test (although this may legally be the responsibility of the audiologist or school nurse)
9. a case history (obtained from the parents of younger children and possibly from both the child and the parents in the case of older children).

The speech-language pathologist may also want to observe the child in the classroom or on the playground. Additional information, such as the child's cognitive functioning or home environment, that is obtained by other school personnel may be helpful in interpreting the findings.

Therapy

Other appropriate terms for therapy include remediation and delivery of services. Therapy may be direct, with the speech-language pathologist working directly with the child, or indirect, with the speech-language pathologist working with others in the child's environment, such as the academic teacher or parent, in order to better enable them to help the child. In a set of guidelines regarding caseload size, ASHA (Guidelines for Caseload Size for Speech-Language Services in the Schools, 1984) recommended the use of four types of service programs in the public schools. Ranging from most to least involvement, these include (1) self-contained programs, (2) resource room programs, (3) itinerant programs, and (4) consultation programs. A fifth type of service delivery gaining recognition is classroom-based (Asha, 1992).

Self-Contained Programs
(Academically Integrated Direct Service)
This alternative is most frequently used with children who have severe or multiple communicative problems. Such a child is placed in a special class for the majority of the school day. He or she may be mainstreamed for some educational or social (e.g., recess) activities. The speech-language pathologist in this setting must be certified as a teacher, or else the class must be team-taught with a teacher in order to meet state teacher certification standards. An aide may also be present in this program setting.

Resource Room Programs (Intensive Direct Service)
In this model the child spends most of the day in his or her regular classroom placement (this may be the regular classroom or a special education classroom), but also spends one or more periods per day in a resource room staffed by a speech-language pathologist. Generally, there is a group of up to five children in the resource room. This program is most frequently used with children whose problems are severe, but it may also be used with children whose problems are mild or moderate. Self-paced instruction modules and aides are frequently utilized. Although the classroom teacher is primarily responsible for academic goals, it is to the child's advantage if the classroom teacher and speech-language pathologist cooperate so that the speech-language pathologist can incorporate and reinforce classroom goals, curricula, materials, and procedures.

Itinerant Programs (Intermittent Direct Service)

This is the delivery of service model that has traditionally been used for all children regardless of type of problem or degree of severity. Those of you reading this book who were once enrolled in speech therapy probably were served via this model. You, most likely, left the classroom to go to therapy twice a week for 20–30 minute sessions. This *pull-out* model includes sessions up to one-hour long and therapy as often as five times per week, depending on the needs of the child. The child may be seen individually or in a small group. ASHA (Guidelines for Caseload Size for Speech-Language Services in the Schools, 1984) recommends that the small group include no more than three children. The teacher and speech-language pathologist may consult with each other so that the speech-language pathologist can incorporate classroom materials into the child's communicative program.

Consultation Program (Indirect Service)

ASHA views this program as an emerging one in which the speech-language pathologist is responsible for planning appropriate services and directing others in carrying them out. The Consultation Program could be appropriate for children with very mild to very severe problems. For example, a child who has a stuttering problem may be served via the Intermittent Direct Service approach until he or she demonstrates the ability to use appropriate "controls" to facilitate fluent speech. The speech-language pathologist may then choose not to dismiss the child entirely from therapeutic services but to follow the child via indirect service (the consultation program) in order to insure that the child has the necessary environmental support for maintaining the current communicative status. At the other end of the severity continuum, severely involved children may need virtually continuous speech-language stimulation in their own environment as well as training in the use of alternative communicative devices (see Chapter 8). The speech-language pathologist plans this program; instructs others in carrying it out; and periodically reevaluates progress, modifying the program as necessary. If children can be appropriately served by the consultation program, they should be, as it meets the legal mandate of the least restrictive environment.

Classroom-Based Programs

In this program, the speech-language pathologist goes into the regular or special education classroom and works with the child. In this model, it is much easier to integrate communication skills with academic content, (e.g., vocabulary and concepts in the various curriculum areas). However, the speech-language pathologist may need to know more about curriculum and instruction than is typically the case (Asha, 1992). This model provides a more natural environment for services, and so *carryover* (the habitual use of what has been taught and learned in the child's natural environment) may be more quickly and easily achieved. Advocates of this model also presume that the student is less stigmatized by it than by pull-out programs.

High-Tech Adaptations to Delivery of Services

Computers are now used in both assessment and therapeutic procedures in what today might be considered very ordinary ways. However, in less ordinary ways, technology is providing the opportunity to attain services in remote rural areas with extremely low population densities. Computer-assisted communication lines along with micro-electronic technology have eliminated travel barriers in some remote areas, primarily in areas where the Inuit or Eskimos and the Aleuts live (Asha, 1989; Asha, 1992).

Why Are Some Children Selected for Therapy and Others Are Not?

School districts should have a set of criteria that must be met before a child is considered speech handicapped and in need of services. However, this does not mean that a child who is enrolled in speech therapy in School District A would necessarily be enrolled in speech therapy in School District B or C. Each school district can set its own criteria for determining a handicapping condition. Within these criteria, the actual decisions concerning provision of speech-language services for a child rests with the IEP or IFSP committee. This last statement makes a very important point: whether or not a child meets certain, arbitrary criteria for language remediation, articulation therapy, etc., it is still the prerogative and responsibility of the IEP or IFSP committee to decide whether or not services will be provided.

How Is the Type of Program, Frequency, and Duration of Therapy Chosen?

For school-aged children the delivery of services model and the frequency and duration of each therapy session are selected and approved by the IEP committee and are recorded on the child's IEP. For preschoolers, this information is part of the IFSP. It should be emphasized that the model of remediation chosen as the mode for delivery of services should be the model best suited to the needs of the child, not just the most convenient. For example, age and the severity of the disorder should be considered when making decisions regarding frequency and duration of therapy. Attention span may dictate that two 15 minute sessions per day would be preferable to one 30 minute session (Work, 1985).

What Does the Speech-Language Pathologist Do With the Child, or What Really Goes on in Therapy?

In the succeeding chapters, which focus on particular communicative problems, therapeutic procedures will be briefly described so that the reader has an understanding of the general procedures that may be used for each disorder. Teachers are encouraged to discuss with a speech-language pathologist the possibility of observing a therapy session, particularly a session involving students in their own classrooms. Most speech-language pathologists would eagerly welcome such a request.

When Is a Child Dismissed from Therapy?

Obviously, if the speech-language pathologist felt that a child was performing a new speech or language behavior 100 percent of the time, the child could be dismissed. However, dismissal from therapy is frequently arranged at some point before the 100 percent criterion is reached (generally in the 90 to 95 percent range), since past experience has shown that children usually continue to make progress. Such children will be periodically assessed to confirm that progress does continue. Children are also dismissed from therapy when objective measures indicate that they have reached their maximum potential considering their organic, physiological, or cognitive status. Long-standing lack of motivation and progress may also be a reason to discontinue therapy, at least for a period of time. The IEP or IFSP committee is responsible for making such decisions.

Philosophy of Speech-Language Therapy

A brief comment regarding philosophy of speech-language therapy would be pertinent at this point. Just as there are varying philosophical viewpoints in education, so, too, are there in speech-language pathology. We feel that communicative differences or disorders can affect the whole child: his intellectual development, social development, psychological development, educational attainment, and future goals. Therefore, a speech-language pathologist is not responsible for merely treating a speech-language disorder but is also responsible for working with the whole child. In the same vein, teachers might ask themselves whether they teach reading or whether they teach children to read. The latter choice focuses on the child rather than on the behaviors to be taught. Furthermore, we believe that although there may be exceptions—notably the beginning stutterer—the majority of school-aged children (and their parents) should know why they go to therapy. They should have some understanding of (1) their short-term and long-term goals (in general the child will be striving to achieve a new speech or language behavior and to make that behavior a habit), (2) how they will attempt to achieve these goals, (3) what the criteria are for goal achievement, and (4) why it is important to make changes or improvements in the way they communicate; in other words, they need to be motivated.

In a recent survey of speech-language pathologists (Eger, Chabon, Mient, & Cushman, 1986), over one-half (57.5%) reported that they felt that children with articulation problems who successfully achieved goals in articulation therapy did so because of the motivation and positive attitude exhibited by the children or by their parents. Secondary school youth may be particularly hard to motivate (Fellows, 1976); however, those who hope to enter occupations or professions that demand good communication skills may be easier to convince of the need for therapy.

Scheduling

A schedule is a way of effectively and efficiently planning the use of time and of letting others know what will be (or is) going on at any particular time. A speech-language pathologist may serve one or many schools. One of the writers of this text has served as many as seven schools at a time. Needless to say, travel between schools can consume considerable time, especially when schools are far apart or if travel must occur near noon when traffic is heavier. The number of schools that can be served will vary with the following factors:

- The size of each school: It would be expected that the larger the school, the larger the number of students in need of therapy.
- The time required for travel: The more time spent traveling, the less time is available for providing services.
- The type of programs housed within a particular school: Generally, a larger percentage of students in special education classrooms require speech-language therapy than in regular classrooms. Schools housing several special education classrooms may need a greater proportion of the speech-language pathologist's time in comparison to the total number of students.
- The speech-language pathologist's other duties and responsibilities: If the speech-language pathologist is involved in district-wide assessment, there will be less time available for providing services to individual schools.
- The type of program that the speech-language pathologist will provide: In general, more students can be served via the consultation program than via the itinerant program. The itinerant program, in turn, utilizes less of the speech-language pathologist's time per student than the resource room program. Obviously, only one school and a limited number of students would be served if the

speech-language pathologist works with children in a self-contained program.

The speech-language pathologist has at least one half day, and in some school districts a full day, of coordination time (when regularly scheduled services are not provided) for such activities as assessment (both screening and individual diagnosis); consultation with parents, teachers, and others; preparation for and attendance at IEP conferences; paper work; and preparation of therapy plans for the next week.

Prior to the passage of PL 94-142, most public school speech-language pathologists had a list of students being served and a list of students waiting to be served. Now, in order to comply with federal law, there can be no waiting list (Healey & Dublinske, 1978). Each fall, the speech-language pathologist will identify students and preschoolers with IEPs and IFSPs, note individual time requirements per the IEPs and IFSPs for each child, and construct a new schedule of children, times, and schools. Generally, the speech-language pathologist will utilize more than one type of program to deliver the necessary and most appropriate services to various students. Schedules are not easy to complete and can be a potential source of controversy. Therefore, if a teacher has a request concerning the schedule, it is extremely helpful if that request is made to the speech-language pathologist as soon as possible and *before* the schedule is completed. Otherwise, to accommodate a change for one teacher, the speech-language pathologist must change another teacher's schedule, who may in turn dislike the new schedule. This does *not* mean, however, that a schedule will not change during the school year; schedules must be flexible. As a schedule changes, the therapy times of students in a particular class may be affected. Changes will occur as students are dismissed from therapy, newly identified and assessed children with completed IEPs or IFSPs are placed into therapy, and children are changed from one type of service delivery to another. For example, as a child improves, the duration or frequency of therapy may be decreased; if satisfactory progress does not occur, the duration or frequency of therapy may be increased. The original schedule and each new schedule will be distributed to the teachers. If a teacher needs to contact the speech-language pathologist at other school buildings, the complete schedule should be available in the principal's office.

Will the Children in Need of Speech Therapy from a Single Classroom Go to Therapy at the Same Time?

It is possible but not probable. Some children will be seen individually and some will be seen in small groups, depending on their needs. A child might even be seen both individually and in a small group each week.

Group work may be especially apropos as a social situation with peers can be simulated. The majority of speech-language pathologists will group children homogeneously; that is all the children in a group will work on the same problem, such as stuttering or the "s" sound. A few speech-language pathologists will group heterogeneously, grouping children together who are working on different types of problems; then it is more likely that children in a classroom will all be scheduled for therapy at the same time.

Consultation

Consultation is a process that "involves the interaction between two or more professionals for the purpose of mutually preventing or solving problems" (Heron & Harris, 1982, p. 1). Some school professionals have a consultant's role as their primary job responsibility. However, in the context of this book, the consultation process occurs as just one responsibility of the speech-language pathologist and any other person who can bring to bear information, ideas, and techniques that can potentially and positively affect the communicative status of the child in question. The other person could be the regular classroom teacher, a special education teacher, a resource room teacher, a physical education teacher, a music teacher, an art teacher, a school nurse, a school psychologist, a counselor, the principal, a parent, or any other community resource personnel. The reader is right in interpreting this as an appeal for all concerned to think in terms of an interdisciplinary approach. The participants need to learn what each can contribute. It is of paramount importance that this team process be two-way, a give and take of information and ideas. Consider the following as examples of some of the possible interactions with which the speech-language pathologist might be involved.

Interactions with Parents
Contact with parents is mandatory as the approval for individual diagnosis is obtained and as the IEP or IFSP is completed, but this should be only the first of a series of contacts that should occur before the annual reappraisal and the update of the goal statement. Parents need to be informed periodically of their child's progress and may even be able to help reinforce at home the various achievements that have been made in therapy. They may also be able to provide information about how the child performs communicatively outside the school environment. During parental counseling, McFarlane, Fujiki, and Brinton (1984) suggest that the parents be encouraged to accept their child. They should be helped to understand that their child's communicative problem does not reflect on their value as parents or on the child who needs just as much love and acceptance as any other child.

Interactions with the Classroom Teacher

The speech-language pathologist and teacher need to consult with each other about their goals for a child, how they expect to accomplish these goals, and what success has been achieved. This can be accomplished formally, informally, or by the speech-language pathologist providing the teacher with copies of written speech therapy progress reports that are sent home to the parents.

The classroom teacher usually has more contact with parents and spends more school hours with a child, who may talk about his or her feelings, wants, and life at home. Some information that a teacher receives from a child or parents may be important to the speech-language pathologist. For example, if parents complain that they still cannot understand a child who has shown such remarkable gains in intelligibility that the speech-language pathologist, teacher, and classmates now have little concern about intelligibility, the speech-language pathologist may want and need to discuss this matter with the parents. As another example, suppose that a teacher has as a student, a stutterer, who was in therapy and had learned to control the stuttering except occasionally in stressful situations. If the teacher is informed of stressful situations at home, especially if the situation will be of some duration as a separation or divorce of the parents, and informs the speech-language pathologist, the speech-language pathologist with the parents' permission may confer with the student and review strategies for controlling the stuttering. In this manner, increased stuttering may be averted or, at least, minimized. The stutterer may also be reminded to contact the speech-language pathologist for help at any time.

The teacher is also in a position to provide the speech-language pathologist with information about a child's speech and language skills in the classroom and in informal situations, such as in the hallway, in the lunchroom, or on the playground. The teacher can also provide reminders to the child during the habit-forming stages of therapy, when the child can produce the targeted speech behaviors but still must make them a habit in all communicative situations. As noted earlier in this chapter, this stage of therapy is referred to as carryover.

In return, the speech-language pathologist can serve as a resource for the teacher since the speech-language pathologist may have more experience with language disorders or methods for promoting auditory-visual skills necessary for reading. Specifically, the speech-language pathologist may provide and even demonstrate activities for the teacher, such as ways to develop auditory-verbal skills. This ability to act as a resource is, in essence, the premise that the indirect consultation therapy program is based upon.

Another example of consultation between the classroom teacher and speech-language pathologist involves the use of classroom materials as a source for therapeutic materials. This may be more appropriate at some stages of therapy than at others. However, especially for students experiencing learning difficulties, this could provide more exposure to classroom material in a somewhat different environment. Once the speech-language pathologist and classroom teacher have developed a working relationship, the time spent in communicating about use of appropriate classroom materials in the therapy situation should be minimal and could certainly be worthwhile. The carryover stage of therapy provides many possibilities for reinforcement of classroom materials. For example, a child with a distorted "r" sound might read a portion of a lesson to the speech-language pathologist while practicing a correctly produced "r" sound. A group of children working to establish a correctly produced "s" or working to eliminate the hoarse quality in their voices might discuss a social studies unit with the speech-language pathologist. This could provide the students with an opportunity to determine which sections of the unit each especially needed to review for an upcoming test. Fellows (1976) suggested that utilization of classroom materials works even at the secondary level, giving as examples the use of textbook glossaries or a drivers' education manual for therapeutic materials.

Interaction with Other School Personnel
The physical education teacher, the art teacher, the principal, the office secretary, and others can learn from the speech-language pathologist what to do when a stutterer stutters or how to better and more easily communicate with a hearing impaired child. The speech-language pathologist can utilize the information provided by other school personnel while contributing to that other professional's work. For example, the psychologist and speech-language pathologist might discuss how the results of speech and language tests can be interpreted with respect to the psychologist's findings of cognitive and emotional status or how intelligence tests that rely heavily on linguistic ability should be interpreted for the child who is language impaired. Just as in the case of the classroom teacher, the speech-language pathologist and resource room teachers also need to consult in order to appropriately help a child. For example, since expressive and receptive verbal abilities are prerequisite to learning to read (Freeman, 1985), the speech-language pathologist and reading specialist may both work with some of the same children and will need to communicate and coordinate their goals, techniques, and materials.

Community Resources
The speech-language pathologist may also utilize community resources in providing the best services. The otolaryngologist's report concerning the physical status of the vocal folds of a child with a hoarse, breathy voice will

determine whether or not that child is an appropriate candidate for voice therapy. For the child with an unusual problem, the speech-language pathologist might want a second opinion. A nearby university speech, language, and hearing clinic might be an ideal place to obtain more information or a second opinion. The speech-language pathologist may initiate referrals for therapy during the summer months. This might involve therapy at local resources or at camps specializing in various speech problems, such as the Shady Trails Camp, associated with the University of Michigan, which incorporates speech therapy into a traditional summer camp. The speech-language pathologist may maintain contacts with state and local agencies and with community philanthropic organizations that might provide financial assistance for adaptive communication devices (discussed in Chapter 8).

SUMMARY

Some Important Points to Remember

- All teachers can expect to have children with communicative disorders in their classrooms.
- The emotional and social adjustments of children as well as their educational achievement are related to communication skills.
- The speech-language pathologist is the professional who is prepared to work with children having communicative problems.
- The American Speech-Language-Hearing Association is the professional organization that sets standards for speech-language pathologists and audiologists.
- The audiologist is concerned with hearing and hearing disorders and their remediation.
- Public Law 94-142 addresses the needs of all school-aged handicapped children.
- An Individualized Educational Program (IEP) must be completed for each handicapped school-aged child, and the education must be provided in the least restrictive environment (LRE).
- The IEP is drawn up by a team of school personnel and the child's parent(s).
- An Individualized Family Service Plan (IFSP) focuses on both the preschooler who is age three or above and the child's family.
- Communicative disorders are among the most prevalent handicapping conditions in the United States.
- The term *communication* implies a transfer of ideas, opinions, and feelings via *language*, which is a formalized system by which we communicate.

- *Speech* is the spoken production of language.
- The components of language include: (1) syntax, (2) semantics, (3) morphology, (4) pragmatics, and (5) phonology.
- The responsibilities of the speech-language pathologist involve: (1) assessment, (2) therapy, (3) scheduling, and (4) consultation.
- Five types of service programs for children in the public schools are: (1) self-contained programs, (2) resource room programs, (3) itinerant programs, (4) consultation programs, and (5) classroom-based programs.
- Teachers should discuss observing speech therapy sessions with the speech-language pathologist.
- Speech-language pathologists are interested in the total development of a child's communicative skills.
- It is important that children and parents understand why the child is in therapy.
- The scheduling of therapy for any child must be jointly accomplished by the teacher and the speech-language pathologist.
- Generally, the speech-language pathologist serves more than one school building.
- If more than one child from a classroom receives therapy, they might not all leave and return to the room together—this depends on the nature of the disorders.
- The speech-language pathologist frequently confers with teachers, other professionals, and parents.

SELF-TEST

Fill in the blank:

1. In 1990, the Education for All Handicapped Children Act and the Education of the Handicapped Children Act Amendments were renamed _____

2. All schools must have speech, language, and hearing services available since _____.
3. The purpose of screening is to _____

4. IEP stands for _____.
5. LRE stands for _____.
6. A frequently used term associated with the concept behind LRE is ____

7. The five dimensions of language are _____, _____, _____, _____, and _____.

8. The ability to produce a sound with or without specific directions is referred to as _____.
9. The five service delivery models discussed include _____, _____, _____, _____, and _____.
10. Work with other professionals to prevent or solve problems has been referred to as _____.

True or False:

1. Speech, language, and hearing services may be considered special education under the Education for All Handicapped Children Act. ____
2. Parents are a part of the IEP team. ____
3. Reading and writing are examples of expressive language. ____
4. A communicative disorder exists when the listener pays more attention to how the message is communicated than to what is being communicated. ____
5. The cause of the communicative disorder must be determined before therapy is initiated. ____
6. Parents must give permission for their children to be screened for communicative problems. ____
7. Kindergartners are always screened for communicative problems. ____
8. Secondary teachers do not need to be concerned with making referrals to the speech-language pathologist. ____
9. Remediation, therapy, and delivery of services are synonymous terms. ____
10. Children on a waiting list will receive speech therapy just as soon as there is an opening in the speech-language pathologist's schedule. ____

REFERENCES

Bolton, W. F. (1981). Language: An introduction. In V. P. Clark, P. A. Eschholz, and A. F. Rosa (Eds.), *Language* (3rd ed.) (pp. 1–17). New York: St. Martin's Press.

Chezik, K. H., Pratt, J. E., Stewart, J. L., and Deal, V. R. (1989). Addressing service delivery in remote/rural areas. *ASHA, 31,* 52–55.

Eger, D. L., Chabon, S. S., Mient, M. G., and Cushman, B. B. (1986). When is enough enough? *ASHA, 28,* 23–25.

Fellows, J. B. (1976). The speech pathologist in the high school setting. *Language, Speech, and Hearing Services in Schools, 7,* 61–63.

Freeman, G. G. (1985). Consultation. In R. J. Van Hattum (Ed.), *Administration of speech-language services in schools* (pp. 22–53). San Diego: College-Hill.

Gantwerk, B. (1985). Assessment issues in decision making. In *Caseload issues in schools* (pp. 25–34). Rockville, MD: American Speech-Language-Hearing Association.

Garbee, F. E. (1985). The speech-language pathologist as a member of the educational team. In R. J. Van Hattum (Ed.), *Organization of speech-language services in schools* (pp. 58–129). San Diego: College-Hill.

Guidelines for caseload size for speech-language services in the schools. (1984). *ASHA, 26*(4), 53–58.

Healey, W. C., and Dublinske, S. (1978). Notes from the school services program. *Language, Speech, and Hearing Services in Schools, 9,* 203.

Heron, T. E., and Harris, K. C. (1982). *The educational consultant: Helping professionals, parents, and mainstreamed students.* Boston: Allyn & Bacon.

Matthews, J. (1986). The professions of speech-language pathology and audiology. In G. H. Shames and E. H. Wiig (Eds.), *Human communication disorders* (2nd ed.) (pp. 3–26). Columbus, OH: Charles E. Merrill.

Matthews, J. (1990). The professions of speech-language pathology and audiology. In G. H. Shames and E. H. Wiig (Eds)., *Human communication disorders* (3rd ed.) (pp. 2–27). Columbus, OH: Charles E. Merrill.

McDermott, L. (1985). Service alternatives. In *Caseload issues in schools* (pp. 18–24). Rockville, MD: American Speech-Language-Hearing Association.

McFarlane, S. C., Fujiki, M., and Brinton, B. (1984). *Coping with communicative handicaps.* San Diego: College-Hill.

Moore, P., and Kester, D. C. (1953). Historical notes in speech correction in the pre-association era. *Journal of Speech and Hearing Disorders, 18,* 48–53.

Neal, W. R., Jr. (1976). Speech pathology services in the secondary schools. *Language, Speech, and Hearing Services in Schools, 7,* 6–16.

Neidecker, E. A. (1980). *School programs in speech-language: Organization and management.* Englewood Cliffs, NJ: Prentice-Hall.

Paul-Brown, D. (1992). Alternative service delivery models. *Asha, 34,* 12.

Phillips, P. P. (1976). Variables affecting classroom teachers' understanding of speech disorders. *Language, Speech, and Hearing Services in Schools, 7,* 142–149.

Sommers, R. K., and Hatton, M. E. (1985). Establishing the therapy program: Case finding, case selection, and case load. In R. J. Van Hattum (Ed.), *Organization of speech-language services in schools* (pp. 130–223). San Diego: College-Hill.

Task force report on school speech, hearing, and language screening procedures. (1973). *Language, Speech, and Hearing Services in Schools, 4,* 109–119.

Taylor, J. S. (1980). Public school speech-language certification standards: Are they standard? *ASHA, 22,* 159–165.

Van Hattum, R. J. (1985). Introduction. In R. J. Van Hattum (Ed.), *Organization of speech-language services in schools* (pp. 1–23). San Diego: College-Hill.

Van Riper, C., and Emerick, L. (1984). *Speech correction: An introduction to speech pathology and audiology.* Englewood Cliffs, NJ: Prentice-Hall.

Work, R. S. (1985). The therapy program. In R. J. Van Hattum (Ed.), *Organization of speech-language services in schools* (pp. 286–337). San Diego: College-Hill.

2

ARTICULATION AND PHONOLOGICAL DISORDERS

It is probably safe to make two wagers. The first is that everyone reading this book has heard a young child make errors in speech sound production. The child may have called a rabbit a "wabbit" or said "Mith Thmith" instead of "Miss Smith." In the first instance a "w" sound was substituted for an "r" sound, and in the second instance a "th" sound was substituted for an "s" sound. Both of these are very typical errors. The second wager is that the reader has also heard an adult make speech sound errors. Possibly the "s" sound was distorted, sounding either slushy and indistinct or as though it were combined with a noisy whistle. Some speakers are able to overcome the negative impressions that such errors create through strong personal assets. However, other speakers who make speech sound errors are thought to be less intelligent, less well-educated, less physically attractive, or less socially attractive (Crowe Hall, 1991; Mowrer, 1974, cited in Shriberg, 1980; Mowrer, Wahl, & Doolan, 1978; Perrin, 1954; Silverman, 1976; Silverman, 1986; Silverman & Falk, 1992; Silverman & Paulus, 1989). Children and adults exhibiting such errors are often called names, teased, or laughed at. Children (and unfortunately even adults) sometimes make fun of a person with speech sound problems by mimicking that individual's speech.

WHAT IS A SPEECH SOUND?

A speech sound is generally called a *phoneme* by speech-language pathologists. Technically, it is the smallest sound segment in a word that we can hear and that, when changed, modifies the meaning of a word. For example, the words "bit" and "bid" have different meanings yet differ in their respective sounds by only the last sound of each word (i.e., "t" and "d"). These two sounds are phonemes since they are capable of changing meaning. Speech sounds or phonemes are classified as vowels and consonants. In English, as most readers are aware, the letters of a word and the sounds of a word do not always have a one-to-one correspondence. This will be clearer with an example. Consider the word "squirrel." It has eight letters but only five sounds: "s"–"k"–"w"–"r"–"l."

To avoid some of this confusion, speech-language pathologists use symbols from the International Phonetic Alphabet (IPA) to represent each speech sound. Many of these IPA symbols, which are enclosed in slashes or brackets depending on how the symbol is used, are the same as the letters we use, but some are not. However, rather than ask you to learn these symbols, in this book the letters in the alphabet enclosed in quotation marks, such as "s," will be used to represent the various speech sounds as they are discussed. In order to do this, some letters will need additional information attached to them for clarity. For example, to represent the first sound in "jam" the phrase "j as in jam" will be used. (See Table 2-2 and the section on consonants.)

Vowels and Diphthongs

The vowels and diphthongs (a *diphthong* is the sound that results when the articulators move from one vowel to another within the same syllable) used in American English are listed in Table 2-1. Each one of these vowels and diphthongs is a speech sound or phoneme. When asked how many vowels there are in the alphabet, the answer may be a, e, i, o, u, and sometimes y, but when referring to speech, the number of vowels increases. In other words, there are five or six vowel letters but approximately 17 distinct vowel sounds. (Remember that there are some variations in vowel usage due to regional or dialectical differences.)

TABLE 2-1.   The vowels and diphthongs in English (the italicized portions)

h*ea*t	wo*u*ld	h*ai*l
h*i*t	h*u*t	b*oi*l
h*a*t	*a*bout	h*ow*
h*ea*d	*a*ll	h*ur*t
h*o*t	h*o*pe	lett*er*
f*oo*d	h*i*gh	

Consonants

The consonants in English and the way in which they will be referred to are listed in Table 2-2. Speech-language pathologists, speech scientists, linguists, and others interested in speech and language frequently describe consonants by their place of articulation and manner of articulation as well as the presence or absence of voicing. Table 2-3 provides such information. You should note from this table that many consonant sounds are produced alike, except for the voicing factor. For instance, "p" and "b" are both bilabial (made with both lips) stops (the flow of air in the vocal tract is completely stopped and then released at the place of articulation). However, one is produced with voicing (the vocal folds are vibrating) and the other is produced without voicing (the vocal folds are not vibrating). The terms *voiced* and *voiceless* are used to refer to the presence or absence of voicing. When voicing is the only difference in sound production between

TABLE 2-2. The consonant sounds in English

Symbol as used in this book		Examples	
"p"	*p*ig	a*pp*le	cu*p*
"b"	*b*us	ri*bb*on	cri*b*
"t"	*t*oy	bu*tt*on	ligh*t*
"d"	*d*ime	la*dd*er	re*d*
"k"	*ch*oir	bou*q*uet	du*ck*
"g"	*g*host	bu*gg*y	e*gg*
"m"	*m*onkey	ha*mm*er	co*mb*
"n"	*kn*ee	te*nn*is	baco*n*
"ng"		fi*ng*er	ri*ng*
"voiceless th"	*th*umb	too*th*paste	tee*th*
"voiced th"	*th*is	fea*th*er	smoo*th*
"f"	*f*oot	bu*ff*alo	gra*ph*
"v"	*v*acuum	se*v*en	fi*v*e
"s"	*sc*ene	bi*c*ycle	gra*ss*
"z"	*z*oo	pu*zz*le	dog*s*
"sh"	*s*ugar	o*c*ean	mousta*ch*e
"zh"		televi*s*ion	mira*g*e
"ch"	*c*ello	ques*t*ion	mat*ch*
"j as in jam"	*j*et	sol*d*ier	bad*ge*
"l"	*l*ion	pi*ll*ow	bal*l*
"r"	*rh*yme	ca*rr*ot	ca*r*
"w"	*w*atch	to*w*el	
"hw"	*wh*ite		
"h"	*h*ouse	toma*h*awk	
"y as in yoyo"	*y*arn	on*i*on	

TABLE 2-3. Speech sounds in English described by their place of articulation, manner of articulation, and the presence or absence of voicing

Manner of Articulation		Place of Articulation						
		Bilabial	Labiodental	Linguadental	Alveolar	Palatal	Velar	Glottal
Stops	VL	p			t		k	
	V	b			d		g	
Fricatives	VL		f	th	s	sh		h
	V		v	th	z	zh		
Affricates	VL					ch		
	V					j as in jam		
Nasals	V	m			n		ng	
Liquids	V				l	r		
Glides	VL	hw						
	V	w				y as in yoyo		

Place of articulation refers to the location of the constriction that occurs as the consonant is produced: Bilabial—both lips, Labiodental—the lower lip and upper front teeth, Linguadental—the tip of the tongue between the front teeth, Alveolar—the tongue and the ridge behind the teeth, Palatal—the tongue and the hard palate, Velar—the tongue and the soft palate (velum), Glottal—the space between the vocal folds.

Manner of articulation refers to the manner of release and/or the type of constriction within the vocal tract: Stops—sounds produced when airflow is momentarily blocked (stopped) at the place of articulation, Fricatives—sounds produced when airflow is reduced (causing friction) at the place of articulation, Affricates—sounds produced when airflow behind the constriction is first blocked and then constricted, Nasals—sounds produced when airflow behind the constriction is directed through the nose rather than through the mouth, Liquids—sounds that are vowel-like but not produced with an open vocal tract, Glides—sounds produced by the movement of the articulators from one position to another and that occur before vowels or diphthongs.

VL = voiceless, V = voiced.

two sounds, they are referred to as *cognates.* Frequently, when children have difficulty producing one sound of a cognate pair, they also have difficulty with the other sound in the pair. Thus, if they are enrolled in therapy, they will work on both sounds. Note that when uttering a consonant sound, one should not attach a vowel to that sound. For example, the "s" sound says only "s" not "es" and "t" is not "tee" or "tuh."

WHAT TYPES OF SPEECH SOUND PROBLEMS DO CHILDREN EXHIBIT?

Errors may be of the following types:

1. Distortions. A speech sound or phoneme is said to be distorted when it sounds more like the intended sound than any other speech sound yet is noticeably wrong. Example: The "r" in reading is produced so that it sounds strange but is more like an "r" than any other speech sound.
2. Substitutions. A substitution occurs when one speech sound is substituted for another. Example: "f" is substituted for "voiceless th" when a child announces that he has hurt his "fum" instead of his "thumb."
3. Omissions. An omission occurs when a speech sound is simply left out. Example: The "r" is omitted when a child counts to "fo" instead of "four."
4. Additions. An addition occurs when a speech sound that does not belong, and is not replacing another sound, is added to a word. Example: A child may insert the unstressed vowel that occurs in the first syllable of "*a*bout" into the color "blue" between the *b* and *l*, thus saying "buhlue." You should be aware that this type of error can occur, but since it occurs infrequently in the school-aged population, it will not be discussed any further in this chapter.

How Common Are These Errors?

Over and over again, authors (Eisenson & Ogilvie, 1977; McReynolds, 1986; Perkins, 1977; Schwartz, 1983) and speech-language pathologists note that speech sound errors are the most common type of communicative disorder. In fact, speech sound errors account for 50 to 80 percent of all communicative disorders (Fein, 1983).

What Do We Know About These Errors?

Any child may exhibit a combination of errors (distortions, substitutions, and omissions) across sounds or on any one sound. For example, a child may distort one pair of sounds, such as the "sh" and "zh," and exhibit substitution errors on another pair of sounds, such as "voiceless th" for "s" and "voiced th" for "z." For example, this child would distort "zh" in television, distort "sh" in she, say "bathket" for "basket," and say "thithorth" for "scissors." Yet another child may substitute "w" or the vowel in "would" for "l" in initial and medial positions, and may omit "l" in final positions and in blends (a blend consists of two or more consecutive consonants in the same syllable, such as *bl*end or *str*ipe), so that more than one type of error is produced for an individual sound. This child would say "wesson" instead of "lesson," say "sawad" for "salad," say "ba" for "ball," and "fashwight" for "flashlight."

Sometimes speech sound errors cause the meaning of the intended word to be changed, so that unless the listener can determine from the context what the intended word is, *intelligibility* (how easily listeners can understand what a speaker is saying) is decreased. Imagine a teacher's momentary confusion when, on the first day of school, a child announces, "My daddy is a coat." The child, who substitutes "t" for "ch," was really intending to say, "My daddy is a coach." A teacher may not fare much better in understanding a child who, out of the blue asks, "Do you see?" However, if this question was asked in the context of a discussion about the first big snowfall, a teacher would probably be quick to catch on to the fact that the question refers to skiing. Although the child could produce "s" correctly, she could not produce the "sk" blend in the word "ski." Another child may sound as if he is asking "Is this white?" when he means "Is this right?" A "w" for "r" substitution occurred in the initial position of the word "right." A teacher might respond "tear what" to a child complaining, "He won't tear," when really the child is trying to say "He won't share."

Intelligibility is affected by the type of error. Distortions are the most easily understood, followed by substitutions, and then omissions, which are considered the most immature sounding of these errors. Common substitutions, such as "voiceless th" for "s," "voiced th" for "z," "w" for "r," "w" for "l," and "f" or "t" for "voiceless th," are easier to understand than unusual substitutions, such as "l" for "r." For example, the statement "We glow loses" would be more difficult to understand than "We gwow woses" for "We grow roses."

The number of errors made is also related to intelligibility. Think about the child who has many such errors in speech. Such a child might say "Aah nie mama n I hah tuh geh my ih . . uh . a new aah . . ke . cau umbah . . ee tol huh ol one" for "Last night Mama and I had to get my sister a new jacket because somebody stole her old one" (periods are used to indicate a degree of prolongation of the preceding sound). A stranger, or someone who has no idea of what the child might be talking about, may find this communication unintelligible. Compare this to "At retheth today, can Tharah and I go outthide of the fenth to pick thome flowerth?" for "At recess today, can Sarah and I go outside of the fence to pick some flowers?" Even though there are many errors in this request, all errors are consistent substitutions occurring on "s" or "z" sounds. A stranger might have to listen closely but should be able to understand what the child is saying.

Children should be intelligible to strangers by the time they are three to four years old (Shriberg, 1980). That does not mean that they have no errors in their speech; it simply means that they can be understood fairly easily. In fact, it has been estimated (Pendergast, 1966) that one-fourth of the first grade population misarticulates one or more speech sounds. Teachers who work with younger children (preschoolers, kindergartners, and first graders) are the ones most likely to deal with children whose speech is sometimes unintelligible. Even parents report that they do not always understand what their child says. If listeners can contextually narrow a child's message by asking the child to point to what he or she is referring to, or by asking questions that can be answered with one word responses, they are more apt to be able to understand what the child is trying to say.

Traditionally, all speech sound errors were labeled as problems in articulation and were considered to be relatively simple (McReynolds, 1986). However, since the late 1970s research has demonstrated that speech sound errors are more complex than previously thought, thus causing changes in how errors are classified. New classifications include errors of articulation and errors of phonology. The reader will first be introduced to articulatory disorders and then to phonological disorders. Sections on assessment and treatment of both types of disorders will follow.

ARTICULATION

What Is Articulation?

Articulation refers to the actual movements of the speech organs that occur during the production of various speech sounds. Successful articulation requires (1) neurological integrity, (2) normal respiration, (3) normal action of the larynx (voice box or Adam's apple), (4) normal movement of the articulators, which include the tongue, teeth, hard palate, soft palate, lips, and mandible (lower jaw), and (5) adequate hearing.

When Should a Child No Longer Have Articulatory Errors?

In other words, by what age should a child achieve the accepted "adult" standard of articulation? Research has shown that there tends to be a natural developmental sequence to speech sound acquisition and that it is reasonable to expect different sounds to be produced correctly in a child's speech at different ages. Most researchers (Poole, 1934; Prather, Hedrick, & Kern, 1975; Sander, 1972; Smit, Hand, Freilinger, Bernthal, & Bird, 1990; Templin, 1957) have, in general, identified the same sounds as occurring early. The primary differences have been in the ages that are associated with the acquisition of each sound. Many of these differences have been related to how ages were calculated (e.g., the age when 75 percent of the children in a study had acquired the sound in all word positions versus the age when 50 percent of the children had acquired the sound in two out of the three word positions). Although several speech sound acquisition charts could be reported here, most school districts will use an acquisition chart that identifies the acquisition of sounds at later ages. Figure 2-1 (Sander, 1972) is presented as a "rule of thumb" or a guideline to consonant acquisition. For each sound, the solid bars in the Figure begin at the age at which 50 percent of the children correctly produced the sound in two out of three word positions (initial, medial, and final) and extend to the age at which 90 percent of the children correctly produced the sound in all three word positions. Many school districts will use an age somewhere near the upper limit of the bar (and may add a year for blends that contain that sound) as the age at which maturation will no longer be expected to play a role in a child's acquisition of a particular sound. A child would then be eligible to work in therapy on that sound. (Remember, though, that the IEP or IFSP committee makes the final decision.) You will notice that overall maturity for articulation may not be complete until a child is at least eight years old, which for many children corresponds to the third grade. Some school districts may administer prognostic tests to children under eight years of age before decisions are made regarding eligibility and need for therapy. These prognostic tests are intended to separate those children who cannot be expected to "outgrow" a problem from those who probably will. The latter problems may be called *maturational* or *developmental articulation errors*. A teacher should accept such errors as a normal part of childhood.

According to Shriberg (1980), vowel acquisition is normally expected by three to four years of age. The exception to this statement is when the stressed and unstressed "er" sounds (as in "hurt" and "letter") are classified as vowels, since these sounds will be acquired about the same time as the consonantal "r." Some authors (Ingram, 1976) prefer to discuss "er"

AGE

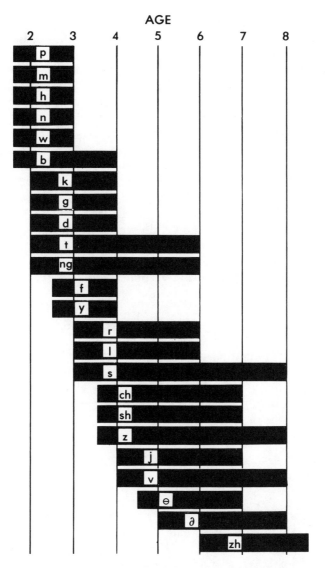

FIGURE 2-1. Average age estimates and upper age limits of customary consonant production. The solid bar corresponding to each sound starts at the median age of customary articulation; it stops at an age level at which 90 percent of all children are customarily producing the sound. From Sander, E. K. (1972). When are speech sounds learned? *Journal of Speech and Hearing Disorders, 37,* 62.

NOTE: ɵ is the international Phonetic Alphabet symbol for the voiceless "th" sound, while ∂ is the symbol for the voiced "th" sound.

sounds as syllabic consonants. The remaining vowels will not be discussed any further in this chapter, since the majority of children will have mastered them by school age. However, it should be noted that school-aged bilingual children and children with organic problems, such as cerebral palsy, cleft palate, and hearing impairments, may have difficulty articulating vowels as well as difficulty with consonants. This will be referred to again in appropriate chapters.

Teachers may be asked to use a consonant acquisition chart similar to the one presented as one guideline for determining how concerned they should be about a child's articulation and whether or not they should make a referral to a speech-language pathologist. For example, according to this chart, a child in second grade who continues to have articulation errors on the "l" sound should be referred to a speech-language pathologist. However, a kindergarten or first grade child who substitutes the "th" sounds for the "s" and "z" sounds would fall well within the maturational time span for these sounds. These errors would be considered typical for the age, and a teacher might rightfully choose not to refer this child to a speech-language pathologist for testing. However, a word of caution. Teachers should not rely on such a chart exclusively. For example, a six year old could correctly produce all sounds corresponding to his chronological age and could err on all other sounds which, upon examining the chart, means that some nine sounds might be misarticulated. Such a child would be expected to be difficult to understand at times, if not unintelligible. This child should be referred. In fact, any child who is difficult to understand should be referred to a speech-language pathologist, regardless of any guidelines to the contrary.

What Sounds Are School-Aged Children Most Apt to Have Difficulty With?

Speech-language pathologists working in schools indicate that the most frequently misarticulated sounds are "r" (including the syllabic consonant "er") and "s" (along with its cognate "z"). In fact, it has been reported that errors on the "r" and "s" sounds are the most common errors made in speech by both children and adults (Shriberg, 1980). Typical errors on "r" include substituting a "w" or the vowel in "would" for "r" and distorting the "r." Various substitutions, notably "voiceless th" for "s," "voiced th" for "z," and sometimes "t" for "s" and "d" for "z," occur along with distorted "s" and "z" sounds. The "voiceless th" and "voiced th" substitutions for "s" and "z" are frequently referred to as a *frontal lisp*. The term *lateral lisp* is sometimes used to refer to distorted "s," "z," "sh," and "zh" sounds. Producing this slushy sound can be approximated by attempting to say "s" while the tongue is in the position for a "l" sound

(Shriberg, 1980). Try it, and feel how air is emitted on either side of the tongue (laterally) rather than down the center of the tongue. Other commonly misarticulated sounds in the school-aged population include "l," "ch," "j as in jam," "sh," "voiced th," and "voiceless th." Young children who are unintelligible are also likely to exhibit errors on "k," "g," and "f."

Churchill, Hodson, Jones, and Novak (1988) found that children between the approximate ages of four and six with histories of recurrent otitis media during their first two years had a higher incidence of "s" errors than did children without histories of recurrent otitis media. They hypothesized that the "s" errors could be accounted for by early hearing loss associated with otitis media.

PHONOLOGY

Phonology is one component of language. It involves the study of speech sounds and the rule system for combining speech sounds into meaningful words. Children must perceive and produce speech sounds and acquire the rules of the language used in their environment. Some familiar rules involve permissible sequences of speech sounds. For example, in American English a blend of two consonants such as *s* and *t* is permissible at the beginning of a word but blending the two consonants *k* and *b* is not; *ng* is not produced at the beginning of words; and *w* is not produced at the end of words (words may end in the letter *w* but not the sound "w"). Marketing experts demonstrate their knowledge of phonology when they coin words for new products; product names chosen are recognizable to the public as rightful words. Slang also follows these rules. For example, consider the word "nerd." It is recognizable as an acceptably formed noun. Game lovers demonstrate such knowledge when they play hangman. Given a word where the next to the last letter is *r*, they know that some letter combinations, such as *rh* at the end of a word would not be logical; sequences, such as *ry*, *rn*, *rs*, or *re*, would be better guesses. Children acquire these underlying rules and principles as normal phonological development occurs.

As children experience normal phonological development, they may use certain processes which allow them to simplify adult forms of speech until they are capable of correct production. In other words, it is assumed that children naturally simplify adult forms that are difficult for them at that point in their development (Ingram, 1976; Schwartz, 1983). The terms *processes* or *phonological processes* have been coined to represent these simplifications (Edwards & Shriberg, 1983; Hodson, 1980; Ingram, 1976; Stoel-Gammon & Dunn, 1985). Each phonological process is applicable to several

sounds at the same time (McReynolds, 1986). Examples of common phonological processes include:

1. deletion of final consonant (e.g., "bat" becomes "ba__")
2. deletion of unstressed syllable (e.g., "about" becomes "__bout")
3. cluster (blend) reduction (e.g., "stove" becomes "__tove")
4. various types of assimilation, in which one sound in a word affects
   another sound (e.g., "dog" becomes "gog" as the last sound in the
   word affects the first sound)
5. fronting, in which sounds made in the back of the mouth are
   replaced by sounds made toward the front of the mouth (e.g.,
   "back" becomes "bat" as the front sound "t" replaces the back
   sound "k").

As children mature, these processes should disappear and be replaced
with the adult form of sound production. When such processes do not
disappear and continue past the time that they should be eliminated, a
child is said to have a phonological disorder. Haelsig and Madison (1986)
found that the greatest decrease in the use of phonological processes
occurred between three and four years of age. Interestingly, this coincides
with the age at which children are expected to be intelligible to strangers.

WHAT CAUSES ARTICULATORY OR
PHONOLOGICAL ERRORS TO OCCUR?

For young children, articulatory errors may represent a stage in the normal
development of speech. However, when certain milestones have passed
and a child continues to make certain errors, questions as to why should be
formulated and answers sought. *Etiology* refers to the study of causes.
Etiological factors can be considered to be either organic or functional.

Organic causes are ones that relate to structural or physiological
abnormalities. These are identifiable causes, such as hearing loss (see
Chapters 6 and 7), cleft palate (see Chapter 5), missing or malformed oral
structures, muscular problems such as paralysis or weakness, or neurological problems. These might be related to hereditary factors, factors that
occurred during pregnancy, birth trauma, accidents, or diseases. If possible, remediation will directly address the organic problem. For example,
surgery may correct a cleft palate. However, if an organic problem cannot
be corrected, therapeutic goals and procedures must take into account the
structural or physiological condition.

Causes are labeled *functional* when no apparent organic or physiological problem is present. Imitation of a poor speech model, little opportunity

to speak, and faulty learning fall into this category. Often the word "functional" acts like a wastebasket term when a cause is simply unknown. Most speech sound problems are functional in nature; that is, no cause can be found and a child does indeed respond to therapy, learning to produce "normal" speech.

In their search for causes, researchers have investigated a wide variety of factors. Following is a list of some of these factors and a brief statement about each (Bernthal & Bankson, 1981; McReynolds, 1986; Shriberg, 1980; Webster & Plante, 1992; Winitz, 1969).

- Intelligence. There appears to be little relationship between articulation and intelligence when intelligence falls within the normal range. However, children with intelligence quotients (IQs) below 70 will be more apt to have articulatory or phonological problems than those with IQs above 70. Therefore, special education teachers may expect a larger percentage of their children to exhibit speech sound errors and to possibly require speech therapy.
- Motor skills. There appears to be no causal relationship between motor skills and speech sound production.
- Auditory discrimination. There is evidence indicating that there is a relationship, although it may not be causal, between auditory discrimination (the ability to discriminate between speech sounds) and the ability to correctly produce speech sounds.
- Phonological awareness. Children who are moderately to severely unintelligible may have poorer phonological awareness abilities, e.g., awareness of language segments (number of words in a sentence, number of syllables in a word, and number of sounds in a word), than do children who are intelligible.
- Sex. Some studies have indicated that at certain ages, girls have better speech sound production than boys, but few of these differences have been statistically significant.
- Dentition, such as misaligned teeth. Overall, there appears to be no consistent relationship between dentition and poor sound production. Certain types of lisps may be associated with poor dentition, but children have a capacity for compensating for poor dentition. Loss of baby teeth does not seem to affect the production of sounds that have already been learned because compensatory movements are quickly and unconsciously learned.
- Oral structures. There does not seem to be a relationship between size and shape of the tongue, lips, or hard palate and speech sound production unless the abnormality is extreme. As with dentition, children appear to be able to compensate for differences.
- Socioeconomic status. Some studies have indicated that there may

be more children from lower socioeconomic levels with speech problems than there are from higher socioeconomic levels. However, it is possible that the findings have been confounded by the type of language stimulation and reinforcement received by these children.

- Personality. Within the broad range of normal psychological profiles, personality does not appear to have a causal relationship to speech sound production. However, there are some indications that children with severe speech sound disorders have more adjustment and behavioral problems than other children do.

In summary, causes generally are not readily found for speech sound errors. Therefore, they do not usually play an important role in therapy (McReynolds, 1986). However, as will be noted in the following section, causes continue to be searched for during an assessment in case a correctable cause does exist.

ASSESSMENT

What Happens During an Assessment?

If a child has failed a screening, the next step (with parental permission) is an individual diagnostic session. Such an assessment for speech sound errors might include (1) a case history, (2) an oral peripheral examination, (3) a hearing screening, (4) an articulation test, (5) a phonological assessment, (6) a conversational speech or oral reading sample, (7) a measure of auditory discrimination, and (8) a measure of stimulability. These measures may be assessed by standardized tests or by materials and/or local norms developed by the speech-language pathologist. A speech sample may be tape recorded for later analysis, particularly if abnormal phonological processes are suspected. Phonological analyses can be very time consuming and can be particularly difficult to score if more than one process occurs in the same word. Generally, they are only conducted when multiple speech sound errors are present. To save time, some speech-language pathologists will use a computer program to help analyze data.

Does It Really Make a Difference Whether a Problem Is One of Articulation or Phonology?

Yes, because therapeutic goals and procedures are different.

Then How Can Articulatory Disorders Be Differentiated from Phonological Disorders?

The information gathered during an assessment will be analyzed and a decision will be made as to whether a problem, if indeed a problem does exist, is articulatory or phonological in nature. It is not the purpose here to delve into details of such an analysis, but it should prove useful to discuss several general indicators (McReynolds, 1986; Schwartz, 1983; Shriberg, 1980):

1. Children with phonological disorders are more apt to make multiple sound errors (resulting in reduced intelligibility), whereas children with articulatory problems are more likely to err on only a few sounds.

2. Children who have phonological disorders are likely to misarticulate a given sound, and then produce that very sound in the process of misarticulating another sound. For example, a child may substitute a "voiceless th" for an "s," saying, "I have *th*ome *th*and in my shoe," for "I have some sand in my shoe," and then in the next sentence substitute an "s" for a "voiceless th" saying "I *th*topped *th*ucking my *s*umb," for "I stopped sucking my thumb." Children with phonological disorders may be capable of saying a particular sound, but they may not always know where to use the sound appropriately. In contrast, children with an articulatory problem may be able to produce the error sound correctly in one or two words, but will otherwise consistently misarticulate the sound.

3. The errors exhibited by children with phonological disorders generally fall into a pattern that is explained by the phonological process. For example, a child might consistently omit several sounds, such as the "t," "d," "k," "g," "s," and "z," in the final position of words (final consonant deletion) but produce them correctly in other positions. Such children demonstrate that they can motorically produce the correct sounds but they do not produce them in all of the proper places.

4. Children with phonological disorders are likely to have other language delays. (Remember that phonology is the sound component of language.) These other concomitant language delays will be discussed in Chapter 3.

Will a Child Outgrow a Problem?

There is no sure way of determining this. Nevertheless, an attempt is made to determine whether or not a problem exists for a particular child with regard to that child's chronological age (refer back to the sound acquisition chart) and cognitive status. If it is determined that errors are within normal limits, the child may be said to have maturational or developmental speech sound errors. Generally, the child will be retested at a later date(s) in order to provide documentation of any changes that occur in speech behavior. Sometimes this is called *tracking* (McDermott, 1985). If a problem does exist, then to comply with the law, an IEP or IFSP committee conference must be held and services must be provided within specified time limits. Some additional measures (even though there is some controversy surrounding these) that are frequently used to help determine how likely a child is to outgrow a problem include consistency of error and stimulability for the correct production.

A consistent articulatory error (i.e., the erred on sound is essentially always wrong) is less apt to be affected by maturational processes (outgrown) than is an inconsistent error. The fact that the error is inconsistent may signify that the sound is being acquired.

Auditory and visual clues may be used, along with specific directions, to test stimulability. For example, in order to stimulate a child to produce the "s" sound, the child may be directed to watch and listen carefully as the speech-language pathologist says the sound. The child is then asked to produce the sound. If the sound is still not correct, instructions, such as "place your tongue tip near the ridge behind your front teeth, loosely bite your back teeth together, and blow gently," may be given. A child who is not stimulable (i.e., with help still cannot produce a sound correctly) is less apt to acquire a sound without intervention than a child who is stimulable. However, if the child is stimulable, it is no guarantee that the sound will be acquired without therapy (Schwartz, 1983). On the other hand, stimulability can be an important prognosticator; if a child is stimulable and is enrolled in therapy, success and progress may be relatively rapid.

It is possible that the more problems children have in other developmental areas, such as motor, cognitive, and social areas, the less likely they are to "outgrow" speech sound errors (Shriberg, 1980).

TREATMENT

Articulation

What Is the Goal of Articulation Therapy?

The goal in articulation therapy is for a child to learn to motorically produce correct speech sounds in all speaking situations. In other words, a child must learn how to position and move the articulators to produce a sound. Therapy can be broadly conceptualized as having two subgoals: (1) the acquisition of (or the ability to produce) the correct sound and (2) the habituation of that correct sound in all contexts and speaking situations (sometimes referred to as *carryover* or *generalization* of the sound).

Some speech-language pathologists will add a third subgoal that can be referred to as *maintenance*. This refers to the time period after a child has been dismissed from therapy. In other words, some speech-language pathologists distinguish between the time that a child is habituating a sound(s) while still enrolled in therapy and the time that a child continues to habituate a sound(s) after dismissal from therapy. In the interest of simplification, only the two subgoals will be used in this book.

What Sound Should a Child Work on First?

If a child has more than one error sound, the speech-language pathologist will decide which sound to begin with by considering a number of factors that may include the following:

- The normal progression of speech sound development. This refers to the relationship between speech sound acquisition and age.
- The sounds used most frequently in children's speech. The more frequent an error is, the more noticeable it is.
- A sound that is important for personal reasons. The sounds in a child's name may be given preferential consideration. The parents or teacher may request that a particular sound be worked on in therapy.
- Visible sounds. Sounds that are more visible are easier to learn than sounds that are less visible.
- A sound that a child can produce correctly in at least one word. The speech-language pathologist may be able to use this word to stimulate correct production in other words.
- The sound that will contribute the most to increased intelligibility. This may be closely related to the frequency of occurrence of a sound in a child's speech, although type of error (omission, substitution, or distortion) may also be a factor.
- The sound for which quickest success is anticipated. This will relate to some of the above factors, primarily visibility of sound and ability to produce the sound in at least one word.
- Cognates. Pairs of sounds that differ only by the presence or absence of voicing will be worked on simultaneously. Frequently, as children learn to produce one sound of a pair correctly, they naturally become able to produce the other.

Just What Goes On in Therapy?

Traditional articulation therapy involves discrimination and production. Discrimination is the ability to differentiate (1) between different sounds and (2) between correct productions and distorted productions of sounds. Depending on the philosophy and training of the speech-language pathologist and the needs of the child, differing degrees of emphasis and time in therapy may be placed on discrimination tasks. Production refers to the ability to produce a sound either alone or in various contexts.

Therapy involves a gradual progression from less to more difficult and lengthy contexts, and can be divided into various stages including:

1. Isolation (all alone, with no other sound)
2. Syllables
3. Words (first one syllable words containing only one target sound, i.e., the sound to be corrected, then multisyllabic words and words containing more than one target sound; e.g., for the "s" sound, "soap" would be followed by "lesson" and "seesaw")
4. Phrases or short sentences containing only one word with the target sound (e.g., for the "s" sound, "I want some")
5. Longer sentences containing more than one word with the target sound (e.g., for the "s" sound, "Did you see the six new posters in Mrs. Brown's office?")
6. Reading
7. Structured conversation (the child is provided a topic to discuss)
8. Unstructured spontaneous conversation.

Following this sequence, a child would first learn to produce a sound all alone with no other sound, then progress to production of the sound in syllables, and so forth.

Teachers may hear a speech-language pathologist refer to the ability of a child to produce sounds in the initial (prevocalic), medial (intervocalic), or final (postvocalic) position (e.g., "ch" is in the initial position of "choose," the medial position of "teacher," and the final position of "which"). Most speech-language pathologists feel that, with the possible exception of "r" and "er," production is easiest in the initial position and hardest in the medial position. Thus, after production in isolation, they have a child attempt to produce a sound in syllables, first in the initial position, then in the final position, and last in the medial position. Some speech-language pathologists begin work on the production of "r" in the initial position and the syllabic consonant "er" in the final position.

There are a number of specific therapeutic approaches to articulation therapy. Most speech-language pathologists are eclectic, pulling from various therapeutic approaches the techniques they feel will work best for a particular child at a particular time.

Are Some Sounds Harder to Learn Than Others?

It certainly takes longer to teach some sounds than others. Part of the reason may lie in the amount of visual, tactile (sense of touch), and kinesthetic (sense of movement and posture) feedback that is present for a given sound. This may sound complicated, but consider the "voiceless th" and "r" sounds.

Frequently, the production of the "voiceless th" sound in isolation can be taught in just a few minutes with a mirror and the directions: "Watch me and listen to the way I say this sound." (Then say "voiceless th") "Now look in the mirror and you try it. Stick the tip of your tongue out between your teeth and blow gently."

On the other hand, say "er" and think about the instructions that could be given to a child who can not say the sound. The sound is not really visible, so watching the instructor or looking in the mirror will not help much. Say "er" and think about where your tongue is. Compared to the "voiceless th," placement is much more difficult to describe. Most of the tongue, including the tip, is not even touching another part of the mouth. To further confuse the issue, there are two possible tongue positions that will result in a correctly produced "er" sound and, generally, one of these is much easier for a child to use than the other. However, there is no way to know for sure which set of directions to start with for any one child.

Phonology

What Is the Goal When a Problem is One of Phonology?

Since many of a child's errors fall into one process, the goal of remediation is to eliminate that process. For example, the goal may be to eliminate the final consonant deletion process. Rather than the goal being to correct just one sound or a cognate pair of sounds, as it is in articulation therapy, the goal is for a child to correctly produce all of the sounds that are involved in a particular process.

Just What Goes on in Therapy?

To continue with this example, assume that a child deletes eight different sounds when they occur in the final position of words. Even though the goal is to eliminate the process of final consonant deletion, in therapy the child will not work on all eight sounds but a subgroup of these eight. The assumption is that the child will learn (1) that there is a rule that says that final consonants should not be omitted or, in effect, that final consonants are important, and (2) that this rule will generalize to the other consonants not directly included in the therapy lessons. This is presumed to be more efficient than working on each of the eight sounds separately.

One approach to this problem would be to use what is called *minimally contrastive words* or *minimal contrasts*. (A pair of such words might be called *minimal pairs*.) A list of such words could include "sea, seed, seal, seam, and seat." Therapy is set up so that in order to respond correctly, children must use the information contained in the final consonant. For example, children are rewarded when (1) they follow directions (e.g., when confronted with a group of pictures, they respond correctly to an instruction, such as "put the *(seal)* in your pile of cards") or (2) they speak plainly enough that the speech-language pathologist follows their directions (e.g., a child instructs the speech-language pathologist to "give me the *(seed)*"). Notice that work did not begin with the sound in isolation, as it usually does in articulation therapy, but began in a meaningful linguistic context. In this way, children use information about a correct sound in a language context and learn that there are consequences related to their language behavior. (Remember that phonology is one component of language.)

Work on discrimination as well as production may be necessary. Furthermore, therapeutic procedures for articulatory and phonological disorders are not necessarily incompatible. Both may be used simultaneously with a particular child. For example, some children may need instructions about how to produce a sound to be able to produce it correctly in a particular context (even though they produce it correctly in other contexts).

A child may demonstrate more than one phonological process in speech. If so, the speech-language pathologist will need to determine which ones, if any, might normally still be present for a particular child.

In determining this, ASHA (Cole, 1983) recommends that the speech-language pathologist consider not only guidelines or norms established from published research, which tends to use predominately white children as subjects, but also local norms which the speech-language pathologist has established. For example, Haynes & Moran (1989) found that rural black children in Alabama who spoke the Black English dialect of that region continued to use final consonant deletion in a normal manner beyond the time that would be expected for children speaking Standard American English. However, if there is more than one phonological process that should no longer be present, then decisions about which process to target first in therapy will need to be made. Several factors will be considered, including how frequently the process occurs in the child's speech, which ones interfere most with intelligibility, which ones should have been deleted first (i.e., the ones which reflect the most immaturity), and those which the child would have the quickest success eliminating. Sometimes therapy is planned so that two processes are targeted at the same time; half of the therapy session is spent working on one process and half on the other.

WHEN SHOULD CHILDREN BE DISMISSED FROM THERAPY?

To some degree this is a judgment call. A speech-language pathologist could wait until children made absolutely no errors before dismissing them from therapy. However, research has indicated that a child need not be performing at the 100 percent criterion in order to be dismissed. When children are dismissed while still making some errors, they generally continue to improve. This is certainly more time and cost efficient. However, whether a particular child should be dismissed when able to produce a sound correctly 80 percent, 90 percent, or 95 percent of the time, or some other percentage, has not been conclusively determined.

Toward the end of therapy, a speech-language pathologist may recommend that the number of sessions be decreased. After dismissal, the speech-language pathologist may continue to periodically (frequently up to a year) monitor a child for regressing or backsliding. This may be accomplished by talking to the child for a few minutes, by checking with the teacher or parents, or by unobtrusively listening to the child.

ARE THERE CHILDREN WHO SHOULD NOT BE IN THERAPY?

Sometimes a child who has been in therapy for several years but is no longer progressing seems "burned out," tired, and bored with therapy. The child may be very verbal in saying that he or she does not want to attend therapy or may consistently "forget" to show up. Such a child probably needs a break from therapy, and the IEP committee should consider giving the child a break. Therapy can always be reinitiated, and progress may once again be satisfactory.

There is also the occasional child who, after considerable time and the use of a variety of procedures, still shows no progress. Appropriate referrals that might discover a reason for the lack of progress should be considered. However, continuing a child in therapy when there is no reason to expect success is not ethical and serves no positive purpose.

HOW CAN A TEACHER HELP?

A teacher can be supportive of a child's efforts in therapy by:

1. encouraging a child to go to therapy and to be on time.
2. showing an interest in what a child is doing in therapy. This is

especially easy if a child has a speech therapy notebook that can be shared with the teacher.

3. not demanding (or even asking) that a child say a word correctly before the speech-language pathologist has told the teacher that the child is ready to produce the necessary sound(s) correctly. In other words, it takes time before success in therapy is translated into better speech in the classroom, and a teacher does not want to demand better speech before a child is capable of it.

4. recognizing that even after a child is capable of producing a sound in some contexts, the child may still be unable to produce it in other contexts. For example, just because a child can say a good "s" in the word "so" or even in the longer word "summer" does not mean that the child can say the "s" sounds in "mistakes," "Mississippi," or "scarce." Do not accuse a child of not trying unless you know from the speech-language pathologist that the child is capable of the task.

5. helping a child remember to use correct sounds during carryover. The teacher and speech-language pathologist should consult to determine exactly how this help should be rendered in the case of each child. Possibilities include just listening and praising a child for good speech, or an occasional unobtrusive signal when the teacher hears a child misarticulating. Under no circumstances, however, should the teacher attempt to correct a child everytime an error is made. For one thing, the teacher does not have the time to do this and, more importantly, the child may easily become embarrassed, frustrated, and self-conscious. This could result in the child talking less, which is certainly not a goal.

6. being aware of increased numbers of errors (blacksliding) after a child has been dismissed from therapy and contacting the speech-language pathologist who can follow-up on the problem.

7. accepting young children who have maturational or developmental speech sound errors. If prognostic tests indicate that the odds are with a child "growing out" of a problem, therapy would be superfluous. On the other hand, if a child does not outgrow a problem, some research indicates that the child may learn sounds more quickly in third or fourth grade than in earlier grades (Diedrich & Bangert, 1980).

IS THERE A RELATIONSHIP BETWEEN SPEECH SOUND ERRORS AND ACADEMIC SUBJECTS, SUCH AS READING AND SPELLING?

It makes sense to expect that a child who says "wain" for "rain" might also spell "rain" with a *w*. Considerable research time has been spent examining the relationships among reading, spelling, and articulation. However, the evidence is not clear. In our experience, such problems do not often exist for children with only a few articulatory errors. Teachers are encouraged not to expect such relationships but, on the other hand, not to allow themselves to overlook them if they do exist. However, there does seem to be some support for the expectation that a child with multiple speech sound errors and delayed phonological development may also have difficulty with other language-based tasks, such as learning to read and spell.

ARTICULATION, PHONOLOGY, DIALECTS, AND ENGLISH AS A SECOND LANGUAGE

The numbers of multicultural children are increasing, and is expected to continue beyond the year 2000 (Adler, 1990). In fact, a projection based on census data indicated that by 2000, one-third of all school-aged children will belong to an ethnic or racial minority (Cole & Taylor, 1990). Therefore, speech-language pathologists will continue to experience a real challenge in becoming knowledgeable about different dialects and foreign languages. However, their efforts are necessary so that children can be assessed based on the rules of their own dialect or language and not solely on the rules of Standard American English. Also, if children are in need of remediation, desire to learn Standard American English in addition to their own dialect, or are learning English as a second language (ESL), the speech-language pathologist needs to be able to compare and contrast the two dialects or languages to make learning easier for the child. The following examples will highlight some (but not all) of the common articulatory and phonological differences between Standard American English and Black English and between Standard American English and Spanish.

Black English may be characterized by:

- "d" substituted for "voiced th" at the beginnings of words, such as dem for them, and "d" or "v" substituted for "voiced th" in the middle or at the ends of words, such as mudder for mother
- "t" or "f" substituted for "voiceless th" especially in the middle and at the ends of words, such as toof for tooth
- "l" deleted in some contexts, such as hep for help
- unstressed initial syllables deleted, such as member for remember
- "r" weaker or deleted depending on the context, such as cah for car
- "b" substituted for "v," such as bery for very
- final consonants weakened
- "skr" substituted for "str," such as skreet for street
- gonna substituted for going to

Spanish is characterized by:

- five vowels and four diphthongs compared to 12 vowels and five diphthongs in English so errors on English vowels may occur
- an absence of final consonant clusters, such as st in last and lk in milk, so the final consonant cluster in English may be omitted or distorted
- a different *prosody* (the melody of speech perceived as stress and intonation) in which all vowels have the same length instead of vowel length being determined by syllable stress

Native Spanish speakers are most apt to make substitution or distortion errors on "ng," "j as in jam," "sh," "ch," "y as in yoyo," "voiced th," "voiceless th," and "v."

CASE HISTORIES

Jill

Jill, a third grader, had been enrolled in speech therapy for approximately four months. She had problems with the articulation of the "r," "s," and "z," sounds. The word "ride," for example, was spoken as "wide," "soup," as "thoup," and "zoo," as "thoo." Sounds were misarticulated consistently and in all positions. Jill was a bright girl and did excellent work in the classroom. She was well adjusted and accepted by her peers.

Jill was cooperative in speech therapy sessions, but there seemed to be almost no progress toward correcting the misarticulated sounds. Not until a second conference was held with the parents and teacher to review the IEP was it learned that correct articulation was being negatively reinforced. Specifically, it was learned that Jill's father and an older sibling had been imitating Jill's faulty articulation since she began to talk. For some reason they thought this was of no harm and rather "cute," as the mother expressed it.

Several weeks after the imitation of Jill's misarticulation ceased, Jill started to make good progress toward correcting her faulty sounds. At the end of the school year Jill actually had attained almost 100 percent mastery of the "r," "s," and "z," sounds in spontaneous speech.

John

John, a fourth grader, has had speech therapy for several years. The initial approach was an articulatory one. Progress was minimal. A reevaluation of John's problems when he moved to another state revealed that he sustained a phonological problem consisting of several processes, including cluster reduction, syllable reduction, and liquid and glide deviations.

A phonological approach to these problems has been highly rewarding as John has accomplished each successive task. It is too early to determine the length of time it may take before John can be considered for dismissal from therapy. However, John's general adjustment to the school environment has seemed to improve. He seems willing to volunteer more in classroom activities requiring speech. His teacher has been extremely helpful in reinforcing the progress that John and his speech-language pathologist have made in therapy sessions.

SUMMARY

Causes

- Faulty learning
- Hearing loss
- Brain damage
- Cleft palate
- Dental problems
- Neurological problems

Some Important Points to Remember

- A speech sound is called a phoneme and is the smallest segment of a word.
- IPA is the International Phonetic Alphabet and represents sounds.
- A diphthong is made when the articulators move from one vowel to another within the same syllable.
- There are approximately 17 vowel sounds.
- Some consonants are produced with voice and others without voice, as in "b," and "p."
- Children make several types of speech sound errors: distortions, substitutions, omissions, and additions.
- Speech sound errors account for 50 to 80 percent of all communication disorders.
- Speech sound errors can affect the intelligibility of the message.
- Some speech sound errors are consistent whereas some are inconsistent.
- There are articulatory errors and phonological errors.
- There is a natural developmental sequence in speech sound development.
- Commonly misarticulated sounds are "s," "z," "r," "l."
- Phonology involves the study of speech sounds and the rules for combining them.

- Assessment of a speech sound problem might involve a case history, an oral peripheral examination, a hearing screening, an articulation test, a phonological assessment, an auditory discrimination test, a stimulability test, and a conversational speech or reading sample.
- Phonological disorders are likely to be characterized by multiple sound production problems.
- There is no sure way of determining the extent to which a child will outgrow a sound production problem.
- Inconsistent errors are more likely to be outgrown than consistent ones.
- Stimulability is a good prognosticator of whether or not a child will outgrow a sound production problem.
- The more developmental problems a child has, the less likely he or she is to outgrow a speech problem.
- Consideration of several factors determine which sound or phonological process is worked on first in therapy.
- Articulation therapy progresses from shorter units, such as sounds, to longer units, such as sentences.
- The more severe the articulatory or phonological problem, the more likely the child will have difficulty with other language-based tasks, such as reading and writing.
- Some sounds are more difficult to learn than others; "r," for example, is more difficult than the voiceless "th."
- The aim of phonology therapy is to work on a sound process rather than to correct a particular sound.
- The speech-language pathologist must determine when intervention has brought about sufficiently correct production that warrants dismissal from therapy.
- The goals of articulation therapy are to produce correct sounds and to stabilize use of correct sounds in all speech.
- A speech-language pathologist must consider several factors in determining which sounds a child works on first, such as visibility of production, normal progression of sound development, most frequently used sounds, sounds most easily corrected, and sounds most likely to increase intelligibility.
- Therapy is tailored to individual needs.
- Phonological therapy utilizes linguistic contexts.

Do's

- Refer a child who is difficult to understand to a speech-language pathologist, regardless of the child's age.

- Work closely with the speech-language pathologist when working with a child with a speech sound problem.
- Attempt to reinforce in the classroom what a child has mastered in the therapy sessions.
- Cooperate fully with a speech-language pathologist when he or she wishes to recheck a child who has been in therapy.
- Encourage the child.

Don'ts
- Don't permit ridicule of a child with a speech sound problem.

Referral Resources

- Speech-language pathologist
- Audiologist

SELF-TEST

True or False

1. In this chapter IPA stands for the Independent Phonetic Alphabet. ____
2. A phoneme is a speech sound. ____
3. A diphthong is a sound that results from articulatory movement ____ from one vowel to another vowel within the same syllable.
4. When a child says "wed" for "red" the type of error made is one of ____ substitution.
5. Intelligibility of speech is not affected by disorders of articulation. ____
6. As many as one-fourth of all first graders may misarticulate one or ____ more speech sounds.
7. Maturational or developmental articulatory errors is a term that ____ refers to those speech sound errors which may be "outgrown."
8. Phonology is a component of language. ____
9. Phonological development is not rule-based. ____
10. Auditory discrimination has little or nothing to do with either articu- ____ latory or phonological problems.
11. Phonological disorders can be distinguished from articulatory dis- ____ orders.
12. An error of articulation that is consistent in the speech of a child is ____ less likely to be outgrown than an inconsistent error.
13. "Sea, seed, seal, seam, and seat" are examples of minimally con- ____ trastive words.
14. A child should not be dismissed from therapy until 100 percent of the ____ phonological or articulatory problems are corrected.
15. Children who speak English as a second language should be tested ____ in their native language as well as English.

REFERENCES

Adler, S. (1990). Multicultural clients: Implications for the SLP. *Language, Speech, and Hearing Services in Schools, 21,* 135–139.

Bernthal, J. E., & Bankson, N. W. (1981). *Articulation disorders.* Englewood Cliffs, NJ: Prentice-Hall.

Churchill, J. D., Hodson, B. W., Jones, B. W., & Novak, R. E. (1988). Phonological systems of speech-disordered clients with positive/negative histories of otitis media. *Language, Speech, and Hearing Services in Schools, 19,* 100–107.

Cole, L. (1983). Implications of the position on social dialects. *ASHA, 25* (9), 25–27.

Cole, P. A., & Taylor, O. L. (1990). Performance of working-class African-American children on three tests of articulation. *Language, Speech, and Hearing Services in Schools, 21,* 171–176.

Crowe Hall, B. J. (1991). Attitudes of fourth and sixth graders toward peers with mild articulation disorders. *Language, Speech, and Hearing Services in Schools, 22,* 334–340.

Diedrich, W. M., & Bangert, J. (1980). *Articulation learning.* San Diego: College-Hill.

Edwards, M. L., & Shriberg, L. D. (1983). *Phonology: Applications in communicative disorders.* San Diego: College-Hill.

Eisenson, J., & Ogilvie, M. (1977). *Speech correction in the schools* (4th ed.). New York: Macmillan.

Fein, E. J. (1983). The prevalence of speech and language impairment. *ASHA, 25,* 37.

Haelsig, P. C., & Madison, C. L. (1986). A study of phonological processes exhibited by 3-, 4-, and 5-year old children. *Language, Speech, and Hearing Services in Schools, 17,* 107–114.

Haynes, W. O., & Moran, M. (1989). A cross-sectional developmental study of final consonant production in southern black children from preschool through third grade. *Language, Speech, and Hearing Services in Schools, 20,* 400–406.

Hodson, B. W. (1980). *The assessment of phonological processes.* Danville, IL: Interstate Printers & Publishers.

Ingram, D. (1976). *Phonological disability in children.* London: Edward Arnold Publishers.

McDermott, L. (1985). Service alternatives. In *Caseload issues in schools* (pp. 18–24). Rockville, MD: American Speech-Language-Hearing Association.

McReynolds, L. V. (1986). Functional articulation disorders. In G. H. Shames, and E. H. Wiig (Eds.) (2nd ed.) *Human communication disorders* (pp. 139–182). Columbus, OH: Charles E. Merrill.

Mowrer, D. E., Wahl, P., and Doolan, S. J. (1978). Effect of lisping on audience evaluation of male speakers. *Journal of Speech and Hearing Disorders, 43,* 140–148.

Pendergast, K. (1966). Articulation study of 15,255 Seattle first-grade children with and without kindergarten. *Exceptional Child, 32,* 541–547.

Perkins, W. H. (1977). *Speech pathology: An applied behavioral science.* St. Louis: The C.V. Mosby Co.

Perrin, E. H. (1954). The social position of the speech defective child. *Journal of Speech and Hearing Disorders, 19,* 250–252.

Poole, I. (1934). Genetic development of articulation of consonant sounds in speech. *Elementary English Review, 11,* 159–161.

Prather, E., Hedrick, D., and Kern, C. (1975). Articulation development in children aged two to four years. *Journal of Speech and Hearing Research, 40,* 179–191.

Sander, E. (1972). When are speech sounds learned? *Journal of Speech and Hearing Disorders, 37,* 55–63.

Schwartz, R. G. (1983). Diagnosis of speech sound disorders in children. In I. J. Meitus and B. Weinberg (Eds.) *Diagnosis in speech-language pathology* (pp. 113–149). Baltimore: University Park Press.

Shriberg, L. D. (1980). Developmental phonological disorders. In T. J. Hixon, L. D. Shriberg, and J. H. Saxman (Eds.) *Introduction to communication disorders* (pp. 263–309). Englewood Cliffs, NJ: Prentice-Hall.

Silverman, E. (1976). Listeners' impressions of speakers with lateral lisps. *Journal of Speech and Hearing Disorders, 41,* 547–552.

Silverman, F. (1986). Documenting the impact of a mild dysarthria on peer perception (Letter to the editor). *Language, Speech, and Hearing Services in Schools, 17,* 143.

Silverman, F. H., & Falk, S. M. (1992). Attitudes of teenagers toward peers who have a single articulation error. *Language, Speech, and Hearing Services in Schools, 23,* 187–188.

Silverman, F. H., & Paulus, P. G. (1989). Peer reactions to teenagers who substitute /w/ for /r/. *Language, Speech, and Hearing Services in Schools, 20,* 219–221.

Smit, A. B., Hand, L., Freilinger, J. J., Bernthal, J. E., & Bird, A. (1990). The Iowa articulation norms project and its Nebraska replication. *Journal of Speech and Hearing Disorders, 55,* 779–798.

Stoel-Gammon, C., and Dunn, C. (1985). *Normal and disordered phonology in children.* Baltimore: University Park Press.

Templin, M. (1957). *Certain language skills in children: Their development and interrelationships.* The Institute of Child Welfare, Monograph 26. Westport, CT: Greenwood Press.

Van Riper, C., & Emerick, L. (1984). *Speech correction: An introduction to speech pathology and audiology.* Englewood Cliffs, NJ: Prentice-Hall.

Webster, P. E., & Plante, A. S. (1992). Effects of phonological impairment on word, syllable, and phoneme segmentation and reading. *Language, Speech, and Hearing Services in Schools, 23,* 176–182.

Winitz, H. (1969). *Articulatory acquisition and behavior.* Englewood Cliffs, NJ: Prentice-Hall.

3

LANGUAGE DISABILITIES

A variety of terms have been used as labels for children having difficulty with language, including *language impairment, language difference, language delay, language disorder, learning disability* (LD), *language-learning disability* (LLD), *language deviance, language disability,* and *language-reading disorders.* Some authors draw distinctions among these terms, but generally the terms are used synonymously (Newhoff & Leonard, 1983). Teachers will need to become familiar with the terms that are used in their own school districts. In this chapter the terms *language disabled* and *language disabilities* will be used.

Children and youth who have educational difficulties with language (language disabilities) fall under the broader term *learning disabled.* The field of learning disabilities is broad, encompassing more controversy among its authorities than any other field of special education. Thirty-eight definitions and ninety-nine different characteristics of learning disabled children have been enunciated (Cartwright, Cartwright, & Ward, 1985). In defining specific learning disabilities, The Education for All Handicapped Children Act of 1975 (PL 94-142) states: "Children with specific learning disabilities exhibit a disorder in one or more of the basic psychological processes involved in understanding or using spoken or written language. These may be manifested in writing, spelling, or arithmetic. They include conditions which have been referred to as perceptual handicaps, brain injury, brain dysfunction, dyslexia, developmental aphasia, etc. They do not include learning problems which are due primarily to visual, hearing, or motor handicaps, to mental retardation, or to environmental disadvantage" (United States Office of Education, 1977, p. 42478).

In this definition, certain children are excluded from having learning disabilities. For obvious reasons, children who are hearing impaired, visually impaired, mentally retarded, or motorically impaired, or who are reared in a linguistically deprived environment cannot be expected to develop language skills in a normal manner. Even though there is a high probability these children will have problems with language, the term *learning disabilities* cannot be used to categorize these children according to PL 94-142. Such an exclusion is required by state and federal laws for allocation of funding. Nevertheless, some authorities in the field of learning disabilities object to this exclusion, because the implication is that a child does not exhibit learning disabilities along with another disability. They feel that disabled children, such as those with hearing impairments or visual impairments, may be multiply-handicapped and therefore may also be learning disabled. In response to this concern, the National Joint Committee for Learning Disabilities (NJCLD), composed of members of the American Speech-Language-Hearing Association, the Association for Children and Adults with Learning Disabilities, the Council for Learning Disabilities, the Division for Children with Communication Disorders, the International Reading Association, and the Orton Dyslexia Society, recommended use of the following definition: "Learning disabilities is a generic term that refers to a heterogeneous group of disorders manifested by significant difficulties in the acquisition and use of listening, speaking, reading, writing, reasoning, or mathematical abilities. These disorders are intrinsic to the individual and presumed to be due to central nervous dysfunction. Even though a learning disability may occur concomitantly with other handicapping conditions (e.g., sensory impairment, mental retardation, social and emotional disturbance) or environmental influences (e.g., cultural differences, insufficient/inappropriate instruction, psychogenic factors), it is not the direct result of those conditions or influences" (Hammill, Leigh, McNutt, & Larsen, 1981, p. 336).

This definition also mentions emotional disturbances. Some definitions of learning disabilities (e.g., Hallahan & Kauffman, 1976) state that the language problems of those with emotional disturbances do not fall under the umbrella of learning disabilities. To reiterate, the NJCLD contends that children can present multiple handicaps that could conceivably combine an emotional disturbance (or hearing impairment, visual impairment, etc.) with a learning disability. However, on a practical level, it might be difficult to ascertain with confidence which characteristics and behaviors are due to which problems.

The NJCLD definition addresses the issue of the heterogeneity of the learning disabled population. This cannot be overemphasized. Although some problems are common among many learning disabled children and youth, each child will display a unique pattern of difficulty.

JUST WHAT IS THE RELATIONSHIP BETWEEN LEARNING DISABILITIES AND LANGUAGE DISABILITIES?

The answer to this question is clouded with confusion. One review of the literature (Wiig & Semel, 1984) identified at least three independent clusters or syndromes of learning disabilities. The largest group comprises 1.5 to 2 percent of the school-age population and approximately 40 to 60 percent of all learning disabilities. The children within this group have difficulty with language or, more precisely, with language comprehension and expression, word-finding, and speech discrimination. The next largest group, approximately 10 to 40 percent of the learning disabled, exhibits difficulties with articulatory and graphomotor dyscoordination. These children present problems with articulation, writing, and drawing. The smallest group includes 5 to 15 percent of the learning disabled population and involves visuospatial perceptual deficits. Children in this group exhibit difficulties with visual discrimination and visual memory. Combinations of the language group with each of the other two groups have also been reported.

Another writer (Mercer, 1979) identified six clusters within which learning disabled children may have their primary difficulties: academic learning difficulties, language disorders, motor disorders, social-emotional problems, perceptual disorders, and memory problems.

Authorities vary in their opinions about the number and focus of the domains that constitute learning disabilities; however, most agree that language is one domain or subset of the larger problem. Thus, language disabilities fall under the general classification of learning disabilities, but not all learning disabled students have language disabilities.

HOW MANY CHILDREN HAVE DIFFICULTY WITH LANGUAGE?

This is a good question for which there is no definitive answer, partly because there is no universally accepted definition of language disorder and partly because assessment methods and the criteria for categorizing children vary so widely. Some authors appear to include all children with language problems in their estimates while others appear only to talk about children with learning disabilities who have a language problem. Estimates of the learning disabled school-age population range from 1 to 30 percent (Wiig & Semel, 1984) while estimates of the language disabled school-age population range from 3 to 15 percent (Simon, 1985). The United States Office of Education (1979) estimates that 3 percent of the school-age population exhibit specific learning disabilities that are serious enough to be differentiated from other classifications.

Teachers and parents are often perplexed to find that a student will qualify for one set of services in one school district but would qualify for a different set of services in another school district. The child is the same, but the criteria for available services are different. Regardless of the prevalence figures used, regular classroom teachers can expect to have language disabled students in their classrooms.

WHAT CAUSES LANGUAGE DISABILITIES?

The factors, such as mental retardation and hearing impairment, mentioned as exclusions from the definition of learning disabilities can cause language problems. But what causes specific language problems that are a part of learning disabilities? The reader will note that the NJCLD definition addressed this question, stating that learning disabilities are "presumed to be due to central nervous dysfunction" (Hammill et al., 1981, p. 336). Central nervous system dysfunctions may be related to neurological or physiological factors, maturational and developmental lags, or genetic and hereditary factors (Wiig & Semel, 1984). Such dysfunctions have been variously labeled *childhood or developmental aphasia, agnosia, apraxia, minimal brain dysfunction, brain injury,* and *learning disabilities.* However, these terms have been defined in different ways by different writers. Unless they are defined each time they are used, misunderstandings tend to occur. In terms of remediation, classifications based upon causation have not proven to be useful because language characteristics and behaviors within a single causative grouping may vary among children. At the same time, language characteristics and behaviors across causative groupings may prove to be very similar (Leonard, 1986; Naremore, 1980; Newhoff & Leonard, 1983). At this point in medical science, determining causes with confidence is generally not possible, and providing remediation based on causation may not yield satisfactory results. A more viable option is to describe each child's language system and then to use this description to develop remediation goals and procedures.

WHAT IS LANGUAGE?

A Definition

Most people know what language is and can talk about it. Yet it might be difficult for them to give a succinct and complete definition. To some extent, the definition will depend on what one's special interest in language is. Some people compare and contrast languages, others study the history of words, and others study the dialects of a particular language. Since the purpose of reading this book is to learn about the language disabilities that school-age children and youth exhibit, it is necessary to focus on the components (or parameters or dimensions) of language.

The definition of language proposed by the American Speech-Language-Hearing Association (ASHA) helps identify these components of language. The definition states

> Language is a complex and dynamic system of conventional symbols that is used in various modes for thought and communication. Contemporary views of human language hold that:
> • language evolves within specific historical, social, and cultural contexts
> • language, as rule governed behavior, is described by at least five parameters—phonologic, morphologic, syntactic, semantic, and pragmatic
> • language learning and use are determined by the interaction of biological, cognitive, psychosocial, and environmental factors
> • effective use of language for communication requires a broad understanding of human interaction including such associated factors as nonverbal cues, motivation, and sociocultural roles. (ASHA, 1983, p. 44)

You should particularly note the five parameters. The phonologic parameter (speech sounds and speech sound sequences) was discussed in Chapter 2. The other four will be explored in this chapter. Although the terms *form, content,* and *use* coined by Bloom and Lahey (1978) will not be emphasized in this book, readers should be familiar with them because they are often referred to. Form includes phonology, morphology, and syntax. Content includes semantics, and use refers to pragmatics.

Semantics

Semantics deals with the meanings of words (including multiple meanings) and word combinations. The words that we know make up our vocabularies (or lexicons). Words can be thought of as a special code that provides us with a way of labeling things, ideas, and concepts. Each language has its own specific words (labels) that are associated with each possible thing, idea, or concept. We cannot adequately communicate without the labels of common meaning that words provide.

Beginning first graders should have a vocabulary of approximately 2,500 words (Newhoff & Leonard, 1983; Wiig & Semel, 1984). As they progress through elementary school, their ability to differentiate fine meanings between words (e.g., love, affection, fondness, and adoration); to comprehend and classify words based on spatial, temporal, familial, disjunctive, and logical relationships (Owens, 1984); and to comprehend abstract words which can not be perceived by the senses, such as pride, honor, and grief, increases. Children begin to learn modals (can, could, may, might, will, would, shall, and should) around age one and continue to refine their learning of these words until at least eight years of age (Bliss, 1987). Word definitions that are context bound (i.e., tied to a particular sentence) become more abstract (more like a dictionary definition that is not tied to a particular sentence). During their school years, and in particular, adolescence, children also increase their ability to understand and to use figurative language (Nippold, 1993; Owens, 1984), that is, the creative use of words that make up puns, idioms, similes, metaphors, proverbs or sayings, sarcasm, and sometimes the punch lines of jokes.

Syntax

Not all languages rely heavily on word ordering to relay meaning, but the English language does (Tager-Flusberg, 1985). The word *syntax* is used to refer to the ordering of words in such a way that they can be understood. Grammatical rules tell us what the appropriate word orderings are for our intended meaning. The sentence "Jennifer visited Susie" does not carry the same meaning as "Susie visited Jennifer" because of the word ordering. Similarly, the words "Mouse the played catnip cat the with" carry no meaning in that particular order, but they are meaningful if rearranged into "The cat played with the catnip mouse."

Rules also tell us how to transform one sentence construction into another so that compound sentences, negatives, questions, passives, imperatives, and sentences with embedded clauses can be produced. As children advance through school, they learn to understand and to produce more complex sentences. For example, children do not fully understand the passive voice until approximately 11 to 13 years of age (Horgan, 1978). During adolescence, small but significant changes also occur in the length of both oral and written sentences with the increased use of (1) subordinate phrases and clauses and (2) cohesive conjunctions, such as although, anyway, moreover, furthermore, and therefore (Nippold, 1993).

Morphology

Morphology is one aspect of syntax. Some authors only enumerate four dimensions of language (semantics, syntax, pragmatics, and phonology), subsuming morphology under syntax.

Morphology deals with the prefixes and suffixes that are added to words in order to change meaning. Examples include: plurals to indicate number ("chair" versus "chairs"), verb tenses to express time ("laugh" versus "laughed"), markers to indicate possession ("girl" versus "girl's"), -er and -est to indicate comparative and superlative adjectives ("pretty" versus "prettier" versus "prettiest"), and markers to change one part of speech to another (as from an adjective to a noun, i.e., "lonely" to "loneliness"). These prefixes and suffixes are referred to as *affixes* or *inflections* by some authors. The resulting words containing affixes are referred to as *inflectional forms*.

A morpheme is the smallest unit of meaning in a language. There are both bound and free morphemes. A free morpheme may be used alone, whereas a bound morpheme must be attached to a free morpheme in order to have meaning. All words are composed of at least one free morpheme; other words may have one or more bound morphemes attached to the free morpheme. For example, the word "friend" is composed of one free morpheme that has meaning. One or more bound morphemes may be added, making "friendly," "unfriendly," "friendless," "friendliness," "friendship," and "friendlier." There are rules for combining morphemes into words that must be followed (e.g., "disfriend" is not an allowable word and thus has no meaning).

Pragmatics

Pragmatics refers to the use of language in a social context for a particular purpose. The emphasis on pragmatics has been relatively recent in comparison to other components of language. However, its importance should not be underestimated, especially for school-age children. In fact, pragmatics has been called the area of most important language growth during both the school-age and adult years (Owens, 1984).

In order to maximally use language, children must learn how to initiate a conversation, take turns in conversation, maintain a conversational topic, change conversational topics, and close a conversation. Additionally, they must learn how to address different people by modifying their language. For example, research has shown that children as young as four years of age simplify their language when talking to younger children. Learning how to talk in different situations is also important. For example, children would demonstrate knowledge of pragmatics if their language use differed when talking informally to the principal at a football game versus talking to the principal when being disciplined. Language may be used to request, inform, comment, warn, threaten, and promise (Newhoff & Leonard, 1983). Children must learn to phrase all of these uses politely and tactfully. One form of polite construction is the indirect request in which speakers pursue what they want in a roundabout manner. Children may comment, "That sure looks like fun" to someone playing with a videogame, as a hint to the other child to offer them a turn. Indirect requests are first learned in the preschool years (Owens, 1984) and continue to be refined in later years.

Another important pragmatic aspect of language is the ability of children to use language to gain entry into and maintain their position in a peer group. They do so by their ability to use current slang expressions and to employ other strategies to get along with their peers (Nippold, 1993). The slang expressions used differ by gender. Girls are more knowledgeable about slang expressions which refer to clothes and unpopular people, while boys tend to know more expressions for vehicles and money (Nippold, 1993).

Other Terms Relating to Language

Communicative competence refers to one's knowledge of all the dimensions of language. It cannot be assessed directly; instead, inferences are made by observing a child's ability to use language receptively and expressively.

Metalinguistic ability refers to one's ability to think about language. It enables one to decide whether a message is acceptable or successful in its intent.

ASSESSMENT

Deciding if a particular child's language problem requires remediation is not always easy. As with all task performance, variability occurs across "normal" children and within the same "normal" child. In other words, there is a wide range of behaviors that can be considered "normal." Each school district will have criteria that help to make this decision. One problem that arises is that criteria vary from school district to school district.

There are also personal characteristics that affect language. When making referrals and when choosing and interpreting diagnostic procedures, a speech-language pathologist and other concerned school personnel should be careful to consider the effects of the following factors on language:

- Bilingualism. Just as not all languages contain the same speech sounds, not all languages follow the same rules. (See also Chapter 8.)
- Use of nonstandard English dialects. Dialects, such as Black En-

glish, Southern White Nonstandard English, and Appalachian, follow many of the rules of Standard American English but also have some different rules (Labov, 1972). Not all students will want to forsake their dialect for Standard American English. Particularly they may want to continue to use their native dialect with their families and in the communities where they were reared. However, for personal, occupational or professional reasons, some will also want or need to learn Standard American English and become bidialectical. Note that these dialects are referred to as nonstandard and not substandard. Many consider these dialects to be just as "good" as Standard American English. Realistically, however, judgments in many occupations or professions and situations are based on Standard American English.

As was done with articulation and phonology, a few characteristics of these dialects will be highlighted. First, in Black English the following might be noted:
- copula deletion in sentences, such as the paper on the couch for the paper is on the couch
- use of "is" with all persons and numbers in the present tense, such as I is; you (singular) is; he, she, or it is; we is; you (plural) is; they is
- deletion of the plural marker, such as two coat for two coats
- addition of a plural marker, such as childrens for children or that mines
- use of hisself for the reflexive pronoun himself
- use of multiple negatives, such as I don't never want no dog. (number of negatives may indicate strength of negation)
- use of objective pronouns as subjects, such as him for he
- deletion of possessive marker, such as Mary cookie for Mary's cookie

In Southern White Nonstandard English, the following characteristics are common:
- double modals, such as I might could be fixing to
- deletion of relative pronouns, such as the dog bit me for the dog that bit me
- use of double negatives
- use of objective pronouns as subjects, such as him for he

Some characteristics in the Appalachian dialect include:
- double modals
- deletion of relative pronouns
- use of hisself for the reflexive pronoun himself
- addition of a plural marker
- use of his'n for his

- Ethnic background. How an adult approaches a child may affect a child's performance. For example, black and Hispanic children tend to score better when they are familiar with the tester. Therefore, the tester should engage in informal play with a younger child and in verbal interaction with an older one before beginning to test (Adler, 1990).
- Socioeconomic status (SES). Parental education, occupational status, and income are closely associated with socioeconomic status. Because these factors are reflected in language, they must be considered in evaluating a child's linguistic functioning.

Assessment is initiated either through routine screening procedures or through referrals. On a referral form and/or behavior checklist, a teacher will have alerted the speech-language pathologist to any particular areas of language that are causing a child academic or social difficulties. Particular attention in assessment can then be given these areas.

Screening

It has been suggested that every child entering elementary school be screened for language disabilities. Others who should be screened include children who have been referred for possible language problems; children at risk for language problems; children who are having difficulty learning to read, spell, and write; and children who are at critical educational transitions, such as those moving from elementary school to junior high or moving from junior high to high school (Wiig & Semel, 1984).

Diagnosis

What children can do and what they cannot do are both important; assumptions should not be made about either. The purpose of a diagnosis is to describe a child's language status and, if a problem does exist, to determine goals and potential remedial procedures for reaching those goals.

Standardized norm-referenced tests or informal testing procedures, or both, may be used in a diagnostic assessment. In addition to language, some standardized tests also examine memory, the ability to sequence, and auditory processing (the ability to understand oral language in the absence of a peripheral hearing loss; also called *central auditory processing*, it takes place in the brain). However, the way in which these abilities are related to language is still controversial (Newhoff & Leonard, 1983). One informal testing procedure is the spontaneous language sample, which is probably the "most useful approach to examination of older children" (Newhoff &

Leonard, 1983). A language sample involves recording the language that a child uses in a particular situation. The situation should be arranged so that a representative sample can be obtained. For example, if the goal were to obtain the best language performance that a child was capable of in an informal play situation, then the child should be relaxed and comfortable. (Labov, 1972, has recommended that because less privileged children may feel threatened in a formal diagnostic situation with an unfamiliar adult, even if a play situation is being simulated, a more informal situation, perhaps on the floor with at least one other peer, would create a situation in which such children would talk more freely.)

Sometimes a child may be able to help isolate difficulties if questions focusing on each dimension of language are asked. For example, when probing for problems in the area of semantics, a speech-language pathologist might ask children if they notice whether they have difficulty thinking of the right word to use (Wiig & Semel, 1984). It should be noted that in an assessment, it is not always a simple matter to separate the components of language (Newhoff & Leonard, 1983).

The language assessment is certainly not complete without information regarding a child's cognitive status. The school psychologist and a child's teacher would have valuable input in this area. Researchers disagree on the exact relationship between cognition and language, but they do agree that there is a relationship. Two predominant viewpoints include (1) the cognition hypothesis, which states that cognitive ability is a prerequisite for language development, and (2) the correlational hypothesis, which states that linguistic and cognitive development depend on common maturational factors (Newhoff & Leonard, 1983). Piaget's work is often cited when language and cognition are discussed together.

A hearing evaluation should also be conducted on all children suspected of having language disabilities since hearing losses may affect language comprehension and production.

WHAT ARE THE CHARACTERISTICS OF A LANGUAGE DISABILITY?

The range of severity in language disabilities varies from mild to severe. Teachers will recognize that some children entering kindergarten are in need of help, whereas other children, due to the subtleties of their problems, may not be identified as language disabled until upper elementary, junior high, or even high school. School systems should adopt screening policies and procedures, and teachers, counselors, and other school personnel should learn to recognize subtle as well as obvious characteristics of language disabilities. Subtle problems may only be obvious when children meet with difficult situations, such as with difficult academic materials. Sometimes problems seem to wane before becoming noticeable once again (Wiig, 1986).

Kindergartners with more obvious problems may not be able to follow oral directions, count correctly, name the days of the week, match sounds to letters, or sit still long enough to participate in learning experiences. Such children may be called slow, inattentive, impulsive, or obstinate (Wiig, 1986). As language concepts build on each other throughout the school years, these children may lag further and further behind. For example, children who do not grasp the concepts of "more" and "less" in a language arts workbook are apt to have more difficulty than their peers when introduced to "greater than" and "less than" in mathematics. As children pass from grade to grade, instruction becomes more abstract, with fewer instances involving manipulative items and providing concrete experiences. For example, mathematics lessons in the lower grades frequently involve manipulative tasks or pictures of items that can be checked off with a pencil as a child counts them. In the middle elementary grades, these experiences become fewer and fewer, requiring that a child deal with more abstractions.

The remainder of this section will deal with typical problems that are associated with each of the dimensions of language. Remember that language behaviors are not always handily categorized into one of the dimensions and that the behaviors discussed are just some of the typical ones. As a teacher, you will need to further explore language disabilities. We urge you to consider taking courses in learning disabilities and language disabilities, and to learn independently from the books listed in the suggested readings at the end of this chapter.

Semantics and the Language Disabled School-Age Population

Children with language disabilities have smaller vocabularies and use fewer words to express themselves in comparison to their peers. This may mean that they communicate fewer concepts, and what they do communicate, they may communicate less effectively. Word finding or word retrieval problems are common. Even when a child has demonstrated the ability to use a word, he or she may have difficulty recalling it in a practical situation and, instead, may substitute nonspecific words or phrases, such as "stuff," "things," or "you know," for the appropriate word. Older children may substitute a definition of a word for the word itself (e.g., "the thing that you move to get water" for "faucet") or substitute a similar sounding word (e.g., "mural" for "moral"). The fillers that we all use, such as "uh," "um," and "okay," may be used with more frequency. Word and phrase repetitions may also be more prevalent.

When asked to define words, children with language disabilities are apt to use functional definitions, such as "an apple is something that you can eat"; to change the subject; or to use fillers and word repetitions. Such children may also have difficulty understanding words since they have a smaller receptive vocabulary.

Words with multiple meanings typically prove to be perplexing problems that are compounded when the multiple meanings involve more than one part of speech. For example, a child may have difficulty expanding his meaning of the noun "family" to include not only the basic unit in society, but also a family of related plants or animals, a unit of a crime syndicate, and the first family of the United States. However, a word that can be used as different parts of speech, such as a noun or verb, is even more confusing. For example, every child is familiar with the four-legged barking creature that we call a "dog." However, to expand the meaning of the word "dog" and to understand it in the contexts of "you lucky dog," "don't dog my every step," "dog in the manger," "go to the dogs," "put on the dog," "he's a dog," or "my dogs are killing me," may simply not be possible for the language disabled child without a good deal of help. Other examples should come to mind. Most people would probably agree that the word "draw" is a fairly simple word, but *Webster's Beginning Dictionary* (1980), written for students in the elementary grades, lists 16 definitions of the word "draw" as a verb and four as a noun, for a total of 20 different definitions. Moreover, there are the phrases "draw on," "draw out," "draw up," "draw aside," "draw forth," "draw in," "draw near," "draw back," and "draw the line." Not such a simple word after all. In the same dictionary, "set" has 14 definitions as a verb, four as an adjective, and seven as a noun. One of these definitions, "a collection of mathematical elements," will certainly be important for comprehension in mathematics. Some difficulties with sentence comprehension may be due to choosing the wrong definitions for some of the words within a sentence.

Wiig (1986) noted that children with language disabilities had "difficulties interpreting prepositional phrases of location (at), direction (through), or time (before, after)" (p. 345) and difficulties "interpreting sentences with cause-effect or conditional (when . . . then, if . . . then) relationships and those with conjunction of clauses" (p. 346). For example, "we had dinner after we went to the movies" would typically be misinterpreted to mean that dinner occurred first, followed by the movies. She also noted that language disabled children had problems "interpreting sentences with terms of inclusion, such as many, some, or several, or of exclusion, such as none, neither . . . nor, or combinations of these (all . . . except)" (p. 346).

The problems are varied and wide in scope. Children with language disabilities may exhibit trouble with synonyms and antonyms, demonstrative pronouns (this, that, these, and those), correct use of personal pronouns ("her did it"), word endings, verb tenses (and maintaining uniformity of tense throughout the communication), adjectives that provide information about spatial relationships (e.g., "near" and "far"), and forms of the copula "to be." Bracken (1988) did an interesting study of 49 opposite pairs and found that in approximately 70 percent of the opposite pairs the positive pole was learned before the negative pole. The positive pole either represented "more" of the concept quality, for example, "big" versus "little," or contained the root word of the concept, as in "male" and "female." Based on the findings, he advised in general that instruction begin with the positive pole whether working with a concept of just two polar opposites or with a continuum, such as all, most, several, few, and none. Exceptions to this rule included on–off, in front of–behind, large–small, thick–thin, all–none, early–late, always–never, over–under, forward–backward, rising–falling, healthy–sick, into–out, male–female, and arriving–leaving.

Young elementary children have fun with words, having "opposite days" when saying to someone "I hate you" means "I like you." Older children develop their own slang. At neither age are language disabled children able to understand and appropriately use what to them must seem a strange and confusing vocabulary. This causes their peers to laugh at and ostracize them from the group or, at the very least, to ignore them.

Figurative language refers to the creative use of language. Understanding figurative language in the forms of idioms, proverbs, metaphors, similes, sarcasm or jokes may be especially difficult for language disabled children. Generally, they have difficulty not only recognizing that figurative language should not be interpreted literally but also interpreting it (Seidenberg & Bernstein, 1986). To get a sense of the difficulties that these children encounter, consider the following handful of idioms and think about the difficulty that a child would have making sense of whatever context he found them in if he chose the literal interpretation:

- raining cats and dogs
- toe the line
- all thumbs
- butterflies in your stomach
- hit the roof
- burn one's fingers
- read between the lines
- black list
- watched pot never boils
- puppy love
- and, kick the bucket.

Now consider this scenario which was overheard during a carpool of four sixth and seventh graders. "Amy" and "Josh" had been fussing at each other, and finally, Amy burst out with "You're not being nice; you just don't like me." Josh responded, "I do so like you. Just the other day, I stood up for you. Somebody said you weren't fit to eat with the pigs, and I said you were." Poor Amy, who did have difficulty with language, never understood the "slap in the face" (pardon my idiom). Just how early children understand figurative meanings is debatable. One variable affecting children's understanding may be their exposure to various experiences. For example, Abkarian, Jones, and West (1992) gave the example of "skating on thin ice" and hypothesized that the child who has experienced ice skating on ponds where ice is sometimes thin might be more able to understand this idiom. They also point out that children's experiences are often tied to their socioeconomic status.

Syntax and the Language Disabled School-Age Population

The problem evident in the ordering of words may be due to problems with ideation (the process of formulating one's thoughts) or syntax, or both. Details may be sequenced illogically.

A particular problem occurs with the transformation of sentences. This refers to changes (the rearranging, deletions, and substitutions of words) that are made in the base structure of a sentence (such a sentence is a simple, declarative, affirmative sentence written in the active voice) in order to form new sentences. Sentences in which the usual order of words is changed present problems in expression as well as in comprehension. For example, the usual subject-verb-object order is changed in passive sentences, so that "Jason was beaten by Brian in Monopoly" would typically be misinterpreted as subject (Jason)-verb (beat)-object (Brian) or "Jason beat Brian." Sentences that contain both a direct object and an indirect object are also sometimes difficult to interpret. Language disabled children may interpret "Susan showed Mary the monkey" as "Susan showed Mary to the monkey."

Difficulty with "wh" questions (what, why, who, when, which, where, whose) may also be displayed. For example, a child may give a "what" answer to a "why" question (Simon, 1979). "Wh" questions are more difficult to answer when the question refers to events, objects, or people outside of the immediate situation (Parnell, Amerman, & Harting, 1986). Furthermore, ability to ask "wh" questions enables children to learn about the world around them (Schwabe, Olswang, & Kriegsmann, 1986), whether it is the two-year-old asking why or the school-aged child who did not understand the directions for an assignment.

Other problems are created with ambiguous sentences, such as "teasing friends can get you into trouble." The language disabled child might not consider the two possible interpretations: (1) the act of teasing friends may get you into trouble, and (2) friends who tease you may cause you to do something to get into trouble.

In English grammar lessons, children with language disabilities have trouble making up sentences using a particular sentence structure, especially if the sentence is complex. Their sentences tend to be short and lack the syntactical complexity afforded by coordinate and subordinate conjunctions and embedded phrases. For vocabulary lessons, sentences that are formed from the vocabulary words tend to be short, simple, and agrammatical (Wiig, 1986).

Other difficulties include problems with reflexives (e.g., myself, herself, and themselves); the omission of "to" in infinitives; irregular past tense verbs, irregular plural nouns, and difficulties with auxiliary verbs. Words in a sentence may be slurred and run together. Beginning a sentence with "Um, uh, last night, well on yesterday. . . ." is referred to as a *false start*. This is a common problem related to the ability to order thoughts and words and to think of the right words. The difficulties that language disabled children show in repeating, formulating, and comprehending more complex sentences generally represent delays that follow the pattern of normal syntactic development (Wiig, 1986).

Morphology and the Language Disabled School-Age Population

Children with language disabilities frequently ignore word endings, such as plural suffixes, comparative and superlative adjective suffixes, and the -*ly* endings of adverbs, and low stress words, such as prepositions and conjunctions (Wiig, 1986). Difficulties occur with possessives, the past tense of verbs, and prefixes.

The inability of language disabled children to comprehend and use derived words, such as "loveliness" from "lovely," implies that "they do not learn the word formation rules (morphology) at the same rate and with the same consistency and degree of sophistication" as their peers "with normal language development" (Wiig, 1986, pp. 346–347).

Pragmatics and the Language Disabled School-Age Population

Children with language disabilities frequently do not give consideration to who the listener is, the age of the listener, the degree of formality of the situation or environment, the amount of time that they have to convey their messages, and how well they know the listener. These children often use a simpler, more informal style of communication with everyone (Wiig, 1986). They may maintain poor eye contact, infringe on their conversational partner's turn to speak, and fail to maintain an appropriate distance between themselves and their conversational partner.

Children who have difficulty with pragmatics may not consider the listener's verbal and nonverbal responses or the listener's ability to follow the speaker's train of thought. In contrast, effective speakers make note of the listener's responses, attempt to interpret those responses, and, if necessary, change their communication strategies. Consider the following mental scenarios that a speaker faced with a frowning listener might engage in:

Possible problem: Did the listener hear?
Possible solution: Repeat the message loudly.

Possible problem: Did the listener understand the meaning?
Possible solution: Rephrase the message.

Possible problem: Is the listener unhappy, disapproving?
Possible solutions: Provide supporting reasons or temper the message to go along with what the listener evidently feels.

Possible problem: Was the topic of conversation switched without giving the listener any warning?
Possible solution: Inform the listener that the speaker's train of thought changed.

A few other listener reactions include edging away from the speaker, smiling, nodding, laughing, and other emotional responses, such as crying or swearing.

An effective communicator is capable of planning strategies ahead of time. A child who knows he or she is going to be in trouble for a misdeed may plan whether to accept responsibility, to offer an excuse, or to blame another child. Older youth and adults plan how to answer anticipated questions in a job interview. Effective communicators can also change strategies when they recognize that the one being used is not working out well. As children mature, they learn how to negotiate and persuade, how to choose words and tone of voice, and how to appropriately modulate volume and rate of speech.

The language disabled tend not to couch their speech in polite terms or to show consideration for others in their language use. For example, they may make demands (imperative statements), such as "turn off the radio," instead of requests, such as "Will you turn off the radio, please?" or indirect requests, such as "My head hurts" (hint: the radio is causing the headache), or "Are you still listening to the radio?" (hint: the radio is bothering me).

Unfortunately, when language disabled children have difficulty comprehending language, they tend not to ask clarifying questions or to indicate that they did not understand and need help. Thus, they may not respond at all or may respond inappropriately. Obviously, this behavior leads to academic problems. Perhaps less obviously, it leads to social problems.

WHAT EFFECTS DO LANGUAGE DISABILITIES HAVE ON ACADEMIC PERFORMANCE?

Children with language disabilities are at a high risk of failing academically (Wallach & Butler, 1984). Children who do not have a command of oral language will have difficulty learning to read and write. Think about beginning reading experiences. Textbook companies make use of the fact that stories about experiences that are familiar to children are the easiest for children to understand and to learn to read. However, language disabled children may be unable to organize experiences in their own minds. When a teacher asks language disabled children, "What do you think happened next?" or gives them a worksheet with pictures or sentences to order into a story, even if the children have experienced the events in the story, they may be unable to organize and order the events.

Another approach to reading involves asking kindergarten or first grade children to dictate sentences about pictures that they have drawn. After the teacher prints the sentences under the pictures, the children are asked to "read" the sentences. The language disabled child may find it difficult to dictate a sentence, especially a sentence without errors, and then may have a difficult time "reading" the sentence and including any corrections that the teacher may have made. For example, auxiliary verbs, even when added, may continue to be omitted in the "reading."

Problems will arise in mathematics, partly due to the exactness of the vocabulary and partly due to the need to carefully manipulate language, especially in story problems (Simon, 1979).

As a heavier emphasis is placed on social studies, science, literature, and other subjects, basic skills in reading and mathematics do not continue to be taught as they were in lower grades. Children are expected to use those basic skills to learn to reason, to prepare written and oral reports, and to analyze stories in terms of character and plot development. What is automatic for normally developing youngsters is still difficult for the language disabled, and they get left further and further behind.

DO LANGUAGE DISABILITIES AFFECT PSYCHOLOGICAL AND SOCIOLOGICAL ADJUSTMENT?

Parents who react to their children's language problems by being overly protective, demanding, or rejecting may cause their children to develop even poorer interactions (than those caused by the language problem alone) with others, thus exacerbating the problem.

As children approach adolescence, increasing social demands are made by their peers. Language disabilities may prevent children from meeting these demands (e.g., appropriate use of slang terms or coy, flirting behaviors with the opposite sex), resulting in social maladjustment, which in turn may cause increasing academic problems.

Maladjustment may be manifested through anxiety, frustration, lack of motivation, or withdrawal. Action may not be taken, however, until the effects of the maladjustment become more visible through unmistakable aggression, stealing, eating disorders, or obvious depression (Wiig, 1986).

WHAT ABOUT REMEDIATION?

Teachers and parents often know that something is wrong when children with language disabilities enter kindergarten, but it is not always easy to obtain appropriate services. We recently talked to an elementary school principal about a preschooler who had a suspected language disability and would enter kindergarten the following autumn. We were told that no kindergartner in that school was identified as needing special help because the school did not want to start off giving a child a bad label. Although the intent may be sound, the bottom line is that a child in this school loses at least one year before needed help is provided.

The individualized educational program (IEP), drawn up with the parents after a complete assessment takes place, will provide guidelines for remediation. Without doubt, a team effort is needed. Potentially, the classroom teacher, a speech-language pathologist, and a reading specialist or learning disabilities tutor will work with a child. Each needs to know what the other is doing and why. Their efforts need to be coordinated. Goals in the IEP will frequently be stated in percentages. For example, if a child uses appropriate verb tenses 40 percent of the time, then the goal might be that the child, by a certain date, would demonstrate 80 percent accurate use. In order to stimulate carryover of any behavior, a child needs to understand the purpose of what he or she is learning and to produce the behavior easily many times in situations that are as meaningful as possible

(Simon, 1979). Cooperative parents might be asked to provide structured generalization or carryover experiences.

Expressive and receptive language should not be separated from each other. It is recommended that time be spent talking about the relationships among thinking, speaking, listening, reading, and writing. Consider the following logical sequence: What children can think about, they can talk about. What they can talk about, they can learn to write and in turn to read. Moreover, once they can read what they have written, they can also learn to read what others have written (Van Allen & Allen, 1970, cited in Simon, 1979).

Wilson, Lanza, and Barton (1988) have suggested that language disabled children may need help developing thinking skills. They used Bloom's taxonomy of thinking levels (knowledge, comprehension, application, analysis, synthesis, and evaluation) to identify strategies for helping children increase the variety and complexity of their thinking skills. For example, they recommended that children be encouraged to (1) recognize and recall facts from a story or experience, (2) relate the facts in order, (3) explain ideas, (4) relate the experience or story to their own lives or knowledge of others' experiences, (5) compare and contrast events in the story to each other or to personal experiences, (6) create new parts to a story, (7) identify logical next events, and (8) make judgments, such as was it a good idea for the characters to have acted as they did.

When selecting textbooks, teachers should consider the language difficulty of textbooks in relationship to the language proficiencies of the children they have, or expect to have, in their classrooms. Teachers should analyze their own discourse in relationship to the language proficiencies of their charges. Teachers' rate of presentation, complexity of sentence structure (syntax), use of vocabulary (will it be understood by the children), interaction between syntax and vocabulary, length of explanation or direction, and use of visual (body language or seeing the item being discussed) and tactile (feeling the item being discussed) clues should conform to the children's abilities. Teachers can also help by rephrasing their messages rather than simply repeating what they have said; using concrete, direct wording rather than abstractions or subtleties; using nonverbal clues along with verbal messages; asking children to demonstrate nonverbally (pointing, doing what they were told, etc.) that they have understood a message; providing visual examples of what they are talking about; encouraging children to indicate that they do not understand and to ask clarifying questions; and never assuming that children understand.

Pragmatics should be emphasized. Sometimes it is easy to forget what reality is like and to emphasize artificial behaviors. For example, if a child were working on syntax, it would not be appropriate to stress that every sentence the child said be a complete sentence, because that is not how we talk. If asked, "Are you going to your grandparents for Thanksgiving?" one does not answer "Yes, I am going to my grandparents for Thanksgiving." This would sound awkward and stilted. A mere "Yes" would suffice. Politely adding "What are you doing?" would provide an appropriate "extra" that would consider the needs of the original speaker to be recognized.

Adolescents who have language problems are attracting increased, well-deserved, and long-overdue attention. Typically, these youth have gotten lost in the cracks of the educational system, and in many states and school districts still do get lost. It has been common to find that children who received language services in elementary school no longer receive services when they move on to junior (or middle) and senior high schools. These students still have the same needs, no matter which grade they are in, and their continued need is being increasingly recognized. Part of the blame for these students not being served for their language needs may lie in the fact that the traditional pull-out model has been typically used as the service delivery model. Secondary teachers are more apt to object to their students being pulled out; the students are also more apt to object to being pulled out.

When other service delivery models have been implemented, results have been very favorable. Those that have been found to work best include (1) the consultative model where the speech-language pathologist collaborates with the student's teachers to provide extra language help and (2) the resource room where language remediation is offered by the speech-language pathologist as a course (Larson & McKinley, 1993; Larson, McKinley, & Boley, 1993; Work, Cline, Ehren, Keiser, & Wujek, 1993). It has even been reported that the dropout rate for language disabled students decreases in both rural and urban schools when appropriate language remediation along with other special help and programs, such as vocational education, is provided (Larson, McKinley, & Boley, 1993).

WHAT DOES THE FUTURE HOLD FOR LANGUAGE DISABLED CHILDREN AND YOUTH?

The belief that children with language disabilities "catch up" to their peers is seriously questioned (Wallach & Liebergott, 1984). Authorities are in general agreement that although some symptoms of language disabilities will change over time, others will continue into adulthood (Hall & Tomblin, 1978; Wiig, 1986). The adult may continue to be poor at conversation, exhibiting difficulty beginning conversations, maintaining topics, shifting topics, and ending conversations. Difficulties with deictic terms (i.e., words that directly show or point, such as "these," "those," "this," and "that") may continue (Owens, 1984).

Some adults avoid the linguistic situations with which they have the most difficulty. They may also use coping strategies. However, new experiences, such as a new job or a promotion, in which the adult feels uncertain, may prove particularly difficult and may interfere with any learned strategies for coping. It can be expected that adults who have been identified and have received language therapy as youngsters are in better positions to cope as adults.

Case History

Sue

Sue is an active and overly aggressive third grader, who had a poor academic record in the first and second grades. Her adjustment to the school situation has left a great deal to be desired. Her third grade teacher is particularly oriented to meeting the individual needs of children and was curious about Sue's achievement and behavior as she interacted with the other students.

Sue was observed to have a smaller vocabulary than the other children in the class. She seemed to have difficulty recalling specific words she wished to use and would substitute nonspecific, general terms for them. Her skill in defining words also seemed obviously restricted.

Sue had great difficulty comprehending lengthy and complex sentences. She also had difficulty in repeating such sentences when asked to do so.

Sue tended to blurt out whatever she chose to say, irrespective of those around her. These less than meaningful attempts only added to her own sense of apparent frustration and her growing nonacceptance by those around her.

It was these few but astute observations by a sensitive, caring teacher that prompted a referral to a speech-language pathologist. Assessment is currently underway and, without doubt, a program of therapy, focusing on syntax, semantics, and pragmatics, will be developed for this child, who exhibits rather marked symptoms of a language disability.

SUMMARY

Causes

- Central nervous system dysfunction
- Hearing, visual, mental, motor impairment and linguistically deprived environment

Some Important Points to Remember

- Learning disabilities refers to difficulties in listening, reading, reasoning, or mathematical skills.
- Emotional, hearing, and visual problems can coexist with a learning disability.
- Hearing, visual, mental, or motoric impairment can cause language delay.
- Learning disabled children differ from each other.
- Language delay is a subset of the larger problem of learning disability.
- The primary difficulties of learning disabled children are academic learning, language disorders, motor disorders, social-emotional problems, perceptual disorders, and memory problems.
- Three percent of school children have some learning disability.
- Language is a system used in various ways for thought and communication.
- Semantics deals with the meanings words evoke.
- Syntax refers to the ordering of words.
- Morphology, an aspect of syntax, deals with prefixes and suffixes.
- A morpheme is the smallest meaningful unit in a language.
- Pragmatics refers to the use of language in a social context for a particular purpose.
- Parental education, occupation, and income are reflected in a child's linguistic functioning.
- There are standardized tests for assessing language ability.
- Language disabilities range from mild to severe.
- Children with language disabilities may have smaller vocabularies than their peers.
- Words with multiple meanings present particular problems for the semantically involved language delayed child.
- Children with problems of syntax have difficulty in ordering words using a particular sentence structure.
- Children with morphological problems frequently ignore word endings.
- Children with problems of pragmatics often use a simpler style of communication than do their non-language disabled peers.
- Language disabled children with pragmatics problems tend not to use polite terms or show consideration for their listeners.
- Children with language disability are at high risk of academic failure.
- The psychosocial adjustment of a child with language delay may be affected directly by that delay and indirectly by the parent's response to the child's problem.

- The individualized educational program (IEP) should be complete in its provision of guidelines for remediation.
- The effects of language disabilities in childhood are often observed in adulthood, but those who received speech-language therapy in childhood are better prepared to cope than those who did not.

Do's and Don'ts for Teachers

Do's:

- Be alert to the presence of any language disabled children in the classroom.
- Consider the socioeconomic level of parents when evaluating a child's linguistic functioning.
- Refer children suspected of language delay to a speech-language pathologist.
- Recognize that children with oral language problems have difficulty communicating.
- Be sure to understand the provisions of the IEP regarding reading and writing.

Don'ts:

- Do not confuse sensory problems of hearing or vision with learning problems.
- Do not expect all languages to follow the same rules.

Referral Resources

- Speech-language pathologist
- Psychologist
- Neurologist

SELF-TEST

True or False:

1. Language disability and learning disability refer to the same condition. ____
2. According to the United States Office of Education definition, learning problems due primarily to visual, hearing, or motor handicaps, mental retardation, or environmental disadvantage are not to be classified as a learning disability problem. ____
3. Language disability is identified by most authorities as a part of the learning disabilities picture. ____
4. Hearing impairment may cause a speech problem but not a language problem. ____

5. Language development has little, if anything, to do with social and ____ cultural contexts.
6. The components of language include phonology.   ____
7. Semantics is a component of language primarily focused upon pre- ____ fixes and suffixes of words.
8. Pragmatics is simply another term for morphology.   ____
9. Language development is rule based.   ____
10. Parental occupation and education as well as income are factors to ____ consider in the assessment of language.
11. Auditory processing is of little concern to one who makes assess- ____ ment of language performance.
12. The teacher can make valuable contributions to the evaluation ____ of a child's language status by making information available to the speech-language pathologist concerning the child's cognitive capabilities.
13. A language disability rarely retards the scholastic progress of a child. ____
14. Synonyms and antonyms are particularly troublesome for the lan- ____ guage disabled child whose primary problem is one of syntax.
15. Difficulties of repeating, comprehending, and formulating complex ____ sentences are usually related to a problem with semantics.
16. Children who have problems with oral language usage will most ____ likely have difficulties with reading and writing.
17. Parental attitudes can have a profound influence on the progress of a ____ language disabled child.
18. Psychological adjustment may be affected by a language disability. ____
19. The teacher should refer to the speech-language pathologist any ____ child suspected of having a language problem.
20. There are systematic approaches used by the speech-language ____ pathologist with the language delayed child.

Suggested Readings

Gleason, J. B. (Ed.). (1985). *The development of language.* Columbus, OH: Charles E. Merrill.

Holland, A. L. (Ed.). (1984). *Language disorders in children. Recent Advances.* San Diego: College-Hill.

Leonard, L. (1986). Early language development and language disorders. In G. H. Shames & E. H. Wiig (Eds.), *Human communication disorders* (2nd ed.) (pp. 291–330). Columbus, OH: Charles E. Merrill.

Lund, N. J., & Duchan, J. F. (1988). *Assessing children's language in naturalistic contexts* (2nd ed.). Englewood Cliffs, NJ: Prentice-Hall.

Mercer, C. D. (1979). *Children and adolescents with learning disabilities.* Columbus, OH: Charles E. Merrill.

Mercer, C. D., & Mercer, A. R. (1985). *Teaching students with learning problems* (2nd ed.). Columbus, OH: Charles E. Merrill.

Newhoff, M., & Leonard, L. (1983). Diagnosis of developmental language disorders. In I. J. Meitus & B. Weinberg (Eds.), *Diagnosis in speech-language pathology* (pp. 71–112). Baltimore: University Park Press.

Owens, R. E., Jr. (1984). *Language development. An introduction.* Columbus, OH: Charles E. Merrill.

Simon, C. S. (1979). *Communicative competence: A functional-pragmatic approach to language therapy.* Tucson, AZ: Communication Skill Builders.

Simon, C. S. (Ed.). (1985). *Communication skills and classroom success. Assessment of language-learning disabled students.* San Diego: College-Hill.

Simon, C. S. (Ed.). (1985). *Communication skills and classroom success. Therapy methodologies for language-learning disabled students.* San Diego: College-Hill.

Wallach, G. P., & Butler, K. G. (1984). *Language learning disabilities in school-age children.* Baltimore: Williams and Wilkins.

Wiig, E. H., & Semel, E. (1984). *Language assessment and intervention for the learning disabled* (2nd ed.). Columbus, OH: Charles E. Merrill.

REFERENCES

Adler, S. (1990). Multicultural clients: Implications for the SLP. *Language, Speech, and Hearing Services in Schools, 21,* 135–139.

ASHA Committee on Language. (1983). Definition of language. *ASHA, 25*(6), 44.

Bliss, L. S. (1987). "I can't talk anymore; my mouth doesn't want to." The development and clinical applications of modal auxiliaries. *Language, Speech, and Hearing Services in Schools, 18,* 72–79.

Bloom, L., & Lahey, M. (1978). *Language development and language disorders.* New York: John Wiley and Sons.

Bracken, B. A. (1988). Rate and sequence of positive and negative poles in basic concept acquisition. *Language, Speech, and Hearing Services in Schools, 19,* 410–417.

Cartwright, G. P., Cartwright, C. A., & Ward, M. E. (1985). *Educating special learners* (2nd ed.). Belmont, CA: Wadsworth Publishing.

Hall, P., & Tomblin, J. (1978). A follow-up study of children with articulation and language disorders. *Journal of Speech and Hearing Disorders, 9,* 193–207.

Hallahan, D. P., & Kauffman, J. M. (1976). *Introduction to learning disabilities: A psychobehavioral approach.* Englewood Cliffs, NJ: Prentice-Hall.

Hammill, D. D., Leigh, J. E., McNutt, G., & Larsen, S. C. (1981). A new definition of learning disabilities. *Learning Disability Quarterly, 4,* 336–342.

Horgan, D. (1978). The development of the full passive. *Journal of Child Language, 5,* 65–80.

Labov, W. (1972). *Language in the inner city: Studies in the Black English Vernacular.* Philadelphia: University of Pennsylvania Press.

Larson, V. L., & McKinley, N. L. (1993). Clinical forum: Adolescent language—An introduction. *Language, Speech, and Hearing Services in Schools, 24,* 19–20.

Larson, V. L., McKinley, N. L., & Boley, D. Service delivery models for adolescents with language disorders. *Language, Speech, and Hearing Services in Schools, 24,* 36–42.

Leonard, L. (1986). Early language development and language disorders. In G. H. Shames & E. H. Wiig (Eds.), *Human communication disorders* (2nd ed.) (pp. 291–330). Columbus, OH: Charles E. Merrill.

Mercer, C. D. (1979). *Children and adolescents with learning disabilities.* Columbus, OH: Charles E. Merrill.

Naremore, R. D. (1980) Language disorders in children. In T. J. Hixon, L. D. Shriberg, & J. H. Saxman (Eds.), *Introduction to communication disorders* (pp. 137–175). Englewood Cliffs, NJ: Prentice-Hall.

Newhoff, M., & Leonard, L. (1983). Diagnosis of developmental language disorders. In I. J. Meitus & B. Weinberg (Eds.), *Diagnosis in speech-language pathology* (pp. 71–112). Baltimore, MD: University Park Press.

Nippold, M. A. (1993). Developmental markers in adolescent language: Syntax, Semantics, and Pragmatics. *Language, Speech, and Hearing Services in Schools, 24,* 21–29.

Owens, R. E., Jr. (1984). *Language development. An introduction.* Columbus, OH: Charles E. Merrill.

Parnell, M. M., Amerman, J. D., & Harting, R. D. (1986). Responses of language-disordered children to wh-questions. *Language, Speech, and Hearing Services in Schools, 17,* 95–106.

Schwabe, A. M., Olswang, L. B., & Kriegsmann, E. (1986). Requests for information: Linguistic, cognitive, prgamatic, and environmental variables. *Language, Speech, and Hearing Services in Schools, 17,* 38–55.

Seidenberg, P. L., & Bernstein, D. K. (1986). The comprehension of similes and metaphors by learning-disabled and nonlearning-disabled children. *Language, Speech, and Hearing Services in Schools, 17,* 219–229.

Simon, C. S. (1979). *Communicative competence: A functional-pragmatic approach to language therapy.* Tucson, AZ: Communication Skill Builders.

Simon, C. S. (1985). The language-learning disabled student: Description and therapy implications. In C. S. Simon (Ed.), *Communication skills and classroom success. Therapy methodologies for language-learning disabled students* (pp. 1–56). San Diego: College-Hill.

Tager-Flusberg, H. (1985). Putting words together: Morphology and syntax in the preschool years. In J. K. Gleason (Ed.), *The development of language* (pp. 139–171). Columbus, OH: Charles E. Merrill.

United States Office of Education. (1977, August 23.) Implementation of Part B of the Education of all Handicapped Children Act. *Federal Register, 42,* 42474–42518.

United States Office of Education (1979). *Progress toward a free appropriate public education: A report to Congress on the implementation of P.L. 94-142.* Washington, D.C.: Department of Health, Education and Welfare.

Wallach, G. P., & Butler, K. G. (1984). *Language learning disabilities in school-age children.* Baltimore: Williams and Wilkins.

Wallach, G. P., & Liebergott, J. W. (1984). Who shall be called "learning disabled": Some new directions. In G. P. Wallach & K. G. Butler (Eds.), *Language learning disabilities in school-age children* (pp. 1–14). Baltimore: Williams and Wilkins.

Webster's beginning dictionary. (1980). Springfield, MA: G. & C. Merriam Co.

Wiig, E. H. (1986). Language disabilities in school-age children and youth. In G. H. Shames & E. H. Wiig (Eds.), *Human communication disorders* (2nd ed.) (pp. 331–383). Columbus, OH: Charles E. Merrill.

Wiig, E. H., & Semel, E. (1984). *Language assessment and intervention for the learning disabled* (2nd ed.). Columbus, OH: Charles E. Merrill.

Wilson, C. C., Lanza, J. R., & Barton, J. S. (1988). Developing higher level thinking skills through questioning techniques in the speech and language setting. *Language, Speech, and Hearing Services in Schools, 19,* 428–431.

Work, R. S., Cline, J. A., Ehren, B. J. Keiser, D. L., & Wujek, C. (1993). Adolescent language programs. *Language, Speech, and Hearing Services in Schools, 24,* 43–53.

4

STUTTERING

Stuttering has been observed across cultures by teachers, scholars, clinicians, and scientists for centuries. It is a speech disorder that has afflicted the rich and poor, the young and old, males and females, persons of high intelligence, those of average intelligence, and also those who possess only modest intellectual capacities. It has been observed that more males stutter than do females.

Probably no other speech disorder catches the attention of the listener as quickly as *stuttering* does. This is most likely due to the sudden and often dramatic breakdown in the timing feature of speech and the prolongations of the various speech elements on certain aspects of an utterance. Normally we expect that although speech is characterized by pauses and some repetitions, it will usually move ahead easily and quite rhythmically. The surprise aspect to the listener is that some of the speech of the stutterer moves along well and sounds just fine, while other parts of it are fractionated by blocks, pauses, repetitions, and prolongations, such that the speech becomes unintelligible.

There are many young children-preschoolers who show disruptions in their speech patterns that might or might not one day turn out to be the beginning of stuttering behavior. Parents frequently become quite concerned about the "stuttering" of their preschool children and some parents seek counseling for their children. Unfortunately, some parents, other family or neighbors are quick to label hesitant speech by some preschoolers as stuttering, when actually it is not. More will be said about this a little later on.

The *classroom teacher* like no one else is best able to observe the stuttering of school-age children. It is also the classroom teacher who manages the stuttering child in the classroom. The teacher is in a pivotal position for establishing the interface between the speech-language pathologist and the child, the child and other children in the classroom, and the parent and the speech clinician. Additionally, the teacher is responsible for establishing the most productive relationship with the stuttering child and an attitude and atmosphere in the classroom that promotes optimum cognitive and emotional development of the child.

WHAT IS FLUENT SPEECH?

Before embarking on a discussion about stuttering and the causes of stuttering, we should examine briefly what is generally regarded as *fluent speech*. Speech that flows along unimpeded like a stream of water, uninterrupted and easily without undue hesitations, pauses, or breaks is considered as fluent. The speech of one who stutters does not meet these criteria and is therefore considered as nonfluent.

Starkweather (1986) pointed out that the notion of fluency was first associated with the use of a second language and that nonfluency, in this context, is the inability to produce the proper word (semantic nonfluency), pronounce words properly (phonological nonfluency), arrange them in proper order (syntactical nonfluency), or use words appropriately for the situation (pragmatic nonfluency). Stutterers may be very fluent linguistically and if so their nonfluency is their inability to utilize the speech mechanism smoothly to transport what they intend to say to the listener.

The classroom teacher or anyone else for that matter, should not automatically attribute the lack of smoothness to a lack of linguistic proficiency on the part of the stutterer's speech. However, it should be noted that there is some evidence (Kline & Starkweather, 1979) suggesting that linguistic proficiency in some cases of young stutterers can be associated with stuttering. Although there is need for continued study of the characteristics of fluent speech and nonfluent speech, there are sufficient data and clinical observations to allow for the development of an operational definition to work with.

So, with reference to the question posed at the outset of this section, "What Is Fluent Speech?" we might answer best as follows. It is speech that is

- relatively effortless,
- not punctuated with many irregularities such as repetitions and prolongations,
- relatively free of abnormal pauses or discontinuities,
- and moves forward quite rhythmically and easily.

WHAT IS STUTTERING?

To define stuttering is not an easy thing to do. For to define anything places limits on that which is being defined. The implication is that what has been said is *all* there is to be said about the defined term. It is probably best to view definitions of stuttering as *operational definitions* that provide points of reference against which to explain causation and a rationale for interventions. Descriptions of the stutterer's behavior, however, are still another way of answering the question "what is stuttering?"

Admitting to the difficulty of defining stuttering, Starkweather (1987) chose to describe primary symptoms of stuttering as being characterized by abnormally high frequency and long durations of sound, syllable, and word repetitions and also long durations of sound prolongations and pauses. He also suggested that the abnormal efforts in producing speech along with the possible avoidance of sounds, words, situations and listeners, coupled with increased anxiety in response to speech and certain social situations, may be a part of the picture.

Ainsworth (1988) suggested in his advice to parents that stuttering is more than just the disruptions in the smooth flow of words by the stutterer but is also composed of the reactions to the trouble the child is having in producing the words. He further suggested to parents that they refrain from being too conscious of them.

These definitions of stuttering are but a few of the many previously set forth by clinicians who have or are presently working with stutterers Unquestionably, all definitions have something important to offer and are helpful for understanding more fully the behavior of the stutterer.

In his analyses of the various definitions of stuttering, Ham (1990) concluded that even though there is a lack of a general agreement on a definition of stuttering, untrained listeners as well as trained listeners can usually identify stuttering quite accurately. This observation supports the efforts of the classroom teacher who is called upon to identify and refer those children who stutter to the speech-language pathologist.

CAUSES OF STUTTERING

Careful and rigorous observations of multiple causes of stuttering have been made by both clinicians and scientists. These have been documented in journals and books throughout the years by speech-language pathologists and others here in the United States. The historical interest in stuttering, however, goes back several centuries. The literature of speech-language pathology is replete with hypotheses and theories that attempt to explain the causes of stuttering. It is somewhat easier to describe how stuttering occurs and when it occurs in individuals than it is to determine what causes the stuttering to occur.

Johnson (1948) developed a diagnosogenic theory that stated that the act of labeling a child a "stutterer" because of dysfluencies caused the one who did the labeling, those surrounding the child, and eventually, the child to respond to the nonfluent speech as *stuttering*. Although a popular explanation some years ago and still maintained by some today, most investigators are looking in other directions for causative factors.

Van Riper (1972), a leader for years in the field of stuttering, has subscribed to a more eclectic approach as regards causation. He suggested for example, that stuttering had many origins and that those factors that help to maintain stuttering are more important than the original causes.

Perkins (1986) maintained that stuttering is a result of the discoordination of respiration, voicing, and articulation. He suggested that the discoordination that interferes with the precision of time of air flow and vocalization, necessary for smooth articulation, is not the cause of stuttering but actually is the stuttering. He suggested also that stuttering is caused by some underlying constitutional condition, whereas others have suggested that stuttering is multidimensional and its causes are unknown.

In his comprehensive review of increased dysfluency and stuttering, Gregory (1986) presented findings from various areas that relate to stuttering. They include family history, auditory processes, speech motor processes, voice reaction time, voice onset time, physiology, linguistic processes, language factors, environmental factors, and electroencephalographic results. The enormity and complexity of the problem of stuttering becomes obvious, even to the casual observer. The most important thing to remember is that stuttering is not a disorder with a single cause.

In his review and analyses of theoretical approaches to stuttering, Ham (1990) presented an overview of the many approaches that have emerged thoughout the years. His analyses suggested three categories: psychological, linguistic, and pathophysiological.

The *psychological* category included psychoanalytic considerations wherein the stuttering is perceived as a symptom of some underlying neurosis and also psychosocial considerations wherein stuttering is viewed as learned behavior. It is also important to note that stuttering tends to increase if rewarded (extra attention and concern shown by those in the environment) and to decrease if the stuttering elicits punishment. Of all the approaches that are psychologically based, the learned behavior approach has had the greatest attention by clinicians and researchers.

Linguistic considerations have led to evaluation of the role of language development as it affects stuttering. Syntactic complexity, frequency and predictability of words, linguistic stress, and meaningfulness of words are all important variables to consider as regards the relationship of language development to stuttering (Ham, 1990). Once again the multicausality of stuttering is reinforced.

Pathophysiological considerations of stuttering are deserving of attention (Ham, 1990). Language is most dominant in the left hemisphere of the brain in most people. Some have believed that stutterers had a tendency toward equality of cerebral dominance; thus, when speech was attempted, the coordination of the hemispheres was affected and disruption in the flow of speech ensued. Still others thought that stuttering resulted from a mild form of epilepsy; however, this notion has not been well supported.

Genetic factors related to stuttering have been examined by numerous researchers and tend to support the notion that there well may be an inherited predisposition to stuttering. Some would argue, however, that the apparent familial component is a sociogenic phenomenon. Research continues in this arena (Wingate, 1986).

Respiration of stutterers has been another item for inquiry. It appears that irregularities are associated with stuttering rather than being the cause.

In view of all the inquiries into the psychological, linguistic, and pathophysiological causes of stuttering, it must be reiterated that it seems prudent to assume that stuttering is multifaceted as regards causality. The concept of *multiple factors* that contribute to this speech problem rather than a single cause serves us best as efforts continue to determine those factors that are most important in most cases.

MULTICULTURAL CONSIDERATIONS

One does not have to travel very far in the U.S.A. before realizing that our population is made up of people who have come from various cultures. Some have long since lost their original attachment to their countries of origin and identify as Americans. There are others that maintain a distinct relationship with their countries of origin. Still others lie in close proximity to one another and with tenacity maintain their original languages, values, and traditions (Perspectives, 1990).

When dealing with the handicapped it must be kept in mind that the values held by one group of individuals are not necessarily compatible with those held by other groups. Pride, theological, ethical, and social considerations are important to consider. The role of males, females and children in the family constellation varies. Is it less than masculine to stutter or to have a child, particularly a male, who stutters? It is believed that those cultural groups where great demands are placed upon the achievement of success and accomplishment create greater pressures on their children than those groups who do not hold this value as being quite that important.

Lieth (1986), who has given careful consideration to the matter of cultural influences and stuttering, suggested that the way in which parents and others in the family group react to their stuttering child will indeed be influenced by their beliefs about the cause. They may feel a sense of shame for having a child who stutters and superstitions may play no small part in all of this.

This writer was approached one day in a public school by a rather angry father who had been invited along with other parents to discuss the speech of their children who were receiving speech therapy. His child was a son who stuttered. He challenged the need for any special attention to his son. He obviously felt as though he was being demeaned by having to admit to the fact that his son had a speech disorder. Interested in saving myself from a broken nose, or worse, I marshalled whatever counseling talents I had and was able to explain to him, with the help of his understanding wife, just why his son was receiving special attention in speech. The efforts proved to be successful and from that point forward he was cooperative and supportive. This incident illustrated to me the penalty that the father felt for having a son whose speech was disordered.

The point of this brief discussion is simply to point out that

- we live in a multicultural society,
- there may be those children in your classroom who come from homes where cultural differences set them apart from the majority of the other children,
- there may be among them those children who need special attention because of their stuttering,
- before making judgments as to next steps, make an appraisal as best you can of the cultural background of the child,
- sensitivity to the dictates of cultural background is important when dealing with the child, and
- one should exercise caution against stereotyping; be aware that there are subcultures within cultural groups and that there are individual differences.

CAN THOSE WHO STUTTER BE HELPED?

Yes. For our purposes here let us consider two general age categories of children who stutter, namely the preschooler and the child of school age.

The preschool child who begins to show disfluencies often does so as language begins to emerge to the point where attempts are being made to speak in short meaningful phrases (Curlee, 1991). Curlee suggested that most people who are ever going to stutter will begin stuttering before their fifth birthday and that virtually no one does after age twelve, unless they have sustained serious head trauma.

Discussion by Guitar and Peters (1985) suggested that certain diagnostic signs are helpful to the clinician in determining whether or not the speech behavior of the child is simply normal disfluency or whether it is indicative of a developing problem of stuttering. If parents report that the hesitant speech is seemingly not noticed by their child, the probability is that what is being seen and heard is normal disfluency. In this case the parents should be relieved of their concern and helped to understand that these disfluencies do occur in normal development of some children and that they will in all likelihood disappear as the child matures in language and general development. Parents should also be made aware of the fact that they can be of assistance to their child by concentrating their attention on "what" the child is saying and not "how" the child is talking.

If, however, the disfluencies described by the parents are characterized by many repetitions and prolongations, accompanied by obvious signs of tension and struggle behavior, then the clinician will make a further check of the child's speech. This appraisal will include an assessment of the frequency of the disfluencies, when they occur, the rate at which the child speaks, the feelings of the child toward the disfluent speech, and how the child feels about speaking in general. Also important to the appraisal is an evaluation of the parents' attitudes about the speech of the child. Are there feelings of guilt? Are they embarrassed by the child's speech? Are they frustrated and somewhat unsympathetic with the behavior they witness, believing that somehow the child could and should do much better with speech? This is important information for the clinician because attitudes held by parents are not easily hidden from the child (Guitar & Peters, 1985).

The speech-language pathologist may arrange for the preschool child to have a trial period of therapy at which time further exploration of speech disfluencies can be made. The primary therapeutic effort might be toward increasing the fluency of the child's speech, or depending upon the circumstances, toward the modification of stuttering. In some instances a combination of the two might be used. The techniques employed have some similarities and both aim toward developing greater fluency or, perhaps, stuttering more easily.

Gone are the days when professionals in stuttering management tiptoe around the stuttering of a child for fear of calling attention to the problem. Two things should be taken into consideration: (1) if the child is experiencing stuttering as a problem, then indeed there is already an awareness of it; and (2) the sooner a child receives help for stuttering, the better, for it has been shown that early treatment yields the best results (Perkins, 1991).

As for management of the stutterer of school age, the approaches are highly similar to those employed with the preschooler. The age range of this group is, however, far greater than that of the preschooler. At the lower end of the range the school child in the primary grades is much more like the preschooler and at the upper end of the range much more like the adolescent or adult.

Interacting with the disfluent or stuttering child of school age usually comes before the clinician has an opportunity to hold an interview with the parents. This makes for a different starting point when talking with the parents for the first time. It must be emphasized that success with therapy for children within this age range necessitates bringing the parents into the picture and providing for them the opportunity to express their concerns. Of importance as well is to give them a chance to share their attitudes toward the child and the child's speech behavior.

As with the preschooler, assessment is made of the disfluencies and perhaps trial therapy will be undertaken. As for the therapy, it has been observed that a combined approach of fluency shaping and stuttering modification is most suitable (Guitar & Peters, 1985). It is in this combined approach that the child is able to see his/her stuttering behavior in perspective, determine the ways in which it is affecting him as a person, reduce the anxiety brought about by stuttering, lessen fears associated with stuttering, and ultimately through skillful treatment by the clinician become desensitized to the stigma associated with stuttering.

For the younger elementary school child it is not unrealistic to expect that the child will produce fluent speech spontaneously. The goals for children who are older, however, might be set more realistically at achieving controlled fluency or acceptable and easy stuttering.

The classroom teacher plays a vital role in the lives of children and particularly in the lives of those who exhibit disfluent speech or who stutter. These children are vulnerable to the misconceptions, attitudes, and responses of others, both children and adults. With adequate understanding and management within the classroom, the teacher can go a long way toward promoting an environment in which the child can, with the help of the speech clinician, make tremendous progress. Teachers should encourage the child to talk irrespective of the fact the he or she stutters. If negative reactions become apparent on the part of the other children, such as laughing or teasing, this is the perfect opportunity for the teacher to explain to the other children that the disfluent child is having some trouble with talking and that they could be of real help to him or her by listening carefully to what is being said even though it might take a bit longer to do so. Most children with proper understanding will be cooperative, accepting and helpful both to the child and the teacher.

The perspective of Perkins (1991) regarding the likelihood of the persistence of stuttering is well noted. He suggested that if stuttering persists into adulthood, both professionals and those who stutter may look only to improvements in their stuttering. For the most part, their speech might sound normal most of the time, but yet they may perceive themselves as stutterers. If children are helped before they begin to fear stuttering and have other secondary kinds of reactions to it such as facial grimaces, blinking, etc., the chances are good that they will become reasonably normal speakers. Preventing a self image as being a stutterer is of great importance.

CASE HISTORIES

Jack

Jack was a second grader who did very well in school. Both of his parents were active professional people, and he had no brothers or sisters. About five months into the school year Jack developed a rapid-fire machine-gun-like stuttering over the course of two weeks. He had blocks, repetitions, and facial grimaces. His father (a speech-language pathologist) was concerned because in Jack's bedtime prayers, Jack prayed that he would be able to complete his work the next day in school. It was also noted that Jack had been watching many hours of television each day. At a parent-teacher conference, Jack's father and teacher discussed Jack's progress in school and the hope expressed in Jack's bedtime prayers. When asked about Jack's ability to complete his work, the teacher (young and inexperienced) said, "Oh yes, he completes his work far ahead of the rest of the students, so I simply enrich his activities with more work than he can complete." Because of the "enrichment" Jack was never able to go to the sand table and play with others who had completed their routine assignments. At the father's request, Jack's assignments were reduced to normal; and Jack was rewarded by being able to play at the sand table upon their completion.

Additionally, Jack and his parents decided together the television programs he would watch and for how long. The parents curtailed some of their own activities and spent more time with Jack individually in play activities. It was not more than three weeks until the "stuttering" subsided and was never observed again. Sensitive parents, a good analysis of the probable causative factors, and a cooperative classroom teacher played vital roles in the restoration of fluency in this youngster. The situation might have been far different if prompt action had not been taken.

Susie

Susie was an easy, relaxed stutterer. Her fourth grade teacher decided that Susie should talk more fluently and set about to correct her speech by having her stop and start over each time she repeated a syllable or word. Additionally, the teacher appointed "watchdogs" from among the students to assist her not only in the classroom but on the playground as well. Susie was miserable. At age eighteen and ready to graduate from high school, Susie was a well-entrenched stutterer with all the frustrations, fears, and anxieties that might have been avoided had there been a speech-language pathologist in the school that could have worked with Susie and her parents in close cooperation with the classroom teacher.

David

David was a delightful preschool four year old child. His parents, both professional people, father a surgeon and mother a psychologist, brought the child to the clinic for evaluation of his "stuttering." The father was the one who insisted that the child needed evaluation and was quite concerned about the status of his only son who was seemingly developing normally in all other respects except for his stuttering when attempting to speak. This had been confirmed by the father who had a neurological examination made of David prior to the visit at the Speech and Hearing Clinic. The father appeared to be a "high-strung" and perfectionistic sort of person. This was not only an observation of the speech-language pathologist, but the mother reinforced indirectly these impressions several times throughout the interview. The mother appeared calm and relaxed and not overly concerned about David's speech disfluencies and alluded to the fact that they might be a part of the picture of normal development.

David was seen briefly in play situations both with and without the parents being present. From the observations that were made, it appeared to the clinician that the child was showing easy disfluencies in speech that were not accompanied by any sense of fear of speaking or struggle in the production of words or sentences. He interacted well with the speech-language pathologist and seemed to be completely at ease and happy.

In the first of a total of three interviews that were held over the course of three months with the parents it was suggested to them that what they were noting were normal disfluencies and that it would be well for them to refrain from reacting to them as stuttering. It was further suggested, however, that they continue to observe David's speech and note when the disfluencies were most apparent. Additionally it was suggested that if there were pressures on David that could be alleviated, the needed adjustments should be made. They were counseled as well to spend more time with David, listen honestly to what he said to them, and to become engaged meaningfully with him in play, reading of stories, etc.

By the third interview both parents were seemingly well pleased with the suggestions made and reported that they thought they noticed much greater fluency in David's speech. Also it became quite apparent to the clinician that the father had really begun to enjoy his preschool son as a person. It was agreed upon by the speech-language pathologist and the parents during the third interview that further interviews were not necessary unless they felt the need for them.

About three months following the last interview, around Christmas time, the florist delivered a large poinsettia plant to the home of the speech-language pathologist with a note from the parents expressing their gratitude for helping David along the way to fluent speech. (It might be added, parenthetically, that what was said by the speech-language pathologist over the course of three interviews was essentially what was said in the first interview. It was noted, however, that there was a reluctance on the part of the father to accept the fact that the child's speech was probably characterized by normal disfluency and not "stuttering." By the end of the last interview it was quite apparent that there was acceptance.)

SUMMARY

Causes

- Current thinking suggests that stuttering has multiple causes.
- Many theories of causation of stuttering exist.
- Some suggest that labeling a child a stutterer causes stuttering.

Some Important Points to Remember

- There are important differences between normal speech disfluency and stuttering.
- Discoordination of respiration, voicing and articulation are frequently associated with stuttering.
- Most stuttering begins with easy syllable repetitions.
- Facial grimaces and struggle behaviors sometimes accompany stuttering.
- Fear, frustration and hostility frequently accompany stuttering.
- Disfluency is often overcome.
- It is important to know which children will probably outgrow stuttering.
- More boys stutter than girls.
- Children who stutter do not all respond alike to the stress connected with it.
- Stuttering interferes with the forward flow of speech.
- Children often stutter more in some situations than in others.

- Children who stutter often feel anxious.
- Children with speech disfluencies or stuttering should not be complimented for fluent speech.

Do's and Don'ts for Teachers

Although some of the following suggestions have been made or alluded to in the preceding pages, the following list summarizes important ways in which the classroom teacher can be of help.

Do's

- Accept the child who stutters just as you would any other child.
- If you observe that a child has marked disfluencies, contact the speech-language pathologist serving your school. Describe your observations of the child's speech and provide all of the pertinent information that is requested. Following the evaluation by the speech-language pathologist, find out how you might be of assistance to the child in the classroom.
- Try in every way to build the self confidence of the child.
- Provide ample opportunity for the stuttering child to participate successfully in oral activities.
- Monitor periodically the free play of the child who stutters to determine the level of peer acceptance and to detect any overt behavior by others that might be associated with the speech problem.
- Maintain eye contact when a stuttering child speaks; be a good listener, even though it may take longer.
- If appropriate, take the opportunity to educate classmates of the stuttering child about stuttering and to help them develop accepting attitudes.
- Reward a child who stutters for things done well, just as you reward any other child.
- Hold the standards high for good manners in talking in the classroom as in other areas of social interactions.
- Stuttering affords no reason why a child should not abide by all of the rules set for other children in the classroom.
- Provide the child who stutters the opportunity to say what he/she has to say.
- Always be a good listener.
- Let the child know that you really care.

Don'ts

- Do not speak for the child when stuttering occurs.
- Do not compliment a child for fluent speech.

- Do not allow interruptions of a stuttering child's attempt to speak.
- Do not allow other children to try to furnish a word or sentence that the stuttering child is trying to say.
- Do not ask the stuttering child to slow down, stop, or start over.
- Do not give the disfluent or stuttering child special privileges with the exception of special assistance in oral recitation when needed.

Referral Resources

- Speech-language pathologist
- Audiologist
- Psychologist

SELF-TEST

True or False:

1. The speech of normal talkers shows no disfluencies.   ____
2. There are multiple causes of stuttering.   ____
3. There are numerous theories of stuttering.   ____
4. The diagnosogenic theory refers to the labeling of a child as stutterer.   ____
5. More girls stutter than boys.   ____
6. Stuttering is essentially a problem of rhythm and timing.   ____
7. Easy repetitions most frequently characterize the beginning of stuttering in children.   ____
8. Some stutterers regain fluent speech.   ____
9. Classroom teachers, after identifying a child who seems to be stuttering, should contact the speech-language pathologist.   ____
10. Building self-esteem in a child who stutters is a primary responsibility of the classroom teacher.   ____
11. Stuttering is a serious speech disorder that should receive immediate attention.   ____
12. When a child blocks on a sound or word, the classroom teacher should speak for the child.   ____
13. Research in stuttering continues.   ____
14. Praise from the classroom teacher should follow a stutterer's fluent speech.   ____
15. The classroom teacher should help shape attitudes of others toward the child who stutters.   ____
16. Only in recent years has stuttering been noticed as a speech problem.   ____
17. Cultural diversity should be of concern to teachers.   ____
18. Stuttering affects only those with average intelligence.   ____
19. Linguistic disfluency and stuttering may be related.   ____
20. Stuttering is not only disfluency but also the stutterer's reaction to it.   ____
21. Only highly trained listeners can detect disfluent speech.   ____

22. Some say there might be an inherited predisposition to stuttering. ____
23. Teachers should be sensitive to cultural backgrounds of children ____
    who stutter.
24. Diagnostic signs help to differentiate stuttering from normal dis- ____
    fluency.
25. Children with speech disfluencies should be encouraged to partici- ____
    pate in oral recitations.

REFERENCES

Ainsworth, S. (1988). *If your child stutters*. (3rd ed.) Memphis, TN: Speech Foundation of America, p. 13.

Curlee, F. F. (1991). Does my child stutter? In *Stuttering and your child: questions and answers*. Memphis, TN: Stuttering Foundation of America, p. 9.

Gregory, H. H. (1986). Stuttering: A contemporary perspective. *Folia Phoniatrica, 38,* 89–120.

Guitar, G. G. & Peters, T. J. (1985). *Stuttering: An integration of contemporary therapies*. Memphis, TN: Speech Foundation of America, 79 pages.

Johnson, W. (ed) (1948). *Speech handicapped school children*. New York, NY: Harper and Brothers, p. 198.

Ham, R. E. (1990). *Therapy of stuttering*. Englewood Cliffs, N.J.: Prentice-Hall, Inc.

Kline, M. L. & Starkweather, C. W. (1979). Receptive and expressive language performance in young stutterers. *ASHA, 21,* 797.

Lieth, W. R. (1986). Treating the stutterer with atypical cultural influences. In St. Louis, K. O. (Ed.), *The atypical stutterer*, Orlando, FL. Academic Press, Inc., p. 15.

Perkins, W. (1991). Should we seek help? Chap. 7 in *Stuttering and your child: questions and answers*. Memphis, TN: Stuttering Foundation of America.

Perkins, W. (1986). Discoordination of phonation with articulation and respiration. Chap. 4, Postscript in Shames, G.H. & Rubin, H. *Stuttering then and now*. Columbus, Ohio: Charles E. Merrill Pub. Co.

Perspectives (1990). The ASHA Office of Minority Concerns Newsletter. Rockville, MD: American Speech & Hearing Association, 11.4.

Starkweather, C.W. (1986). The development of fluency in normal children. Chap. 4 in *Stuttering therapy: Prevention and intervention with children*. Memphis, TN: Speech Foundation of America.

Starkweather, C.W. (1987). *Fluency and stuttering*. Englewood Cliffs, NJ: Prentice-Hall, p. 13.

Van Riper, C. (1972). *Speech correction principles and methods*. Englewood Cliffs, NJ: Prentice-Hall.

Wingate, M. (1986). Physiological and genetic factors. Chap. 3 in Shames, G. H., & Rubin, H., *Stuttering then and now*. Columbus, OH: Charles E. Merrill.

5

VOICE DISORDERS

The voice is a measure of one's self-identity. Just think of the number of times that you have made a telephone call and have known as soon as the speaker said, "Hello," whether or not you had reached the person you wanted to talk to. Conversely, when you have answered telephone calls with a "Hello," the caller may recognize your voice and start talking without first asking "Susie?" or "May I talk to Susie, please?" and may not identify himself or herself on the assumption that you will recognize your caller's voice. Moreover, consider the number of politicians, singers, celebrities, and other well-known public figures whom you can recognize by their voices alone.

The voice also imparts other information about us besides identity. It mirrors our emotions. By the sound of a voice, even an unfamiliar voice, listeners have some notion of the speaker's emotional status. For example, the listener might detect nervousness, fear, elation, disbelief, or anger in a speaker's voice. Actors and actresses learn how to control various vocal characteristics in order to better portray the emotions of their characters. Furthermore, our voices may reflect our physical health. The most frequent and obvious example involves the listener who says, "You sound as if you have a cold." The voice may reflect other serious medical conditions.

We depend on our voices. People who have had severe cases of laryngitis know how frustrating and inefficient it can be not to be able to contribute to conversation or to have to use other modes of communication to get what they want. An individual's voice may affect his or her social acceptance and type of work. Someone with an inappropriately high pitch for his or her sex, age, and size may be nicknamed "Squeaky," a not very flattering nickname and one that surely causes hurt feelings. The person who speaks with a hoarse voice that is prone to pitch breaks (uncontrollable shifts in pitch, generally upward but sometimes downward) or a hypernasal voice (a voice which comes through the nose) may not be perceived as someone whom others would want to listen to, as is required from professionals such as teachers, ministers, news broadcasters, announcers, and disc jockeys. One study (Blood, Mahan, & Hyman, 1979) of college students found that listeners responded negatively to the appearance and personality of speakers with voice disorders. It concluded that the disordered voice may be a handicap to which others will react negatively.

DO MANY CHILDREN EXHIBIT VOICE DISORDERS?

The incidence of children exhibiting chronic voice disorders (not just the temporary hoarseness that may accompany respiratory infections) reported by a number of studies has varied considerably from as low as 0.1 percent to as high as 23.4 percent (Deal, McClain, & Sudderth, 1976). Wilson (1987) has stated that most incidence surveys have found that 6 to 9 percent of all children exhibit voice disorders. This means that, on the average, out of every thirty children that a teacher has in the classroom, at least one or two children will exhibit a voice disorder. Incidence is higher in the primary grades and in boys (Silverman & Zimmer, 1975). The concern many have is that traditionally the numbers of children who exhibit voice disorders have not been proportionally represented in the caseloads of public school speech-language pathologists. This may be due partially to the fact that there is a certain tolerance among listeners for voice disorders that are mild or moderate; thus, speech-language pathologists who rely on referrals may not know about children with less severe voice problems. In fact, Andrews (1975) noted that a child's voice is frequently so closely identified with his or her personality that parents and teachers do not recognize that the child sounds different from other children. School personnel may feel that a voice disorder does not adversely affect educational performance. However, when adverse effect is defined in the broader context of acquiring effective oral communication, as suggested by the Department of Health, Education, and Welfare (Garbee, 1985), one can more easily see that an adverse effect may in fact be occurring. It may also be easy to ignore hoarse voices on the assumption that the speaker has a cold, allergies, or other respiratory infection that will in time go away (Baynes, 1966).

In order to address the issue of underreferral of children with possible voice disorders, studies, such as that of Deal, McClain, and Sudderth (1976), have shown that inservice education programs for classroom teachers have been successful in helping teachers identify and refer children with possible voice disorders. You are urged to attend such programs whenever possible.

IF VOICE PROBLEMS ARE UNDETECTED, CAN THEY REALLY BE ALL THAT SERIOUS?

They certainly can be, because voice problems may be a symptom of a more serious medical condition. This is one reason why the speech-language pathologist generally insists that the person with a voice problem be seen by an otolaryngologist (a physician who specializes in the treatment of the ear, nose, and throat) before voice therapy begins. The vocal folds cannot be seen by looking into the mouth, but a physician can visually examine them by using a laryngeal mirror in a fairly simple procedure called indirect laryngoscopy or by using more sophisticated procedures, such as rigid endoscopy or flexible fiberscopy (Colton & Casper, 1990). A number of conditions are associated with similar sounding voices (Mowrer and Case, 1982), but the otolaryngologist's report will tell the speech-language pathologist the status of the vocal folds and the medical recommendations. Depending on the problem, medical or surgical intervention, voice therapy, or a combination of services may be appropriate. The child who presents a voice disorder will receive the best care when the physician, the speech-language pathologist, and the classroom teacher work together. If voice therapy is indicated, knowing the condition of the vocal folds prior to therapy also provides a baseline against which therapeutic success can be measured. In other words, as therapy progresses the otolaryngologist can determine whether or not the vocal folds are becoming more normal in size, appearance, and color.

A medical examination also helps to determine whether or not a voice disorder may be secondary to another medical condition, such as a congenital anomaly of the larynx (Smith & Catlin, 1984); psychiatric problems (Giacalone, 1981; Hartman & Aronson, 1983; Kaplan, 1982); Reye's syndrome (Reitman, Casper, Coplan, Weiner, Kellman, & Kantner, 1984); juvenile arthritis (Goldberg & Kovarsky, 1983); lipoid proteinosis (Pursley & Apisarnthanarax, 1981), sarcoidosis (Chijimatsu, Tajima, Washizaki, & Homma, 1980); or Tourette's disease (Lang & Marsden, 1983). Although these conditions may be somewhat rare and this is not a list that a teacher would want to memorize, children do present these diseases and conditions, and it would indeed be sad to ignore a condition that should be addressed. Cohen, Geller, Thompson, and Birns (1983) stated that vocal changes in children are important as they may be associated with neurological difficulties, congenital and genetic anomalies, tumors, infection and granulomatous disease, trauma, endocrine gland and metabolic disorders, physiological disorders, pyschogenic causes, and iatrogenic causes (ill-advised or injudicious medical procedures).

Thus, it is important for teachers to be aware of and refer children with possible voice problems to a speech-language pathologist for assessment. When a medical referral is appropriate, teachers may be able to use their understanding of the necessity of a child's visit to the otolaryngologist and their rapport with parents, to help the speech-language pathologist persuade unconvinced parents of its need.

WHAT KINDS OF VOICE DISORDERS ARE THERE?

Voice disorders can be divided into problems of pitch, loudness, and quality. Quality can be further subdivided into problems that are associated with vocal fold (synonymous with vocal cord) action and with resonance. A voice disorder exists when a speaker's voice significantly differs from "normal" along one or more of these dimensions (pitch, loudness, and quality) in relationship to his or her age, sex, size, and cultural background (e.g., a nasal twang may be acceptable in some parts of the country but not others). Such a voice draws attention away from the content of the message and to the manner in which the message is being delivered.

Pitch

A speaker's pitch may sound too high or too low for that particular person. For example, everyone has heard a female who sounded like a man because her voice was pitched so low, or heard a male whose pitch was high and effeminate sounding. A speech-language pathologist may mention pitch breaks (defined previously as uncontrolled shifts in pitch).

Loudness

Loudness, like pitch, is a perceptual judgment. A child whose only problem is a voice that is described as too loud or too soft is rarely enrolled in speech therapy. However, sometimes loudness is one factor of a larger problem, most notably increased loudness levels related to vocal abuse (explained later in this chapter). It should also be noted that voices that are too soft or too loud are sometimes indicative of hearing loss.

Quality Related to Vocal Fold Action

Whereas a normal voice can be described as pleasant (or at least not unpleasant) and smooth sounding, poor vocal quality may be described as hoarse, harsh, rough, breathy, strident, grating, too low or too high in pitch, or monotonous.

Quality Related to Resonance

Most resonance problems are related to the perceived degree of nasality that is present in the voice. In the English language only three sounds, the "m" (as in "*make*"), "n" (as in "*not*"), and "ng" (as in "ki*ng*"), are nasalized. Problems may be related to hypernasality (too much nasality) when all sounds seem to come through the nose or to hyponasality (denasality or not enough nasality) when the nasal sounds ("m," "n," and "ng") do not come through the nose, making "The man bought a ring" sound like "The bad bought a rig." A denasal voice sounds as if the speaker is very congested.

WHAT CAUSES VOICE DISORDERS?

Causes can be discussed from two perspectives: phonation and resonance. To better understand each, it is necessary to have some insight into normal voice production.

Phonation

Phonation refers to the production of sound by the vibrations of the vocal folds and is a complex process. Humans have two vocal folds, which are housed in the larynx (the Adam's apple, or voice box, in the neck) and lie side by side in a front-to-back position. As we use our voices, healthy vocal folds vibrate, coming together smoothly along the length of their surfaces at the midline, separating, and then coming together again. This action is very rapid, so rapid that the naked eye cannot follow the individual movements. The rapidity of vibration is determined by the air pressure coming from the lungs beneath the vocal folds, the tension of the vocal folds, the mass of the vocal folds, and the length of the vocal folds. The rate or frequency of vibration is the physical correlate to what we subjectively perceive as pitch. If the frequency is slower than normal, we perceive the speaker's pitch as being low whereas if the rate is faster than normal, we perceive the pitch as being high. If the vocal folds do not come together smoothly along their edges, the quality of the voice (as related to phonation) will be judged abnormal and the words "hoarse," "husky," "breathy," "strident," etc., may be used to describe it. The energy source for phonation or voice production is the air that we exhale. This air stream must be steady and sufficient. For normal respiration and vocal fold movement to occur, there must be normal neural and muscular activity. Any condition that interferes with the neural impulses directed to the respiratory or laryngeal muscles, or with the muscular activity itself, will result in a vocal disturbance. One such condition that teachers will encounter is cerebral palsy, which is discussed further in Chapter 8.

Voice disorders can result from vocal abuse and vocal misuse; trauma to the larynx resulting from accidents or medical procedures, such as intubation (a tube is passed between the vocal folds in the larynx into the trachea); congenital malformations of the larynx; organic diseases or conditions; tumors; emotional problems; or functional causes, such as the limitation of poor speech models, where no known organic causes exist. In this discussion, we will assume that neural and muscular activities are normal and will focus on phonation. Following is a discussion of the terms that a teacher will most likely hear in reference to the school-age child or youth who has a phonatory voice disorder.

Vocal Abuse and Vocal Misuse

Vocal abuse and misuse involve improper use of the vocal mechanism. Examples include screaming; yelling; shrieking; loud talking; excessive use of the voice; grunting; abrupt initiation of voicing (called *hard glottal attack*); loud, forced laughter; loud, effortful singing; loud talking that is necessary in order to be heard in a noisy environment; unusual use of the voice to make animal or machine-like sounds; coughing; throat clearing; and smoking. Most people have experienced some of these behaviors at one time or another, after which they were temporarily hoarse. However, for other people such vocal behaviors may contribute to a voice disorder. These people may spend much of their vocal time abusing their voices. Although all children scream at times, the child who exhibits a voice disorder is apt to scream a bit louder and more frequently than other children (Boone, 1983). Such activity may be related to a child's personality or environment. A child who is very aggressive is more apt to yell and speak loudly in order to command attention. Loud parents tend to beget loud children. A child who has to compete with siblings for attention in a home where the television may be turned on much of the time learns to be loud. Living with a hearing impaired parent or grandparent who can hear fairly well if sounds are loud enough may result in a child who always speaks loudly. Andrews (1986) noted that children who have airborne allergies, asthma, or frequent respiratory infections may be prone to vocal abuse secondary to the respiratory condition, since the mucous membranes of their vocal tracts, including the vocal folds, may already be irritated and swollen.

The term *vocal hygiene* has been used to refer to proper use of the voice. Teachers who discourage screaming and yelling while encouraging their charges to speak at a conversational level with their "inside" voices are not only achieving a quieter, more learning-conducive environment but are also encouraging vocal hygiene. To help their students even more, teachers might consider consulting with a speech-language pathologist and incorporating a unit on vocal hygiene into the health or science curriculum. Sponsors of extracurricular activities which frequently involve improper vocal usage, notably cheerleading, sports, drama, and singing, should also consult a speech-language pathologist. For example, a cheerleading sponsor might ask the speech-language pathologist to teach a lesson on how to cheer and yell less abusively with proper breath support and a lower pitch (Stemple, 1984), since it has been found that many cheerleaders report acute vocal changes after cheering at a game or pep rally (Reich, McHenry, & Keaton, 1986).

Vocal Nodules

People who abuse their voices are apt to develop organic changes in their vocal folds (Arnold, 1962). These changes may begin with swelling (such as vocal fold thickening) and gradually develop into unilateral (on one vocal fold only) or bilateral (on both vocal folds) protrusions known as *vocal nodules*. These nodules are sometimes called *singer's nodules* or *screamer's nodules*. If identified early enough, voice therapy that results in a positive change in vocal habits may be sufficient in reversing vocal nodule development. However, if nodules continue to develop, surgery becomes necessary. Even with surgical removal, voice therapy is necessary to prevent recurrence due to continued vocal abuse. The majority of children referred with possible voice problems in several studies (Deal, McClain, & Sudderth, 1976; Shearer, 1972; Silverman & Zimmer, 1975) were found to have vocal nodules.

Polyps

Polyps may also be the result of vocal abuse or misuse (Arnold, 1962) and may occur after a single instance of abuse, such as screaming at a football game (Boone, 1983). Continued vocal abuse or misuse will cause the polyp to increase in size. Vocal rest, surgery, and voice therapy are possible treatments. If polyps are removed surgically, they are apt to recur unless poor vocal habits are eliminated.

Papillomata

Papillomata (plural of *papilloma*) are the most common laryngeal tumors found in children (Aronson, 1980). Their cause is not known (Moore, 1986). Treatment may involve surgical removal, although papillomata tend to recur. After surgery, a physician may order total vocal rest for seven to ten days, which means that the patient should not talk or even whisper during that time. The teacher will need to provide emotional support, encouragement, and extra consideration for the child during this frustrating time. Voice therapy is generally indicated only when a child needs help in developing the best voice possible.

The identification of children who have papillomata is important, since they grow rapidly and with increasing size may impede respiration and become life threatening (Boone, 1980).

Puberphonia or Mutational Falsetto

The term *mutation* refers to the lowering of a person's pitch that normally occurs during puberty. This process takes the male about three to six months to complete, at which time the voice is pitched on the average about one octave lower. Girls' voices lower about three to four semitones. Andrews and Summers (1988) suggested that for the male the growth of facial hair, which occurs during the latter stages of pubertal maturation, may be used as a guideline for determining whether maturationally a boy's pitch should have become lower. The majority of youth pass through this stage with no problems. However, although the vocal mechanism develops, occasionally the voice does not fully develop into that of a normal sounding adult. The terms *puberphonia* or *mutational falsetto* are used to describe the problem of unnaturally high pitch that is not a result of hormonal disorders. Therapy is generally successful in a relatively short period of time.

Resonance

Air and the laryngeal tone (the sound that is produced by the vocal folds) travel up into the throat, mouth, and nasal cavity. The sizes and shapes of these three structures and the way in which they are connected to each other change the way the laryngeal tone sounds. This change process is referred to as *resonance*. You can easily demonstrate the manner in which size and shape of structures influence resonance by taking several 16 ounce pop bottles; leaving one empty and filling the others with varying amounts of water; blowing across the tops of the bottles much as one would play the flute; and listening to the various pitch sounds that are produced. The most common resonance disorders involve the manner in which the nasal cavity (nose) is connected to the oral cavity (mouth). The *palate* is the structure in the mouth that serves as the roof of the mouth and the floor of the nasal cavity. If you place your tongue on the roof of your mouth immediately behind your top teeth and slowly move your tongue backward along the palate, you will note that approximately the first two-thirds of the palate feels hard (because there is bone beneath the layers of soft tissue), and then the palate becomes soft (there is no longer any bony tissue). The bony two-thirds of the palate is referred to as the *hard palate* and the soft one-third as the *soft palate* or *velum*. The velum is composed partially of muscles, which allow the velum to stretch upward and backward to the back wall of the throat. (Look in a mirror, say "aah," and note this movement.) As the velum moves, the back and side walls of the throat (or pharynx) move slightly forward and inward to meet the velum. These movements together cause the nasal cavity to be shut off from the mouth. A teacher may hear this opening between the nose and mouth referred to as the *velopharyngeal port* and the involved structures referred to as the *velopharyngeal mechanism* ("velo" from "velum"—soft palate; "pharyngeal" from "pharynx"—throat). If there is a problem, a child may be said to have velopharyngeal incompetency or insufficiency. The cause of velopharyngeal incompetency may be functional (no organic cause can be found) or organic (structural or physiological causes can be found). Organic causes will be the focus of this discussion since the majority of resonance problems are organic in nature (Boone, 1983), resulting in either hyponasality or hypernasality.

Hyponasality

Less common than hypernasality, hyponasality (or denasality) occurs when the nasal passages are occluded. This may be due to nasal congestion associated with respiratory infections or allergies; enlarged adenoids, which fill up the space between the soft palate and walls of the throat so that air and sound cannot enter the nasal cavity; tumors; congenital anomalies; or changes in the nasal structures due to accidents that prevent sounds and air from entering the nasal cavity. By necessity, the child who is hyponasal due to organic problems will be a mouth-breather. Treatment may consist of decongestants and other medical-surgical procedures.

Hypernasality

Hypernasality occurs when velopharyngeal incompetency or insufficiency is present, that is, when the nasal cavity cannot be sufficiently shut off from the oral cavity, so that all sounds have a nasal quality. If severe enough, listeners may hear a noisy escape of air from the nose; speakers may noticeably try to pinch together their nostrils in order to reduce this escape of air from the nose (called a *nasal grimace*); articulation errors may occur as the speaker distorts sounds, omits sounds, or substitutes easier sounds for harder ones; and intelligibility of speech may be reduced. Hypernasality may result from an opening in the palate (called a *cleft palate*), lack of bone in the hard palate (called a *submucous cleft*), a short velum that cannot reach far enough back, a throat that is so deep that the velum and pharyngeal walls cannot meet even when these structures are normal, neurological problems that cause the muscles of the velum or pharyngeal walls to be weak or paralyzed, or a hearing impairment that prevents the speaker from monitoring his or her voice. (Cleft lip and palate will be discussed later in this chapter.) Visual inspection alone may not be sufficient to determine the condition of the velopharyngeal mechanism. A medical diagnosis that relies on x-rays and other diagnostic procedures is required. When such organic conditions exist, medical-surgical procedures are indicated to reduce the impact of these conditions on speech, since there is little chance that speech therapy alone will be helpful in significantly reducing hypernasality (Shanks, 1983).

WHAT DO VOICE ASSESSMENT AND THERAPY ENTAIL?

Assessment

A child who is suspected of having a voice disorder will be carefully rated by a speech-language pathologist for quality, pitch, and loudness. More than one rating may be advisable over several weeks since many voice disorder symptoms are temporary, due to colds, seasonal allergies, or other temporary respiratory conditions (Moore, 1986). In order to have a more objective basis of comparison, the speech-language pathologist may record the child's voice during these screenings. If an individual diagnosis is warranted and the parents agree, the speech-language pathologist will want to obtain a medical history and information from the child, parents, teachers, and important others regarding vocal abuse behaviors. Hearing tests and more specific vocal procedures will be conducted. If the judgment is that the child does indeed have abnormal vocal aspects, referrals to appropriate medical specialists, such as to an otolaryngologist for phonation-related problems or to a cleft palate team at a hospital or clinic for problems involving the velopharyngeal mechanism, will be made before the child is scheduled for voice therapy at school.

Therapy

Most people do not hear their own voices as others hear them. Thus, frequently voice therapy will begin with listening skills or ear training intended to teach children to hear their own voices and to compare them with others in terms of targeted vocal attributes, such as pitch or quality. Andrews (1975) advised that negative terms regarding the voice, such as "wrong," "bad," or "unpleasant," be replaced by more neutral terms, such as "different," since the voice is so closely associated with self-identity.

For many children a program of vocal abuse reduction will be initiated in which the types of vocal abuse will be identified, a baseline count of the number of times per day that each type of abuse occurs will be made, and a plan to reduce the number of abuse instances will be formulated with the children and carried out. In establishing the baseline count, a speech-language pathologist may ask the parents and teachers to make independent counts or to help a child count, particularly in environments or situations that would be associated with a high probability of abuse behaviors (e.g., while playing). The speech-language pathologist may also do some counting in situations outside of therapy and may particularly want to talk to the music teacher, the physical education teacher, and even the bus driver and lunchroom supervisor (Andrews, 1986). As baseline information is being gathered, the child will be told how vocal abuse behaviors relate to the present voice condition and how they will affect his or her voice in the future. Time may be spent identifying behaviors that can replace vocal abuse behaviors, such as clapping instead of yelling at an athletic event, walking across the playground to a friend instead of yelling to the friend (Blonigen, 1978), or using a silent cough where air is forced from the lungs in staccato-like bursts with no voicing (Prater & Swift, 1984). The goal will be to first decrease and then eliminate all vocal abuse behaviors. In order to accomplish this, the child will continue to count the number of daily abuses. This information may be plotted on a graph so the child can evaluate visually his or her progress. It has been suggested that a child should be provided with a wrist-type counter during this time (Johnson, 1983). If teachers know these graphs are being kept, they can show their interest by asking to see them and by making appropriate remarks. (It is hoped that the child will be progressing so that these may legitimately be remarks full of praise.)

Andrews (1986) has suggested that although no research evidence of a relationship exists, clinical experience indicates that when a child has a voice disorder associated with vocal abuse, voice use related to social and emotional development should be evaluated. There may be no problem, but some children may need to learn to listen instead of incessantly talking, learn to take turns instead of doing all the talking, and learn when it is appropriate and when it is not appropriate to talk loudly. The school psychologist may be helpful in these situations.

Direct therapy on whatever aspects of voice need remediation may progress while a child attempts to decrease vocal abuse behaviors. Such therapy may involve establishing a new pitch, relaxation exercises and techniques, and elimination of hard glottal attacks. Explanation of voice production and the necessity for these activities and changes will be an integral part of the therapy process. Just as with articulatory problems, a child will begin using his or her new voice in small speech tasks, gradually increasing the length and complexity of each task so that it is only in the latter stages of therapy that the child will be asked to consciously habituate the new voice in all situations.

WHEN SHOULD A TEACHER REFER A CHILD TO A SPEECH-LANGUAGE PATHOLOGIST?

In deciding whether or not to refer a child because of a voice disorder to the speech-language pathologist, a teacher might ask the following questions (Pentz, Jr. & Gilbert, 1983):

- Has the child been hoarse for more than two or three weeks?
- Does the child's pitch seem too high or too low?
- Does the child talk too loudly or too softly?
- Does the child exhibit vocal abuse behaviors?
- Does the child talk through his or her nose?
- Does the child always seem to sound congested?
- Does the child have an unpleasant voice?

WHAT IS CLEFT PALATE?

Many teachers-in-training raise a number of questions about clefts. What exactly is a cleft palate? How often do they occur? What causes a cleft lip or palate? Can cleft palate be corrected? How does a cleft lip and/or palate affect speech?

A cleft, which can involve the lip and/or palate, is an opening in these structures due to their failure to close or fuse during early development of the fetus. These structures normally are fused sometime within the first three months of fetal development. Failure to develop properly may result in a cleft of one or both sides of the upper lip; a cleft of the palate alone; of the lip alone; or of both palate and lip. The extent or severity of a cleft is variable as well. In some instances it may be relatively small and restricted only to the lip or palate, whereas in others it may be extensive and involve both lip and hard and soft palates.

Many causes without scientific basis are attributed to cleft lip and palate. Legend has it that a baby born with a cleft lip or palate is punishment for parents who are in disfavor with the Almighty, or that the child is not really wanted. These and other such attributions are myths. However, scientists are still seeking answers that are based in fact. Currently, the best indications are that this anomaly in development is genetically related and seems to follow in families. It may be that the two variables of genetic predisposition toward a cleft and the environment provided a fetus together conspire to cause this maldevelopment.

One of every 700 newborns has some form of cleft lip and/or palate, the fourth most common birth defect (Beverly-Ducker, 1992). The frequency of occurrence is related to race and gender. Incidence estimates vary as follows: for Caucasians, approximately 1 in 750 to 1,000 births; for Blacks, approximately 1 in 1,900 to 3,000 births; and for Orientals about 1 in 500 births. Clefts are seen more frequently in boys than in girls (McWilliams, 1986).

Correction of cleft palate is best accomplished by an interdisciplinary team composed of representatives from surgery, dentistry, nursing, orthodontics, prosthodontics, psychology, medical social work, speech-language pathology, and audiology. Medical and dental correction involves surgical repair and the fitting of prosthetic appliances. The surgical approach calls for specialized surgical procedures. In some instances, depending upon the nature and severity of the cleft, several operations over many years may be necessary. In those cases where surgery is inappropriate or has not culminated in a complete closure, a prosthetic appliance, called an *obturator,* is used. The obturator fills the opening created by the maldevelopment. It is also possible to fit missing teeth (a not uncommon problem) onto an obturator. As a child grows, the obturator must be replaced periodically. Contraindications to an obturator include severe mental retardation, uncooperative parents or child, and an extremely poor dental situation.

For some children, early medical treatment and a good program of speech-language stimulation in infancy will correct adverse effects on speech by the time a child begins school. However, for many children a cleft lip and palate may affect speech adversely, although surgical repair and prosthetic devices help to provide the structures necessary for acceptable speech. In fact, Bzoch (1979, p. 293) stated that although "effective means of focusing on the prevention or early correction of these serious problems (of cleft palate speech) have been developed and refined . . . the majority of infants born in the United States with clefts involving the soft palate still exhibit the stigmata of cleft palate speech abnormalities throughout most of their important formative and early school-age years." To this end, home training programs involving both parents and child (making use of the speech-language consultation program or indirect service that was discussed under "Therapy" in Chapter 1) have been recommended (Hahn, 1979). Speech, sometimes referred to as *cleft palate speech,* may be characterized by articulatory errors, such as weak sounds, distortions, omissions, substitutions of easier sounds, and use of non-English sounds, including the glottal stop; nasal emission of air; and facial or nasal grimaces made in a compensatory effort to trap the air escaping through the nose to allow better sound production. Cleft palate speech at its worst will be difficult to understand and the grimaces may be visually distracting. However, it should be noted that children with clefts may have speech problems that are not related to the cleft, but that develop much the same as they do for children from the so-called normal population.

Frequently, children with clefts exhibit other congenital problems involving the skeletal, cardiovascular, digestive, genitourinary, or sensory systems (Koepp-Baker, 1979). A problem involving the sensory system is that of middle ear disease, which may be slight or severe. Recent investigation showed that middle ear disease is a factor in loss of high-frequency sensitivity (McDermott, Fausti, & Frey, 1986). This can result in hearing loss, which in turn can have an adverse effect upon speech and language development.

It has been speculated that children with clefts might experience negative parent-child relationships, have poorly developed self-images, and be exposed to fewer social contacts, which would in turn affect language experience and development. In a summary of the literature regarding psychological and sociological adjustment, Clifford (1979) concluded that although there are indications that there may be some subtle effects of the cleft, persons with cleft palates do not demonstrate gross maladjustments either as children or as adults. Shames and Rubin (1979) reported that their review of the literature indicated that children with cleft palates demonstrated a slight, but not significant, reduction in language skills.

It is important that classroom teachers are fully aware of the implications that cosmetic and speech problems can have. It has been recommended that before children with clefts start school, they be taught how to explain their problems, including anticipated future treatment, to peers in a straightforward manner (Hahn, 1979) in an attempt to ward off teasing and other negative comments. A teacher knowledgeable (through discussions with the parents, child, and speech-language pathologist) about an individual child will be able to help the child do this. The teacher should also work closely with the speech-language pathologist and report the child's adjustment to various speech situations (Brown, 1948; Freeman, 1977).

CASE HISTORIES

Jonie

One of Jonie's teachers referred her to the speech-language pathologist because her voice was very husky and low pitched. Upon assessment by the speech-language pathologist, it was learned that Jonie, then a junior in high school, was a very outgoing girl who talked constantly. To further complicate the picture, Jonie was a cheerleader and yelled incessantly at sports events. The case history revealed that on many mornings following a game she was literally voiceless. There was little question but that she was in trouble already, and without help she would most certainly be even more deeply in trouble with her voice.

The speech-language pathologist consulted with Jonie's parents about the seriousness of the situation. The parents agreed to have Jonie seen by an otolaryngologist to determine whether medical or surgical treatment was necessary. Fortunately, neither was, but the otolaryngologist described Jonie's swollen and reddened vocal folds and warned of the danger of developing polyps or vocal nodules if the yelling continued. The otolaryngologist then proceeded to put Jonie on vocal rest for three weeks: no yelling, no talking, no whispering. Jonie continued at games as a cheerleader, but strictly without voice.

Following the period of vocal rest, Jonie's voice was much improved; only a slight trace of huskiness remained. A program of vocal hygiene was outlined for Jonie, and she met regularly with the speech-language pathologist for its implementation. The latest word is that therapy is moving along well and that Jonie, although still a very outgoing girl, is seeing the wisdom of being much more careful about not abusing her voice.

Richard

Richard was a fourth grader who had been born with an extensive cleft of both lip and palate. He had undergone several operations as a preschooler, and both the lip and palate had been repaired. Prior to his direct work in the speech therapy class, he had received no other special help because he lived in a rural area where public school speech therapy had been unavailable prior to the enactment of PL 94-142. Thus, Richard was nine years old before he had any opportunity to improve his speech. Unfortunately, unlike some children with repaired clefts, his speech, even with the excellent palatal repair, was nasal to the point of being unintelligible at times. He was shy and old enough to be quite embarrassed about his unsuccessful attempts at communicating with his teacher and his classmates. To make matters worse, he was the butt of many wisecracks made by some pupils, despite the classroom teacher's attempts to stop them.

Richard's work with the speech-language pathologist was a bright spot in the day for both Richard and his clinician. He not only eagerly accepted help but also made excellent progress in the development of better articulation and a voice that was considerably less nasal. His classroom teacher worked intelligently and enthusiastically with Richard and the speech-language pathologist. She maintained a "transfer sheet" of sounds (set up by the clinician) that Richard could be expected to produce successfully in the classroom. Richard seemed to be gaining more confidence each day, and after a year of special help he had made substantial progress. It appeared, also, that his fellow pupils were including him more in their play and accepting him much better. He obviously was thinking more highly of himself, and they were seemingly regarding him more favorably.

One day the following autumn a youngster was referred to the clinician by the kindergarten teacher. It was John, Richard's younger brother. Evaluation quickly revealed that John had cleft palate speech as well. The only difference was that John had a perfect speech mechanism—no cleft lip—no cleft palate! He had simply learned Richard's cleft palate speech in his five years at home. A real challenge!

SUMMARY

Causes

- Vocal abuse
- Allergies
- Maldevelopment of the vocal mechanism
- Frequent infections
- Trauma
- Emotional problems
- Vocal nodules and tumors
- Vocal changes in puberty

Some Important Points to Remember

- The voice often mirrors the speaker's emotions and physical health.
- Pitch that is too high or too low can affect how others accept a child.
- From 0.1 to 23 percent of children experience some form of voice disorder.
- Based upon frequency of occurrence, children with voice disorders are underrepresented in the caseloads of speech-language pathologists.
- Examination by a physician (otolaryngologist) is frequently indicated for children with voice problems.
- There are disorders of pitch, loudness, and quality (related to both phonation and resonance).
- Hyponasality refers to too little nasal resonance.
- Hypernasality refers to too much nasal resonance.
- Vocal assessment involves a case history and voice examination by the speech-language pathologist, and frequently a medical examination.
- Cleft palate and cleft lip can cause voice and articulation disorders.

Do's and Don'ts for Teachers

Do's

- Be aware of children with unusual sounding voices and refer them to a speech-language pathologist.

- Learn from the speech-language pathologist the nature of a child's vocal disorder and how you can help.
- Reinforce the work of the speech-language pathologist.
- Create an atmosphere of acceptance and understanding in the classroom for the child with a voice disorder.

Don'ts
- Do not attempt to correct a voice disorder except as instructed by a speech-language pathologist.

Referral Resources

- Speech-language pathologist
- Otolaryngologist
- Allergist
- Psychologist
- Audiologist
- Cleft palate team

SELF-TEST

True or False:

1. The voice sometimes reflects the speaker's emotions and physical ____ health.
2. A hypernasal voice is one with too much nasality. ____
3. A hyponasal voice is one with too little nasality. ____
4. An acceptable figure for prevalence of voice disorders in children is ____ from 25 to 30 percent.
5. There is some concern that children with voice disorders have been ____ underrepresented in the caseloads of speech-language pathologists.
6. Voice problems may be indicative of medical conditions. ____
7. The majority of youth pass through puberty without any serious ____ voice problems.
8. The throat, mouth, and nasal cavities contribute insignificantly to the ____ resonance characteristics of the voice.
9. Resonance refers to the production of sound by the vibrations of the ____ vocal folds.
10. When making an assessment of voice, the speech-language patholo- ____ gist is concerned with checking quality, pitch, and loudness.
11. It is a fact that we hear our voices as others hear them. ____
12. Children with voice disorders due to vocal abuse may need to be ____ evaluated relative to their psychological and emotional adjustment.
13. Vocal hygiene refers to therapy for voice disorders. ____
14. The causes for cleft palate and cleft lip have yet to be firmly es- ____ tablished.

15. Cleft palate usually occurs sometime between birth and the end of _____
the first year.
16. Clefts vary considerably in type and severity.   _____
17. Where there is a cleft lip, there is always a cleft palate.   _____
18. Both hard and soft palates may be cleft in some babies.   _____
19. Figures show that the frequency of cleft palates is considerably _____
higher among Blacks than among Orientals.
20. Rarely is surgical repair an option for a child with cleft lip and cleft _____
palate.
21. A prosthetic appliance called an obturator is sometimes used for _____
filling the space created by a cleft.
22. The speech of cleft palate children is frequently hyponasal.   _____
23. More boys are born with a cleft palate than girls.   _____
24. A multidisciplinary team effort is indicated for a child with a cleft _____
palate and lip.
25. An obturator is an appliance used in cases of cleft lip.   _____

REFERENCES

Andrews, M. L. (1975). Some common problems encountered in voice therapy with children. *Language, Speech, and Hearing Services in Schools, 6,* 183–187.
Andrews, M. L. (1986). *Voice therapy for children.* New York: Longman.
Andrews, J. L., & Sumers, A. (1988). *Voice therapy for adolescents.* Boston: Little, Brown.
Arnold, G. E. (1962). Vocal nodules and polyps: Laryngeal tissue reaction to habitual hyperkinetic dysphonia. *Journal of Speech and Hearing Disorders, 27,* 205–217.
Aronson, A. E. (1980). *Clinical voice disorders.* New York: Brian C. Decker Division of Thieme-Stratton.
Baynes, R. A. (1966). Incidence study of chronic hoarseness among children. *Journal of Speech and Hearing Disorders, 31,* 172–176.
Beverly-Ducker, K. (1992). Cleft Palate–Craniofacial Groups. *ASHA, 34*(4), 56.
Blonigen, J. A. (1978). Management of vocal hoarseness caused by abuse: An approach. *Language, Speech, and Hearing Services in Schools, 9,* 142–150.
Blood, G. W., Mahan, B. W., & Hyman, M. (1979). Judging personality and appearance from voice disorders. *Journal of Communication Disorders, 12,* 63–67.
Boone, D. R. (1980). Voice disorders. In T. J. Hixon, L. D. Shriberg, & J. H. Saxman (Eds.), *Introduction to communication disorders* (pp. 311–351). Englewood Cliffs, NJ: Prentice-Hall.
Boone, D. R. (1983). *The voice and voice therapy* (3rd ed.). Englewood Cliffs, NJ: Prentice-Hall.
Brown, S. F. (1948). Cleft palate; cerebral palsy. In W. Johnson, S. F. Brown, J. F. Curtis, C. W. Edney, & J. Keaster (Eds.), *Speech handicapped school children* (rev. ed.) (pp. 330–365). New York: Harper and Row.
Bzoch, K. R. (1979). Rationale, methods, and techniques of cleft palate speech therapy. In K. R. Bzoch (Ed.), *Communicative disorders related to cleft lip and palate* (2nd ed.) (pp. 293–303). Boston: Little, Brown.

Chijimatsu, Y., Tajima, J., Washizaki, M., & Homma, H. (1980). Hoarseness as an initial manifestation of sarcoidosis. *Chest, 78,* 779–781.

Clifford, E. (1979). Psychological aspects of cleft lip and palate. In K. R. Bzoch (Ed.), *Communicative disorders related to celft lip and palate* (2nd ed.) (pp. 37–51). Boston: Little, Brown.

Cohen, S. R., Geller, K. A., Thompson, J. W., & Birns, J. W. (1983). Voice change in the pediatric patient: A differential diagnosis. *Annals of Otology, Rhinology and Laryngology, 92* (5 Part 1), 437–443.

Colton, R. H., & Casper, J. K. (1990). *Understanding voice problems.* Baltimore: Williams and Wilkins.

Deal, R. E., McClain, B., & Sudderth, J. F. (1976). Identification, evaluation, therapy, and follow-up for children with vocal nodules in a public school setting. *Journal of Speech and Hearing Disorders, 41,* 390–397.

Freeman, G. G. (1977). *Speech and language services and the classroom teacher.* Reston, VA: The Council for Exceptional Children. (Publication of the National Support Systems Project under a grant from the Division of Personnel Preparation, Bureau of Education for the Handicapped, U.S. Office of Education, Department of Health, Education, and Welfare.)

Garbee, F. E. (1985). The speech-language pathologist as a member of the educational team. In R. J. Van Hattum (Ed.), *Organization of speech-language services in schools* (pp. 58–129). San Diego: College-Hill.

Giacalone, A. V. (1981). Hysterical dysphonia: Hypnotic treatment of a ten-year-old female. *The American Journal of Clinical Hypnosis, 23,* 289–293.

Goldberg, J., & Kovarsky, J. (1983). Beclomethasone dipropionate in inhalation treatment for chronic hoarseness in rheumatic disease. *Arthritis and Rheumatism, 26,* 1412.

Hahn, E. (1979). Directed home training program for infants with cleft lip and palate. In K. R. Bzoch (Ed.), *Communicative disorders related to cleft lip and palate* (2nd ed.) (pp. 311–317). Boston: Little, Brown.

Hartman, D. E., & Aronson, A. E. (1983). Psychogenic aphonia masking mutational falsetto. *Archives of Otolaryngology, 109,* 415–416.

Johnson, T. S. (1983). Treatment of vocal abuse in children. In W. H. Perkins (Ed.), *Current therapy of communication disorders: Voice disorders* (pp. 3–11). New York: Thieme-Stratton.

Kaplan, S. L. (1982). Case report: Mutational falsetto. *Journal of the American Academy of Child Psychiatry, 21,* 82–85.

Koepp-Baker, H. (1979). The craniofacial team. In K. R. Bzoch (Ed.), *Communicative disorders related to cleft lip and palate* (2nd ed.) (pp. 52–61). Boston: Little, Brown.

Lang, A. E., & Marsden, C. D. (1983). Spastic dysphonia in Gilles de la Tourette's disease. *Archives of Neurology, 40,* 51–52.

McDermott, J. C., Fausti, S. A., & Frey, R. H. (1986). Effects of middle ear disease and cleft palate on high-frequency hearing in children. *Audiology, 25,* 136–148.

McWilliams, B. J. (1986). Cleft palate. In G. H. Shames & E. H. Wiig (Eds.), *Human communication disorders* (2nd ed.) (pp. 445–494). Columbus, OH: Charles E. Merrill.

Moore, G. P. (1986). Voice disorders. In G. H. Shames & E. H. Wiig (Eds.), *Human*

Communication Disorders (2nd ed.) (pp. 183–241). Columbus, OH: Charles E. Merrill.

Mowrer, D. E., & Case, J. L. (1982). *Clinical management of speech disorders.* Rockville, MD: Aspen Systems.

Pentz, A. L., Jr., & Gilbert, H. R. (1983). Relation of selected acoustical parameters and perceptual ratings to voice quality of Down syndrome children. *American Journal of Mental Deficiency, 88,* 203–210.

Prater, R. J., & Swift, R. W. (1984). *Manual of voice therapy.* Boston: Little, Brown.

Pursley, T. V., & Apisarnthanarax, P. (1981). Lipoid proteinosis. *International Journal of Dermatology, 20,* 137–139.

Reich, A., McHenry, M., & Keaton, A. (1986). A survey of dysphonic episodes in high-school cheerleaders. *Language, Speech, and Hearing Services in Schools, 17,* 63–71.

Reitman, M. A., Casper, J., Coplan, J., Weiner, L. B., Kellman, R. M., & Kantner, R. K. (1984). Motor disorders of voice and speech in Reye's syndrome survivors. *American Journal of Diseases of Children, 138,* 1129–1131.

Shames, G. H., & Rubin, H. (1979). Psycholinguistic measures of language and speech. In K. R. Bzoch (Ed.), *Communicative disorders related to cleft lip and palate* (2nd ed.) (pp. 202–223). Boston: Little, Brown.

Shanks, J. C. (1983). Treatment of resonance disorders. In W. H. Perkins (Ed.), *Current therapy of communication disorders: Voice Disorders* (pp. 39–49). New York: Thieme-Stratton.

Shearer, W. M. (1972). Diagnosis and treatment of voice disorders in school children. *Journal of Speech and Hearing Disorders, 37,* 215–221.

Silverman, E. M., & Zimmer, C. H. (1975). Incidence of chronic hoarseness among school-age children. *Journal of Speech and Hearing Disorders, 40,* 211–215.

Smith, R. J. H., & Catlin, F. I. (1984). Congenital anomalies of the larynx. *American Journal of Diseases of Children, 138,* 35–39.

Stemple, J. C. (1984). *Clinical voice pathology: Theory and management.* Columbus, OH: Charles E. Merrill.

Wilson, D. K. (1987). *Voice problems of children* (3rd ed.). Baltimore: Williams and Wilkins.

6

HEARING AND HEARING LOSS

Hearing and speech provide the means through which we communicate ideas and transmit information and emotions. Speech and language are usually acquired through hearing. Hearing loss can cause individual speech and language systems to be disordered. The resultant communication problems are some of the most serious and challenging to confront a classroom teacher. A significant hearing disability not only signals difficulty understanding the sounds of the environment, but also correlates with serious language, voice, and articulation deficits.

Although it is not common for regular classroom teachers to have the responsibility for children with severe hearing loss, it is likely that many children with moderate to mild losses will be assigned or mainstreamed to a regular classroom for at least part of the school day. Therefore, it is essential that a teacher have a basic understanding of the nature of hearing loss as well as the social, communication, and educational problems that are associated with it.

WHAT IS SOUND?

It is difficult for most of us to think of sound as separate from hearing, but they are two distinct concepts. Hearing is like taste, smell, and touch—it is not a physical event; it is a sensation. Hearing occurs in response to a physical event taking place external to our ears. Sound, therefore, is what our hearing mechanism is engineered to perceive. Accordingly, it is a phenomenon to which our ears are capable of responding, with the implication that sound can be heard if we are present to hear it.

When an object moves in our environment, the disturbed air around the object causes an abnormal air pressure that travels from the site of the object in all directions. If an object vibrates, a series of pressure waves with fluctuations below and above normal air pressure will simulate the vibratory pattern, the back-and-forth motions of the object. These fluctuating pressure changes are called *sound waves.* The strength or power of sound waves correlates with the loudness of the perceived sound. The strength of a sound, therefore, is measured in terms of how much the pressure varies above and below normal atmospheric pressure. This can be referred to as *sound pressure level.*

Sound is also characterized by the rate at which an object vibrates. The slower the cycle of vibrations, the farther apart the sound waves will be spaced. Objects that vibrate at a more rapid rate, or *frequency*, will cause shorter (faster) waves to emanate from the sound source. Therefore, a sound's wavelength always increases as its frequency decreases. Shorter wavelengths, characterized by rapid vibratory rates, are perceived as higher pitched sounds. Longer wavelengths are characterized by slower vibratory rates. Frequency is expressed in cycles per second (cps), also known as hertz (Hz).

Sound *intensity* concerns the strength of the sound waves emanating from an object that has moved or has been set into vibration. The convention for expressing sound intensity is the decibel (dB) scale. The *B* is capitalized in the abbreviated expression in honor of Alexander G. Bell because of his work with sound and hearing. The reference point for describing dB changes is usually zero dB. In measurement of hearing sensitivity, this reference typically represents the softest sound we can detect and can be referred to as the *threshold of hearing*. Our upper tolerance for sound intensity is variable, but for practical purposes, any sound level that elicits a painful or tickling sensation in the ears can be considered too intense, and for most of us, this occurs between 115 and 140 dB.

The psychological correlates of these physical phenomena are *loudness* for intensity and *pitch* for frequency. It should be noted that most sounds in our environment are complex in structure. This means that many frequencies with varying intensities are occurring at the same time. Speech is an excellent example of a complex sound.

WHAT IS NORMAL HEARING?

All sounds are air pressure variations, but some of these variations are beyond our ability to hear. For example, bats generate sounds up to a vibratory rate of 30,000 Hz. The pitch level is so high that it is out of the range of human hearing altogether. There are numerous other sounds,

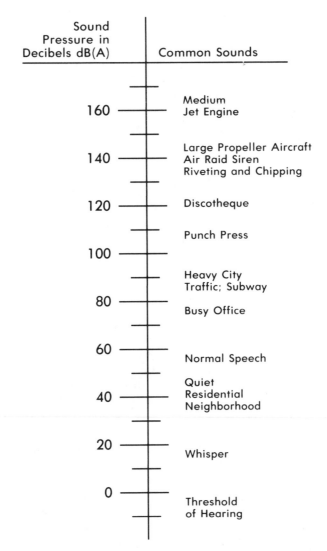

FIGURE 6-1   Sound pressure levels of common sounds in dB.

such as certain dog whistles, that possess intensity and frequency characteristics that humans do not have the capability of hearing.

The frequency and intensity boundaries for human hearing are narrow but variable. The lowest audible frequency for most of us is around 15 Hz, which is generally heard as a low pitched rumble and felt as vibrations throughout the body. The upper boundary is generally around 12,000 to

18,000 Hz. The important frequency range for hearing speech is between 300 to 4,000 Hz.

The physical characteristics of sound can be processed by one ear. Why do we have two? The reason is that one ear does not tell us all we want to know about a sound. For example, the location or origin of a particular sound is not easily traced with one ear. Listeners depend on the difference in time for a sound to reach each ear to make these judgments. When one ear is blocked or damaged to the point that hearing is not possible, localizing sound is difficult, if not impossible, particularly in noisy situations.

HOW DO WE HEAR?

The hearing centers in the brain are essentially isolated from the environment. All the important information about sound that gets to the brain is piped in through the ears. Because the brain functions by diverting electrical impulses from one brain cell to another, the information it processes must be delivered in this form. The ears, therefore, must convert the sound stimulus (air pressure fluctuation) into patterns of electrical impulses that transmit essential information about the sound's intensity, frequency, and location. There are three basic steps in the process. First, the atmospheric pressure changes are converted to vibrations. Next, these vibrations are enhanced into stronger vibrations. Last, the vibrations are converted into electrical energy. The three major components of the ear—the outer, middle, and inner ear—are designed to accomplish these objectives.

The ear flap, or *pinna,* of the outer ear collects the air pressure fluctuations and channels them through the external ear canal to the eardrum, or *tympanum.* The eardrum also prohibits the free flow of air into the middle ear chamber. As a result, the air pressure differences outside of the middle ear and within the middle ear force the eardrum to bulge in and out in accordance with the air pressure fluctuations impinging upon it. Thereby the eardrum is set into vibration and the air pressure fluctuations are changed into vibratory patterns.

The middle ear is a cavity within the mastoid bone on the side of the skull and is about the size of an ordinary thimble. Normal atmospheric air pressure is maintained within the chamber by a small tube, the *Eustachian tube,* which opens into the throat during the act of swallowing or yawning. The middle ear also houses a chain of three tiny bones, *ossicles,* that connect the eardrum vibrations by mechanical motion to the inner ear. These three bones are called the *malleus, incus,* and *stapes,* and they act as a system of levers to enhance the vibratory energy. The stapes, the last bone in the chain, is attached to a small window-type membrane at the wall of the inner ear *(cochlea).*

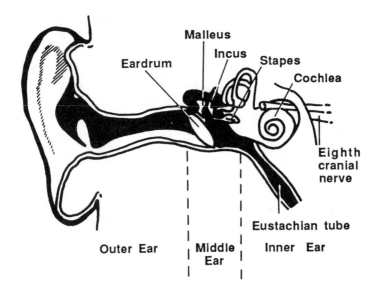

FIGURE 6-2 Structure of the human ear.

The cochlea is filled with fluid and is shaped like a coiled snail shell. The lever action of the middle ear causes pressure changes in the fluid. The movement of the fluid across the nerve endings housed in the inner ear converts the vibrations into electrical impulses. The nerve endings eventually converge into the auditory nerve (there are two nerves, one for each ear) which delivers the electrical impulses to the brain.

HOW DO WE UNDERSTAND WHAT WE HEAR?

The process of hearing relies on the brain to interpret the patterns of electrical impulses delivered from each cochlea. However, the meaning that is attached to the sounds of our environment is learned. At birth an infant can detect sounds within the range of human hearing, but sound, in itself, does not carry associated meaning. Within weeks after birth, however, primitive associations among sounds, events, and behaviors are learned. By the end of the first year, a normal hearing child understands many words and begins to say them. Children with normal hearing typically develop mature articulation of speech sounds between the ages of six and eight. Obviously, hearing plays a critical role in the development of language and speech, because without it a child is incapable of hearing words and thus cannot imitate speech.

HOW IS HEARING MEASURED?

The measurement of hearing loss incorporates the concepts of intensity and frequency. This is accomplished by determining the softest sound the ear can detect. It is necessary that the listener be situated in a very quiet room, preferably a sound-treated chamber conforming to nationally accepted standards for eliminating ambient noise. If a stimulus is complex, comprising several frequencies (as does speech), it cannot be determined which component the listener is hearing. Therefore, the sound should be a single frequency of vibration, a *pure tone*. The machine designed to generate these tones is called an *audiometer*. Each pure tone is presented for brief periods of time, with each successive presentation made louder until the listener detects the sound. This procedure is repeated for several different frequencies, usually 125, 250, 500, 1,000, 2,000, 4,000, and 8,000 Hz. The decibel level (intensity) required for hearing at each frequency becomes the threshold of hearing for each frequency. The intensity and frequency for each pure tone that is heard are plotted on a special form called an *audiogram* (See Figure 6-3). The symbol "X" indicates responses for the left ear, and "O" signifies responses for the right. Any decibel level below the zero line can be referred to as an *x dB hearing loss* for that frequency. As greater decibel levels are required to hear a particular tone, hearing sensitivity is described as poorer. Accordingly, when lower levels elicit a response, hearing is depicted as better.

The important point is what decibel level of hearing loss at each frequency constitutes a problem for the listener. There is no simple, single answer. A significant loss at any one frequency is not likely to cause a problem. But should several frequencies be affected a problem is likely. A further question is whether both ears are affected or only one.

Figure 6–3 depicts an audiogram showing hearing loss in both ears. The sensitivity thresholds for the right ear indicate a profound hearing loss causing a significant problem in understanding speech even with the use of a hearing aid. Fortunately, the threshold levels for the left ear are somewhat better, providing a situation where the listener can perhaps understand speech from the ear when the signals are loud enough.

Northern and Downs (1978) presented compelling data supporting the notion that, for some children, even a minimal hearing loss (around 15 dB) can cause a significant problem with hearing, especially when the deficit is caused by a chronic ear condition. At the same time, other children may show poorer hearing and demonstrate little or no disability. Generally speaking, children with longterm hearing losses in excess of 25 to 30 dB demonstrate communication and learning problems (Table 6-1).

There are several other factors that preclude a simple, accurate description of the nature of hearing loss. For example, losses can affect one or both

AUDIOGRAM

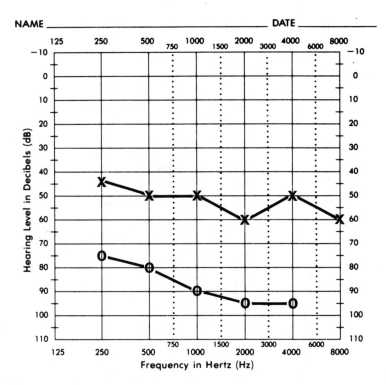

FIGURE 6-3 An audiogram used to plot hearing loss levels.

ears, be mild or profound, worse for some frequencies and better for others, congenital or acquired, temporary or permanent, facilitated with hearing aid use or not facilitated, and disabling to varying degrees. Care should be taken when describing a hearing loss, as simplistic statements can be misleading and not in a child's best interest.

TABLE 6-1 Classes of Hearing Handicap

dB	Degree of Handicap	Ability to Understand Ordinary Speech
0	Not significant	No significant difficulty with faint speech.
15	Slight	Difficulty only with faint speech.
30	Mild	Frequent difficulty with normal speech.
45	Moderate	Frequent difficulty with loud speech.
60		Can understand only shouted or amplified speech.
80	Severe	Usually cannot understand even amplified speech.
	Profound	
100		

WHAT ARE THE TYPES AND COMMON CAUSES OF HEARING LOSS IN CHILDREN?

Hearing losses are generally identified as *conductive, sensorineural,* or *mixed.* Conductive losses refer to any obstruction in the conduction (transmission) of sound from the external ear to the inner ear. In such cases, the inner ear is not damaged and is capable of transmitting information to the brain, providing the transmission link to the inner ear is functioning or can be bypassed. For example, the sound-conducting mechanism of the middle ear can be bypassed by directly stimulating the mastoid bone posterior to the external ear flap. The vibrations are thereby picked up by the fluid of the inner ear and processed without the assistance of the middle ear.

Certain congenital anomalies, childhood diseases, ear infections, and physical injuries to the ear can be responsible for a conductive hearing loss. Middle ear infection, or *otitis media,* is the largest cause of hearing loss in children. Frequently, these infections affect the Eustachian tube function, thereby causing middle ear air pressure to be less than adequate. This, along with the buildup of fluid in the cavity, often causes otitis media to be a very painful experience for a child. The common cold and various viruses are largely responsible for these infections. Decongestants, antihistamines, and antibiotics are frequently prescribed. If the problem persists, a myring-otomy, or surgical incision of the eardrum, may be necessary to allow adequate pressure balance and fluid drainage from the middle ear. In addition to the discomfort associated with the infection, it is not atypical for a child to have a mild-to-moderate temporary conductive hearing loss. All in all, an acute condition of otitis media can be a disconcerting experience for a child. Classroom teachers need to be particularly supportive during these episodes.

Sensorineural hearing loss refers to disorders caused by problems in the cochlea or the cochlear nerve. A pure sensory disorder has its origin in the cochlea, whereas a neural disorder stems primarily from pathology of the cochlear nerve. Sensorineural hearing losses are not "cured" by prescription drugs or by medical intervention of any sort. These losses are typically permanent and in some cases are progressive over time. Hearing losses of this nature are typically moderate to profound, and there are many potential causes. Genetic factors are responsible for many cases of congenital sensorineural hearing loss, but not all cases are congenital. Sometimes a congenital problem does not manifest itself until years after birth. Also, there are some congenital syndromes that include many other anomalies in addition to hearing loss.

Maternal viral infections can cause severe hearing loss and other problems in developing fetuses. Rubella (German measles) is a cyclical phenomenon, occurring in the past about every seven years in the United States. However, a vaccine to prevent rubella has been developed, so we will be seeing many fewer cases of rubella-induced hearing loss. Other childhood viral diseases such as measles, mumps, chickenpox, and influenza also have the potential, albeit not great, to cause hearing loss. When a hearing deficit follows the mumps virus, it is ordinarily seen in one ear only. Cytomegalovirus, anoxia at birth, prematurity, birth trauma, Rh incompatibility, and meningitis are also correlated with hearing loss and brain damage.

Hearing loss is not always categorized as conductive or sensorineural. Children with permanent sensorineural losses are just as vulnerable to transient middle ear diseases as are those with normal hearing, and hearing loss in such children is *mixed*.

Two additional types of hearing loss are of special interest to the classroom teacher: functional and central. A functional loss is not a true hearing loss. That is, a child responds to auditory stimuli at high decibel levels when, in fact, true threshold levels are normal. In most cases, the fake response is intentional, and there is usually some stress-related reason for it. Typically, these problems are not serious, but they usually require professional intervention. Teachers need to be supportive of the child as the problem is being resolved. Less common is the situation in which a child is incapable of responding to auditory events in a normal manner, for various reasons, including emotional problems. School children with functional hearing disorders are rarely seen in regular classrooms.

Central auditory processing problems concern difficulty in the understanding of information received auditorially due to pathologies of the brainstem or hearing centers of the brain. Children with *central auditory processing problems* may have unimpaired peripheral hearing mechanisms but varying degrees of brain dysfunction. Accordingly, they may receive the sounds in the environment but show difficulty in fully interpreting the meaning of the sounds. They encounter their greatest processing difficulties when the listening environment is cluttered with background noise and speech. The problem generally manifests itself by characteristics of limited attention span, inability to follow verbal directions precisely, problems in mastering verbal materials, confusion and verbal communication, occasional aberrant behavior, and reading and writing problems. Parents and teachers often label these students as having behavior problems before they are diagnosed otherwise. It would not be incorrect, however, to apply the label of "special learning disorder."

The existence of a central auditory processing problem is not easily determined. The clinical psychologist, audiologist, speech-language pathologist, and neurologist all may have a critical role in the diagnostic process. The psychologist can determine whether the problem is a specific learning disorder or a generalized learning problem. The audiologist can identify the type and magnitude of the auditory dysfunction. The speech-language pathologist can evaluate the impact the disorder has on receptive and expressive language performance. Finally, the neurologist can verify the presence of a brain dysfunction and, when appropriate, provide medical intervention.

The classroom teacher may wish to initiate the evaluation process with an audiologist. If none is available, referral to a psychologist or speech-language pathologist is suggested. By utilizing special tests that focus on difficult listening tasks, the audiologist often can provide evidence in support of the presence or absence of an auditory processing problem.

Should such a disorder be identified, the speech-language pathologist and the learning disorders specialist typically provide guidance in the design of the intervention program. In any case, the assistance of the classroom teacher and the child's family members is crucial to the success of the remediation.

WHAT ARE THE CLASSIFICATIONS OF HEARING LOSS?

Most adults have observed the significant communication problems of deaf children. Deaf children generally exhibit hearing losses in excess of 90 decibels, have little or no functional hearing and often have limited capability for oral speech. Deaf children are usually diagnosed as such before school age because their receptive and expressive communication problems are more readily observed. There are substantially more children, however, with slight hearing losses whose hearing difficulties are noted only under poor acoustic conditions. Excessively reverberant classrooms and seating at a distance provide listening problems for these students. Their speech, however, is rarely affected. Diagnosis of the child with a slight hearing loss is often elusive because symptomology is not as apparent. Before diagnosis, these students typically are described as inattentive, restless, daydreamers, and as having difficulty in following directions.

Deafness and *slight hearing loss* are terms signifying the extremes of a classification system of hearing impairment. Each category of hearing loss presents a unique constellation of diagnostic, educational, and emotional adjustment considerations. Although varying in numbers, all classifications are encountered in the schools (see Table 6-1).

Hearing impaired is a generic term for all types and degrees of hearing loss. Often, modifiers such as "mild," "moderate," "severe," and "profound" are included to denote the degree of hearing impairment (e.g., "moderately hearing impaired").

The *hard of hearing* category includes all degrees of hearing loss except the classification of deaf. Therefore, children in this group have hearing losses ranging from 15 to 75 dB. Their speech and language skills are developed primarily through the use of *hearing*, although lipreading and hearing aids are often very important as well.

Deaf children, those with severe hearing deficits, do not rely on hearing for learning or for the development of language and speech. They are highly dependent upon visual systems such as lipreading, fingerspelling, and sign language. Most deaf children have some residual hearing, usually in the very low frequencies.

WHAT IS THE PREVALENCE OF HEARING LOSS IN CHILDREN?

There are at least 15 to 25 times more hard of hearing children than deaf ones (Ross & Giolas, 1978). Data from Eagles, Wishik, Doerfler, Melnick, and Levine (cited in Ross & Giolas, 1978), show that 50 children out of 1,000 demonstrate hearing levels outside the range of normal hearing for at least one frequency in one or both ears. Probably a realistic figure for this group of children is about 30 per 1,000 (Ross, 1982). The prevalence of deaf persons is commonly reported as 1 per 1,000 of the population, although many believe this is high (Ross & Giolas, 1978). Regardless, it can be concluded that deafness is relatively rare.

CASE HISTORY

Brian

Brian, a second grader and an excellent student, had just had a week-long illness that included severe earaches and fever. When the pain and fever subsided, his parents had concluded the illness had run its course. Brian had indicated his desire to return to school and had said that he felt good.

During Brian's second day back at school, the teacher gave a spelling test, on which he did poorly. During oral reading sessions with his group, Brian had difficulty following the class recitations. He appeared to be inattentive, followed instructions inconsistently, and eventually provoked the teacher to admonish him for his lack of attention. The above characteristics typified his behavior for the next few days. Brian cried easily and began to withdraw from classroom involvement. The teacher began to be concerned, as Brian was generally a very good student. He did not appear ill, and the teacher was at a loss to explain his atypical behavior. The single, new mannerism she did note was that he tugged at his earlobes often. The teacher decided to have a discussion with him to find out if there was a problem she could help resolve. Brian told the teacher he felt well but that he had trouble listening and understanding. In addition, he said that his ears felt as if they were full of water, but they did not hurt.

The teacher contacted Brian's parents, seeking permission to have his hearing tested by the school speech-language pathologist. Permission was granted, and the test results showed that Brian had sustained a significant conductive hearing loss in both ears. He was referred to a physician and was given medication to reduce the fluid levels in his middle ears. Within a short period of time, his hearing had returned to normal and so had his behavior and school work. The teacher's early awareness and willingness to help a youngster whose behavior signaled a problem may have prevented a chronic middle ear problem from developing.

SUMMARY

Causes

- Physical anomalies of the ear
- Childhood diseases
- Ear infections (especially otitis media)
- Eustachian tube dysfunction
- Common colds
- Certain antibiotics and drugs
- Genetic factors
- Maternal viral infections (especially rubella)
- Anoxia at birth
- Birth trauma
- Blows to the head and acoustic trauma
- Rh incompatibility
- Brain damage

Some Important Points to Remember

- A significant hearing loss can cause serious language, voice, and articulation problems.
- The magnitude of hearing loss is expressed in decibels.
- The more decibels of hearing loss, the poorer one can hear.
- Hearing loss for one or two frequencies does not cause a problem with hearing.
- The interpretation of what is heard is completed by the brain.
- The meaning that is attached to the sounds in the environment is learned.
- Pure tones and speech signals are used in routine audiometry.
- Hearing loss is plotted on an audiogram.
- An "X" signals left ear responses, "O" signals right ear responses.
- The number of decibels below the zero line on the audiogram indicates the decibels of hearing loss.

- Hearing loss in only one ear usually does not mean a child will have a school learning problem.
- Children acquiring hearing losses before the development of language usually present more serious problems.
- Conductive hearing losses, which are often treatable, refer to any obstruction in the transmission of sound to the inner ear.
- Sensorineural hearing losses usually are not reversible.
- Central auditory processing problems are special cases of specific learning disorders.
- Children with central auditory processing problems often have normal hearing sensitivity.
- Diagnosis of the child with a slight hearing loss is often elusive, as symptomology is not apparent.
- The term *hearing impaired* is a generic term referring to all types and degrees of hearing loss.
- *Hard of hearing* children usually rely on residual hearing and lipreading for learning.
- *Deaf* children often rely on fingerspelling, sign language, and lipreading for learning and communication.
- There are about 20 times more hard of hearing than deaf children.
- It is commonly reported that one in every thousand persons is deaf.

SELF-TEST

Circle the correct answer:

1. The rate of vibrations in a sound is expressed in:
   A. decibels
   B. Hertz
   C. intensity
   D. dB
   E. loudness
2. Speech is an excellent example of:
   A. a pure tone
   B. a single vibratory rate
   C. a complex sound
   D. a single sound pressure wave
3. The meaning associated with a sound is processed in:
   A. the middle ear
   B. the brain
   C. the inner ear
   D. the cochlea
4. The frequency of a tone corresponds to its:
   A. loudness

B. intensity

C. pitch

D. decibel level

5. The important frequency range for hearing speech is between:

   A. 300 and 4,000 Hz

   B. 5,000 and 10,000 Hz

   C. 12,000 and 18,000 Hz

   D. 300 and 4,000 dB

   E. 12,000 and 18,000 dB

6. Hearing with two ears is most important for recognizing the:

   A. frequency of the sound

   B. intensity of the sound

   C. complexity of the sound

   D. location of the sound

   E. pitch of the sound

7. Normal atmospheric pressure within the middle ear is achieved through the:

   A. cochlea

   B. stapes

   C. both A and B

   D. Eustachian tube

   E. ossicles

8. Meaning that is attached to the sound of our environment is:

   A. learned

   B. innate

   C. acquired only after 24 months of age

   D. all of the above

   E. none of the above

9. With normal hearing, children typically develop mature articulation of speech sounds between the ages of:

   A. six and eight

   B. two and three

   C. ten and twelve

   D. none of the above

10. While testing an individual's hearing, sensitivity threshold levels for various frequencies are plotted on a form called a(n):

    A. scatterplot

    B. audiogram

    C. audiometer

    D. decibel graph

    E. tone profile

11. The largest cause of hearing loss in children is:

    A. mumps

    B. rubella

    C. otitis media

    D. cytomegalovirus

    E. none of the above

12. Sensorineural hearing losses are:
   A. typically permanent
   B. not readily "cured" by prescription drugs
   C. sometimes progressive over time
   D. all of the above
   E. none of the above
13. Children with central auditory processing problems:
   A. typically receive sound in the environment, but show difficulty in fully interpreting the meaning of the sound
   B. often have most difficulty when the listening environment is cluttered with background noise
   C. have conductive hearing loss problems
   D. both A and B
14. The term *hearing impairment* is:
   A. used synonymously with *deafness* only
   B. used synonymously with *hard of hearing* only
   C. a generic term relating to all types and degrees of hearing loss
   D. none of the above
15. Deaf children:
   A. rely on hearing for the development of speech and language
   B. typically have substantial hearing ability
   C. are highly dependent upon visual systems such as sign language and lipreading

REFERENCES

Martin, F. (1991). *Introduction to audiology.* Englewood Cliffs, NJ: Prentice-Hall.

Northern, J., & Downs, M. (1978). *Hearing in children.* Baltimore: The Williams and Wilkins Company.

Ross, M. (1982). *Hard of hearing children in regular schools.* Englewood Cliffs, NJ: Prentice-Hall.

Ross, M., & Giolas, T. (Eds.). (1978). *Auditory management of hearing-impaired children.* Baltimore: University Park Press.

7

HEARING IMPAIRED SCHOOL CHILDREN

This chapter addresses the management of hearing impaired children under the provisions of Public Laws 94-142 and 99-457 where the traditional boundaries of grades K through 12 are expanded to promote intervention from birth to 21 years of age. As a result, detection and management of hearing loss can occur at a very early age for hearing impaired children and increase their potential for educational achievement and personal adjustment. Early intervention also takes advantage of the formative language development period between six months and four years of age. These laws assure all children will have access to intervention, an opportunity that has been historically limited for many.

HOW ARE HEARING LOSSES DETECTED?

Infants and toddlers cannot reliably indicate whether they can hear a sound or not. Accordingly, various hearing screening procedures have been developed that do not require their cooperation. A widely used technique for infants employs various noise generating sources that are triggered close to the head while the tester watches for reflexive behaviors. An approach appropriate for both infants and toddlers requires highly technical equipment and the placement of electrodes on the head to measure electro-physiological responses to sound stimuli. Other techniques exploit a child's developing ability to localize sound, a skill which emerges around three to five months of age. In this method the child is conditioned to look in the direction of sounds emanating from strategically placed loudspeakers. For example, a tone is generated from a speaker to the right of a child's head position. Immediately following the tone burst a captivating visual reinforcer, such as toy dancing clowns, is activated in the immediate vicinity of the speaker. If the child hears the stimulus, he or she should look in the direction of the speaker. It is assumed the child wants to see the dancing clowns again so that when other sounds are generated there is motivation to look in the direction of the sound source and thereby signal the sound was heard. For discussion of other test techniques for this age group refer to the work by Northern and Downs (1984).

Hearing screening programs for children in grades K through 12 are fairly routine. The screening procedures used usually include a pure tone audiometric screening to determine a child's ability to detect certain frequencies at a preset decibel level. This is not a threshold test but is a "pass" or "fail" technique for each frequency used. In addition, screening tympanometry is ordinarily employed. This test is an indirect measure of the integrity of the middle ear. The procedure evaluates how readily the eardrum accepts energy as small changes in air pressure are induced in the external ear canal. The technique measures not only the mobility of the eardrum but also the function of the Eustachian tube. As a result, slight conductive hearing losses can be identified, which might otherwise be missed by pure tone screening.

If a child performs poorly on either of these tests, a follow-up test with an audiologist is scheduled. Conventional pure tone audiometry, tympanometry, and other tests are employed as needed. Should a child exhibit a hearing loss of any type, a referral to an appropriate physician is usually made.

Can a Teacher Identify Hearing Loss in Students?

There is no sure way to recognize hearing loss in children simply by observing their behavior. Nonetheless, teachers often do suspect hearing loss in students and make the appropriate referrals to confirm or reject their suspicions. Deficient hearing may be suspected if a child (1) asks spoken messages to be repeated, (2) frequently misunderstands what has been said, (3) cups ears or tilts head in the direction of a sound, (4) shows facial expressions suggesting inattention to what is being said, (5) speaks louder than the situation dictates, or (6) withdraws from situations requiring listening.

Teachers are advised to pay particular attention to students who have a history of ear disease or who often complain of ear discomfort. It should be emphasized that the only reliable method for identifying hearing loss is audiometric testing by a trained person.

WHAT TYPES OF SPEECH AND LANGUAGE PROBLEMS DO HEARING IMPAIRED CHILDREN HAVE?

In general, children born with hearing loss have significantly greater speech and language problems than children who incur losses after speech has developed. Typically, children with congenital hearing loss are less intelligible and have less potential for learning articulate speech (Booth-royd, 1978).

Hearing impaired children essentially produce speech as they hear it. They tend to omit consonants, especially voiceless consonants, that occur at the ends of words (Gold & Levitt, 1975). Final consonants are ordinarily unstressed, inherently weaker in speech power than when produced in other parts of words, and are not easily heard by the hearing impaired child. In addition, they often prolong and nasalize the preceding vowels. Consonants using tongue tip placements such as *t* tend to be omitted regardless of relative position within words. Another common problem concerns voicing certain speech sounds that should not be voiced.

Numerous factors, including intelligence, socioeconomic class, parental involvement, age of onset of hearing loss, and effective use of amplification affect language competence more than speech articulation proficiency. There are some trends, however, that are worth noting. Hard of hearing children consistently show about a two-year lag in vocabulary development, and deaf children demonstrate about a four to five year lag (Ross, 1982). Hearing impaired children encounter the most difficulty with idiomatic expressions, colloquialisms, and other uses of words beyond their dictionary meanings and are often deficient in use of synonyms. Syntactical constructions pose problems and, again, there is a correlation with degree of hearing loss; children with mild losses often perform like children with normal hearing, whereas children with severe losses show numerous problems with complex grammatical constructions.

HOW DO HEARING IMPAIRED CHILDREN LEARN LANGUAGE AND SPEECH?

Hard of Hearing Children

Hard of hearing children, those who can understand speech if it is loud enough, learn their language and speech skills much like normal hearing children, primarily through the sense of hearing. The IEP team, usually led by the speech-language pathologist, guides the assistance which may include auditory training, using a personal hearing aid, language stimulation, lipreading, and speech training. Parents have the major role during the early years and as the child approaches formal schooling there is more intensive involvement by the speech-language clinician. In general, children with more significant degrees of hearing loss require more intensive intervention and over a longer time span, often for several years.

A major goal for the child classified as hard of hearing is to learn spoken language. The teaching methodologies, which do not vary significantly, have been labeled *auditory-global* and *auditory-visual-oral*. Both are relatively effective if efficiently employed. Each stresses practice in listening using a properly fitting hearing aid, language stimulation, and training in the production of speech sounds.

The auditory global method relies more heavily on the development of residual hearing, the area of hearing which can be enhanced by an appropriate hearing aid. The method is also referred to as *auditory-oral, aural-oral, auditory,* or *acoupedics.* As hearing and listening are stressed, it is considered unisensory. The development of oralism is treated through hearing, only. The professionals who use this method emphasize that hearing impaired children grow up in a hearing world and therefore must survive the forces of a hearing society. Accordingly, teaching should focus on listening with language and speech development as logical products. They note that humans are neurologically predisposed to learn language and that language is learned ideally by hearing it. While the popular view is that the method is highly appropriate for children who have mild to moderate hearing losses, many proponents insist that it is the treatment of choice, regardless of degree of hearing loss.

The *auditory-visual-oral* method is similar to the auditory global approach. Hearing, listening, and speech are stressed. The difference is in the incorporation of a multisensory approach using lipreading (also referred to as speech-reading), along with listening, and the discretionary use of tactile stimulation. Although lipreading may not be taught systematically, children are encouraged to use all the information available by watching lip, tongue, and jaw movements that coincide with the sounds of speech that are produced. Advocates point out that the speech sounds that are not heard by persons with high frequency hearing losses are often the sounds that are more lipreadable. As a result, lipreading supplements hearing and improves one's ability to more fully understand the spoken message.

For those with severe losses tactile sensory stimulation can be beneficial. Transducers that change acoustic stimuli to vibratory information can be worn as stimulators on the wrists or fingertips. Children receive vibrational patterns that represent speech while it is being spoken. The information is limited, however, as the skin is a very poor substitute for the capabilities of the human ear. The transduced speech is perceived as a series of pulses that occur rapidly or slowly, continuously or discontinuously, strong in force or weak (Haas, 1970). A child is not taught how to use tactile stimulation, rather one is encouraged to use the information without instruction about the nature of stimuli. For some the information is useful, for others the benefits are marginal.

Another method, loosely akin to the methods discussed, is *Cued Speech* (Cornett, 1967). Eight hand configurations and four hand placements used in positions around the speech articulators provide cues about certain speech sounds that are otherwise visually obscure. The availability of this information also promotes teaching hearing impaired children the production of speech sounds. The cueing is totally dependent upon speech and is meaningless out of context. Cued Speech is not a sign language but rather a supplement to lipreading and an aid to teaching speech.

For hard of hearing children with more severe degrees of hearing loss, the *Rochester Method* is a pedagogical option. Named after the school for deaf children in Rochester, New York, the approach uses hearing, lipreading, and fingerspelling simultaneously. As with cued speech, the method purports to provide missing information not accessed through hearing or lipreading, using hand configurations that represent each of the 26 letters of the alphabet. Speakers fingerspell words as they are spoken. The Rochester Method is also referred to as visible speech.

The methodologies that emphasize reliance on hearing and speech share the basic goal of providing means for the hearing impaired child to be integrated and functional in the hearing world. Early identification, early use of amplification, intensive auditory training and speech training, commitment of family, and special educational intervention strategies are important to their success. There is little controversy about the appropriateness of these methods for children classified as hard of hearing.

Deaf Children

There has been controversy about the efficacy of the auditory-oral methods for deaf children, those children with audiograms showing hearing losses in excess of 80 to 90 dBs. For years many older deaf persons and professionals have been concerned about the lack of success in communicating and teaching language to deaf children through speech and hearing. They have urged the educational establishment to accept *manual* approaches (sign language) over *oral* approaches (speech and lipreading). The oralists fear that the use of sign language will impede oral language and speech acquisition, while manualists claim the oral approach is often impractical and too difficult for most deaf persons to master.

The manualists also contend that forcing deaf children to communicate only through speech and lipreading denies them full and successful communication through sign language, an efficient communication mode for them. Data show that deaf adults overwhelmingly prefer sign language and that many vigorously promote the teaching of signs to deaf children as the primary form of language expression and learning (Moores, 1987). The opposing view is that our "brains are wired" to learn language by hearing it and that there is no adequate substitute for hearing and speech. These proponents hold that most deaf children are capable of hearing some speech components with properly fitting hearing aids and that the challenge is to maximize their auditory capabilities.

A compromise approach is the simultaneous use of sign language and auditory-oral methods. For deaf children who acquire deafness before the acquisition of language, this method is touted as highly appropriate and often the only realistic option (Pahz and Pahz, 1978). Some deaf children show a propensity for oralism but for those who do not, sign language serves as an efficient communication option. Oralists, though, complain that *American Sign Language,* the language system preferred by the deaf, has a grammar and vocabulary that is substantively different from English and therefore fosters confusion among deaf children about the nature of English and how to read and write it. To accommodate this concern, some educators have devised modifications to traditional sign language so that it will more closely correlate with spoken English. The following sections compare the merits of *American Sign Language,* the use of *sign codes,* and the philosophy of *Total Communication.*

American Sign Language, also known as *AMESLAN* or *ASL,* is a bona fide language in its own right. It has its own vocabulary structure, grammar, and idiomatic form. It is a non-oral language and therefore has inherent value to a deaf person. In this sense, ASL is often referred to as the native language of deaf persons.

When ASL is taught to deaf children at a very early age, it has been shown that these children learn sign language at about the same rate normal hearing children acquire spoken language (Moores, 1987). Accordingly, effective communication skills are not unduly denied the deaf child during the early preschool years. But a deaf child who does not know English will not be able to read and write English. For this reason many educators acknowledge the importance of compromising the use of ASL for another system of signs that more closely correlates with English vocabulary and grammar. This has led to the development of various sign codes.

Sign codes do not qualify as separate languages, although they are often loosely referred to as sign language systems. While signs are used, the grammar and vocabulary are essentially English. These systems are designed to enhance the educational success of deaf children by providing an opportunity to learn English language skills. As a result, proficiency in the reading and writing of English is more likely to result.

Pidgin is a true compromise between ASL and English. The English grammar is intact, the vocabulary is ASL, and English is spoken with the simultaneous use of signs that carry important meaning. Not all of the spoken message is recoded into signs as there is an assumption that the hearing impaired person will lipread the words that are not signed. There is concern, however, that this system is not ideal for teaching young deaf children, as they may miss many important pieces of information that are not visible. A deaf child who does not know English cannot lipread the words or parts of words that are not signed. Signed English is similar to Pidgin in that the signed vocabulary is drawn from ASL and the word order follows English grammar. But an exact representation of the English language is only possible by using extensive fingerspelling and providing special signs for prefixes, suffixes, plural endings, and the use of articles such as "the," "a," and "an." Users of Signed English appear to adapt to ASL readily and ASL users find Signed English translateable, albeit cumbersome and redundant. The major problem with the system concerns adherence to the conceptually based signed vocabulary from ASL causing many English words to possess the same sign. *Seeing Essential English* (SEE-1) (Anthony, 1971) and *Signing Exact English* (SEE-2) (Gustason, Pfetzing, and Zawolkow, 1972) were developed to circumvent this problem. In these systems many signs have been drawn from ASL but where separate signs were deemed needed new ones were created. Deaf adults who use ASL have been highly critical of these two alternatives. They contend that changes stray too far from the basic tenets of ASL.

Total Communication is not a communication method in itself but rather a philosophy about communication options for deaf children (Pahz and Pahz, 1978). It significantly moderates the opposing views of oralism and manualism. It requires that each deaf child be provided aural, oral, and manual modes of communication in any combination that will best facilitate learning, effective communication, and personal adjustment. The philosophy stresses that each deaf child deserves a communication method that is individualized and considers degree of hearing loss, family support, professional facilities and expertise, social and intellectual abilities, and any other variable that significantly influences the potential for success. Today, this philosophical concept is widely embraced as an appropriate framework for the education of hearing impaired children.

Hearing Aids and Assistive Listening Devices

Hearing aids and assistive listening devices help hearing impaired individuals receive and interpret information presented auditorially. *Hearing aids* are electronic devices which make sounds louder but do not provide corrective hearing the same way eye glasses might correct visual acuity problems. If residual hearing does not exist for certain frequencies, a hearing aid will not provide it. Where residual hearing exists, a hearing aid will make sounds louder in that range of hearing. *Assistive listening devices* are systems engineered for specific listening conditions such as theaters, concert halls, churches, civic centers, various sports arenas, and for special use in the home. In most situations ear phones or ear inserts are electronically connected to an amplifying system designed for the environment. Typically, these systems rely on a direct connection to the intended sound source while blocking out intervening sounds in the environment. As a result hearing impaired persons can circumvent the noise distractions that would accompany listening through a personal hearing aid. Other types of assistive listening devices serve as warning, alerting, or wake-up systems. A vibrator placed under a pillow is an example of a wake-up device. A flashing lightbulb situated over a door might indicate the doorbell is ringing. A large flashing red light can be designed to signal a fire alarm has been triggered. There are numerous such devices that help the hearing impaired function more efficiently in a world filled with auditory signals and alerts. The audiologist or speech-language pathologist can help families secure appropriate devices for a hearing impaired child.

There has been significant progress in improving the fidelity and cosmetic appearance of hearing aids. Regardless of size or appearance, all have three basic components. All electronic hearing aids have a microphone that picks up auditory signals in the environment. The microphone also changes the nature of the signals to electrical energy and channels the signals to an amplifier. The *amplifier* boosts the energy level of the signals and routes them to a *receiver* (miniature loudspeaker) that reconverts the electrical signals back to auditory signals. These basic components are powered by a battery and supplemented by various switches that change tonal characteristics, turn the aid on or off, or manipulate volume control.

Persons with severe hearing loss may be fitted with a *body hearing aid* because they have larger compartments to hold bigger batteries resulting in more power for amplification purposes. Body aids are usually worn in a pocket on a blouse or shirt or in a special holder worn under the outer garments. The metal or plastic compartment houses the microphone, amplifier, and batteries. An electrical cord couples the compartment to the receiver which is worn at ear level and connects to an ear mold. The ear mold is specially fitted for the ear and not only provides a coupling device for the receiver but also directs the amplified sound into the ear canal. Because the body aid separates the microphone from the speaker by several inches there is less likelihood that a problem with feedback will occur.

Another style of hearing aid is the *behind-the-ear* aid. All components are at ear level and while these aids can equal the power of the body aid, the proximity of the microphone and receiver can cause a feedback problem when extra volume is needed. The plastic compartment is worn directly behind the ear or in eye glass stems and houses the microphone, receiver, and battery. The amplified sound is routed through a plastic tube from the compartment to an ear mold. Because these aids have good fidelity and are capable of providing high levels of amplification, they are frequently recommended for children with significant losses.

A newer style of ear level amplification is the *in-the-ear* hearing aid. The entire hearing aid is contained within the plastic shell of an ear mold. There are no connecting wires or plastic tubes. When considering the entire population of persons using hearing aids, these account for over three-fourths of all sales (Mahon, 1987). Technology now makes it possible to miniaturize these aids such that the instrument can fit entirely in the ear canal. These are referred to as *canal* aids. With all types of in-the-ear hearing aids the microphone and receiver are very close in proximity causing a potential for feedback. As a result, audiologists tend to prefer larger devices for young children with severe losses.

The reader should be aware that personal hearing aids are a vital component of auditory habilitation for hard of hearing children. They provide the potential to bring the sounds of speech into the range of hearing, sounds that otherwise would not be readily heard. Also, a student's personal adjustment and success in school can be enhanced with an optimally-fitted instrument. Auditory training is designed to maximize the potential of amplified sound. Deaf children, however, do not benefit as much from amplified sound because the severity of hearing loss prohibits the reception of meaningful speech. Some deaf children, however, enjoy amplified sound even though it is little more than fragmentary information about speech, the fact someone is speaking, and information about the tempo and rhythm of the speech. Others rely on their hearing aids to provide clues about alerting signals in the environment, signals correlated with a car horn, a bell, or a siren. And still others consider a hearing aid more of a nuisance than a benefit.

There has been a significant breakthrough, however, for persons who have been unable to benefit from traditional hearing aids. The development of the *cochlear implant* (House, 1982), a type of hearing aid that is partly surgically implanted in the cochlea, represents an exciting future for many with profound hearing losses. To date, implant recipients report varying accounts about the quality of the sound they receive. Some hear the basic components of speech signals better than others. In some cases, only information about the rhythm, duration, and loudness of speech is received. A considerable number of recipients claim their lipreading skills are significantly enhanced. There is no doubt that the number of school

(a)

(b)

FIGURE 7-1   Examples of three most common personal hearing aids used by hearing impaired individuals: (a) from left to right, behind-the-ear aid compared to an in-the-ear hearing aid; (b) a canal aid compared to a small piece of peppermint candy; (c) an over-the-ear aid fitted to a user's ear; (d) an in-the-ear aid fitted to a user's ear. (Photographs courtesy of Siemens Hearing Instruments, Inc.)

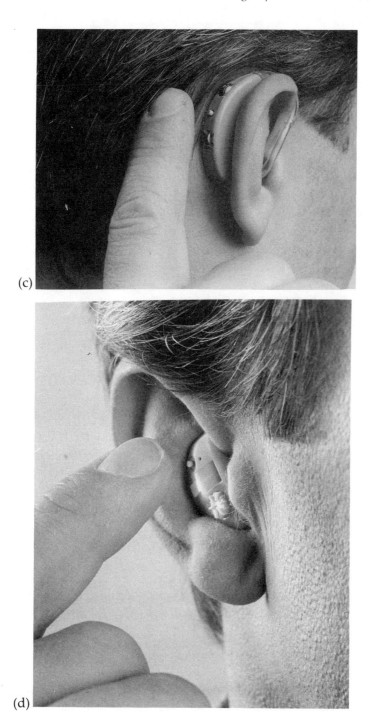

(c)

(d)

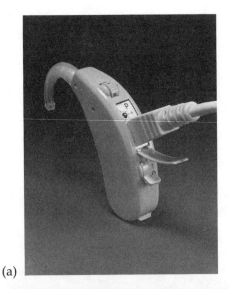

(a)

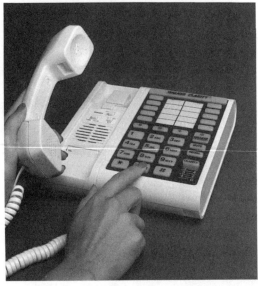

(b)

FIGURE 7-2   Examples of assistive listening devices designed for use by hearing impaired individuals: (a) a hearing aid which is coupled by a direct connection with a sound source to block intervening sounds in the environment; (b) a telephone with special controls to regulate the degree of amplified sound required by the hearing impaired user; (c) an FM transmitter with headset and receiver which can also circumvent the intervention of environmental sounds; (d) a transmitter and combination receiver-headset which uses infrared technology. (Photographs courtesy of Siemens Hearing Instruments, Inc.)

(c)

(d)

children with implants will increase dramatically as the technology develops and surgical risks are minimized over the next few years.

It is important to remember that hearing impaired persons speak their language very much the way they hear it. With appropriate intervention and wearing a properly-fitted hearing aid, most hard of hearing individuals can learn to understand English through hearing and lipreading and can learn to speak effectively. Because deaf children hear very little speech and hearing aids cannot provide hearing where residual hearing does not exist, for many learning through hearing can be a tortuous ordeal.

Intervention strategies that focus mainly on visual communication skills such as fingerspelling, sign codes, and sign language offer a better potential for this group.

What Special School Programs Are Provided for Hearing Impaired Children?

Because learning is dependent upon language skills, and because hard of hearing children are communicatively deficient, guidance from the speech-language pathologist is often critical to the success of these students. This coordinating role does not presume that the work of this professional is more important than that of the classroom teacher. In the final analysis, the classroom teacher has the overall responsibility for learning by all students in the classroom.

Many significantly hearing impaired children are not mainstreamed into regular classroom settings. Special classrooms instructed by specially trained teachers of the deaf are often provided for these students so that their unique learning needs can be met. (Not all children assigned to special classes for the deaf are categorized as deaf.) These classes are usually very small (six to eight students), and rely heavily on various visual aids for instruction. It is not uncommon for sign language to be the primary means of communication. Special language instruction is often provided by a speech-language pathologist.

If a child is mainstreamed into a regular classroom and is dependent upon sign language for communication, it is usually necessary to provide an interpreter for the deaf to assist the classroom teacher. Programs for mainstreamed hard of hearing children usually include substantial assistance by a speech-language pathologist. For those children with moderate hearing (45 to 65 dB) and severe (65 to 85 dB) losses, a hearing resource teacher is often provided. These professionals provide tutoring in support of the regular classroom curriculum, whereas speech-language pathologists focus on listening, language, and speech instruction.

What Is the Role of the Classroom Teacher?

The importance of the classroom teacher in the overall education of a hearing impaired child must not be underestimated. Not all teachers, however, have the disposition or patience to meet the challenge and fulfill the time-consuming responsibilities associated with efficient management of these children. There are numerous special considerations that are vital to the success of the regular classroom experience for the hearing impaired child. A discussion of these considerations follows.

The teacher has a role in assuring that a hearing-impaired child has an optimal hearing and listening environment in the classroom. This means that there should be minimal distance between the teacher's usual physical position and the child's. As listening becomes more difficult, the child will rely more on visual information. Therefore, the arrangement should also consider good lighting, so the child can take advantage of important visual clues such as lipreading. The teacher is urged to keep classroom noise to a minimum, as the effective use of a hearing aid requires a relatively quiet listening environment. The teacher should frequently check to see if the hearing aid is being worn and is functioning adequately. There are so many different types of hearing aids that it is difficult to know how to check their functioning, so close communication with the speech-language pathologist or audiologist in this regard will be of significant value to the teacher.

The teacher has a critical role in the emotional well-being and development of a hearing impaired child. The classroom and playground can be either devastating experiences or they can foster healthy growth and development. It is to everyone's advantage for the teacher to be "up-front" about a child's hearing disability. When the appropriate opportunities surface, the teacher should explain hearing loss to the other children and encourage them to help the disabled child learn and enjoy a rewarding school experience.

The classroom teacher has a responsibility to promote efficient, routine communication with all persons working toward the educational betterment of a child. This includes parents, special teachers, school testing personnel, speech-language pathologists, audiologists, counselors, and school administrators. Information sharing is critical and the teacher often is in the best position to facilitate it.

It is a daily challenge to foster the optimal mainstreaming of a hearing impaired child. It may seem expedient to treat the child as a special observer of the classroom without expecting or encouraging participation, or planning the integration of the child's needs, talents, and learning experiences. However, the teacher should explore workable tactics that truly provide a mainstreamed environment.

The teacher should be fully informed about a hearing impaired child's performance standards and potential. Little realistic planning or teaching can ensue without this information. The most critical information concerns language performance. The teacher must know the level and limits of the child's receptive vocabulary and syntax so that effective communication can take place.

The teacher needs to set realistic educational goals. Many mainstreamed hearing impaired students cannot achieve the same goals as their hearing peers. There is a correlation between degree of hearing loss and language based achievement. To expect or demand unrealistic performance in the classroom can be a source of frustration for the teacher, student, and parents.

Teachers should keep these points in mind when working with a hearing impaired child:

- Face the child during all oral communication.
- Do not exaggerate the pronunciation of words, as this will deter, not facilitate, understanding.
- Frequently check with the child to make sure he or she is comprehending.
- Use appropriate visual teaching aids whenever practical.
- Encourage the child to ask questions whenever necessary.
- Assign a hearing peer to be a "buddy" during extracurricular activities. This should assist the hearing impaired child to be an active participant as well as provide a special helper to support effective communication.
- Learn to "read" the child's facial expressions in order to have feedback about his or her understanding of the material presented.

CASE HISTORIES

Donald

Donald is a six-year-old student at a public elementary school. At the age of four he had a virus which resulted in a bilateral sensori-neural hearing loss of moderate degree with a greater loss for the high frequencies. Before his sickness he was considered to have high verbal skills and had no difficulty using oral language. Donald has been fitted with hearing aids for both ears and he wears them consistently. Test results using the aids show that he has normal hearing sensitivity for all frequencies except for 2000 Hertz and above. In this region his aided audiogram shows a consistent loss of about 30 dB. This causes him to miss many of the voiceless consonants when in noisy listening conditions, especially in the classroom.

Donald is placed in a regular classroom and individually sees a speech-language pathologist three times a week. The speech-language pathologist's objectives include training to help Donald retain articulatory proficiency for those speech sounds which are not clearly heard. In addition, he is receiving auditory training so he can use his hearing aid maximally. The clinician provides coping strategies for him as he meets the challenges of auditory failure during his day-to-day experiences. The clinician also confers with the classroom teacher on a frequent basis so that the classroom environment does not become an educationally restrictive setting for

Donald. Topics such as preferential seating options, noise reduction in the classroom, and the use of special academic resources like visual aids are discussed. The teacher is also apprised of the goals and objectives of the special speech sessions so expectancies for carryover into the classroom can be monitored.

The key members of the IEP team are the parents, teacher and the speech-language pathologist. As Donald represents a case that is not severe nor complicated, there is high expectancy that he will develop, educationally and communicatively, at the same pace as his normal hearing peers. This, however, is contingent upon continued participation and cooperation of all the team members. Should family support and professional services not be available, there is the potential for deviant speech patterns to emerge and some minor language delay to occur. This, in turn, would have a negative impact on academic achievement. The IEP team, however, is optimistic about Donald's potential for academic success.

Theresa

Theresa, a ten-year-old Hispanic deaf child who is being reared by her maternal grandmother, now resides in a residential school for the deaf in her state. Her family lives in a small English speaking community in the south and has very limited financial resources. Although the Spanish language is spoken in a home that shelters six individual family members, the other children have some English speaking skills that were learned in the local public school.

Theresa was not diagnosed as deaf until she was three years of age. Shortly thereafter, the family was provided special assistance by the school through the services of a speech-language pathologist. There was an early attempt to focus on oral language development, but the conflict between using Spanish and English proved to be a problem. Eventually, Theresa was placed in a special education self-contained classroom. While she is not believed to be mentally retarded, the majority of her classmates were so classified. A short time later, it was clear that she was having extreme difficulty in developing useful communication skills. She was failing to acquire language beyond primitive gestures. School officials concluded that the absence of other deaf children in the school program, the nature of the family constellation, and the lack of an alternative communication system for Theresa all contributed to a highly restrictive environment for her educational development. They believed the least restrictive environment was placement in the state supported residential school for the deaf where she could benefit by the association of other deaf children and learn sign language. A visit to the state school by the grandmother led her to support the plan.

Theresa is learning sign language at the state school and now communicates effectively with other deaf children, staff members and her teachers at the school. Her academics are progressing nicely, although she is about one year behind her peers at the school. Teachers believe she will close the gap in time. Also important is the fact that the grandmother and other family members are trying to learn sign language so they can communicate with Theresa when she visits her home.

This case study shows that the least restrictive environment is a relative concept. Clearly, the options for a meaningful, educational experience in this child's home district were unduly restrictive. While other educational alternatives exist, the IEP team with the support of the family prefers the state residential school.

SUMMARY

Some Important Points to Remember

- Early detection and management of hearing loss can increase the potential for educational achievement and personal adjustment.
- The critical period for developing language occurs between six months and four years of age.
- A major goal for a child classified as hard of hearing is to learn spoken language.
- Methodologies for hard of hearing children stress properly fitting hearing aids, auditory training, language stimulation, and speech production training.
- Cued Speech is not a sign language, but rather uses hand signals to provide cues about speech sounds that are produced but not lipreadable.
- The Rochester Method uses fingerspelling of words that are being spoken.
- There is controversy about the appropriate use of auditory methods for children who have been classified as deaf.
- American Sign Language is a bona fide language in itself as it has its own vocabulary and grammar.
- Total Communication is a philosophy that specifies that each deaf child be provided any combination of communication systems that facilitate learning and personal adjustment.
- Hearing aids are electronic devices that make sounds louder but do not provide hearing where residual hearing does not exist.
- Small hearing aids that are worn in-the-ear often present feedback problems when extra volume is needed for persons with significant

losses because the microphone and receiver are too close in proximity.
- School hearing screening tests do not show decibels of hearing loss.
- The only reliable method of identifying hearing loss is audiometric testing.
- Hard-of-hearing children are often mainstreamed, but many deaf children are not mainstreamed due to poor academic achievement.
- Hearing impaired children essentially produce speech as they hear it.
- Hard of hearing children consistently show a two year lag in vocabulary development, and deaf children show about a four to five year lag.

Do's and Don'ts For Teachers

Do's:
- Learn about the child's hearing aid.
- Be aggressive in achieving an ideal emotional climate for the child.
- Facilitate communication between all professionals working with the child.
- Be realistic in your academic expectations for the child; consult other school specialists for advice.
- Become familiar with the child's standardized test performance profile, especially language scores.
- Face the child during all oral communication.
- Frequently check with the child to make sure he or she is comprehending.
- Use appropriate visual teaching aids whenever practical.
- Become familiar with appropriate resource materials, and when practical order such materials for your classroom.
- Encourage the child to ask questions.
- Check with the speech-language pathologist or audiologist about the hearing-listening environment in the classroom.

Don'ts:
- Do not hide the child's hearing problem; be honest and straightforward in dealing with peers of the child.
- Do not exaggerate pronunciation.

Referral Resources
- Audiologists
- Otologists

- Speech-language pathologists
- Hearing resource teachers
- Teachers for the learning disabled
- Clinical psychologists
- Neurologists

SELF-TEST

True or false:

1. Hard of hearing children are more frequently seen in classrooms _____ than are deaf children.
2. Hearing screening procedures utilize a pure tone audiometer to _____ determine a child's ability to detect certain frequencies at preset levels.
3. There are three definitive ways to recognize hearing loss in children _____ simply by observing their behavior.
4. As listening becomes more difficult, the hearing impaired child will _____ rely more on visual information.
5. Good advice for the classroom teacher when communicating with _____ hearing impaired children is to exaggerate pronunciation.
6. Children born with hearing loss show essentially the same types and _____ magnitude of speech and language problems as those who acquire hearing loss after speech has developed.
7. Hearing impaired children often produce speech as they hear it. _____
8. Data show that all deaf children demonstrate about a two year lag in _____ vocabulary development.
9. Almost all deaf children are mainstreamed into regular classrooms. _____
10. Language disorders are rarely caused by hearing loss. _____
11. Ability to localize sounds usually occurs around 3 to 5 months. _____
12. All auditory methods require the study of lipreading. _____
13. Cued Speech is now considered the sign language of choice. _____
14. Most professionals prefer oral methods over manual methods. _____
15. Total Communication includes the use of sign language. _____
16. Many deaf adults prefer the use of sign language over auditory-oral _____ communication.
17. Various devices that help the deaf person understand the auditory _____ events in the environment are called assistive listening devices.
18. Auditory feedback is a common problem for children who wear _____ hearing aids that fit entirely in the ear.

REFERENCES

Anthony, D. (1971). *Seeing essential English.* (Vols. 1 & 2). Anaheim, CA: Anaheim Union School District, Educational Service Division.

Boothroyd, A. (1978). Speech perception and sensorineural hearing loss. In M. Ross & T. G. Giolas (Eds.), *Auditory management of hearing-impaired children* (pp. 131–138). Baltimore: University Park Press.

Cornett, R. (1967). Cued speech. *American Annals of the Deaf, 121,* 3–13.

Gold, T., & Levitt, H. (1975). *Comparison of articulatory errors in hard of hearing and deaf children.* New York: City University of New York, Graduate School and University Center, Communication Sciences Laboratory.

Gustason, G., Pfetzing, D., & Zawolkow, E. (1972). *Signing exact English.* Silver Spring, MD: Modern Signs Press.

Haas, W. (1970). *The vibrotactile reception of spoken English phonemes.* Unpublished doctoral dissertation. Michigan State University, East Lansing, MI.

House, W. F. (1982). Surgical considerations in cochlear implants. *Annals of Otology, Rhinology, and Laryngology, 91,* 15–20.

Mahon, W. (1987). U.S. hearing aid sales summary. The Hearing Journal, 40, 9–14.

Moores, D. (1987). *Educating the deaf: Psychology, principles, and practices.* Boston: Houghton Mifflin.

Northern, J., & Downs, M. (1984). *Hearing in children* (3rd ed.). Baltimore: Williams & Wilkins.

Ross, M. (1982). *Hard of hearing children in regular schools.* Englewood Cliffs, NJ: Prentice-Hall.

Pahz, J., & Pahz, C. (1978). *Total communication.* Springfield, IL: Charles C. Thomas.

8

OTHER POPULATIONS WITH POTENTIAL PROBLEMS OF COMMUNICATION

Mainstreaming children with special problems is becoming more widely accepted in school systems throughout the country. Therefore the classroom teacher must become aware of the special problems of children which affect speech, language, hearing, learning, general communicative effectiveness, and adjustment. Additionally, a basic understanding of some of the alternative modes of communication can serve both the student and the teacher well in effecting social adjustment and academic achievement.

Special communication problems that might be present in some students in the classroom are associated with cerebral palsy, developmental delay, emotional disturbance, neurological disease processes, injury, drugs, AIDS, dialectal differences, and bilingualism. Understanding the ramifications of these is a responsibility of the classroom teacher. A further responsibility is to maximize the child's potential as an individual within the classroom and also for seeing to it that the proper referrals are made to those who can be of assistance, such as the speech-language pathologist, the audiologist, and, when necessary the school psychologist.

Not only are the proper referrals of great importance, but also a close liaison with the parents is of the utmost importance. Through this liaison the classroom teacher can learn about the attitudes that prevail at home concerning the child, the capabilities of the child as seen through the eyes of the parent, the communicative effectiveness of the child at home, and the aspiration that parents hold for their handicapped child. A viable liaison can provide the opportunity for the teacher to keep the parents informed of the problems and progress of the child within the classroom and, when necessary, to help them to be more realistic about the potential for social adjustment and academic achievement. The help provided by the informed and caring classroom teacher can be invaluable to the child not only in the present setting but also for years to come. The classroom teacher is a central figure in the child's progress with a speech, language or hearing problem.

CEREBRAL PALSY

Individuals who have cerebral palsy (CP) are those with neuromotor disorders caused by a nonprogressive brain abnormality (Hardy, 1983). This group presents a wide array of disorders and disabilities. Cerebral palsy can arise from various complications of pregnancy and also of fetal development. The two major causes of cerebral palsy are cerebral hemorrhage and a reduced supply of oxygen to the brain. The most frequent are disorders of the cerebrocirculatory system (Hardy, 1983). Cerebral palsy is neither contagious nor progressive, although in the course of a child's development the symptoms may change. Speech and language problems as well as problems with hearing and vision can accompany cerebral palsy. The intellect can also be affected.

There are different types of cerebral palsy. Spasticity, athetosis, and ataxia constitute the three principal categories. Spastic CP constitutes about 80 percent of cases (Van Riper, 1972). It may affect one limb (monoplegia), both limbs on one side of the body (hemiplegia), both upper or both lower limbs (diplegia), three limbs (triplegia), or all four limbs (quadriplegia). Depending on the degree and severity of involvement, a child may be able to walk unaided, to walk on crutches, or to use a wheelchair. Of course the greatest disabling conditions occur—including speech— when the entire body is involved. Other symptoms involving vision, hearing, retardation of intellectual functioning, orthopedic defects, and emotional development may also be present. Frequently one sees a picture of multiple disability (Perkins, 1971).

All of the processes that are necessary for speech production including respiration, phonation, resonation, and articulation may be affected. The cerebral palsied child often presents delayed development. There simply may be no speech at all. If and when speech emerges, it is frequently characterized by articulation that is labored and slurred, with breaks in fluency. Vowels as well as consonants may be affected. Vocal production is often accomplished only with great effort and struggle. In some instances, when voice is successfully produced, it is weak and hypernasal, particularly for the child with athetosis. Often speech is difficult to understand. However, depending upon the type and severity of the cerebral palsy, there may be no speech problem at all.

Facial grimaces, head movements, and other bodily movements that give evidence of neuromuscular incoordination frequently accompany attempts at speech. Embarrassment and feelings of low self-worth and shame are often related to this disabling condition.

According to reliable estimates, about 750,000 persons in the United States have cerebral palsy. Every year, approximately 9,000 new cases of cerebral palsy are reported (National Institute of Neurological and Communication Disorders and Stroke, 1980). Children with cerebral palsy are not all severely disabled. For some children, the involvement is so mild it goes undetected.

The regular classroom teacher usually will not have severely disabled cerebral palsied children as students, for they are treated in special programs for disabled children where they can be given extra attention. However, mildly and moderately disabled children are often mainstreamed. A classroom teacher will want to maximize the acceptance and academic achievements of such children.

Many children with cerebral palsy are helped by other professionals such as orthopedists, speech-language pathologists, physical therapists, or occupational therapists. It is important for the classroom teacher to communicate with these individuals and to ensure that the cerebral palsied child is performing up to his or her maximum potential without becoming fatigued, is adjusting well to the classroom, and is developing new and necessary skills for daily living and communication. It is likely that a child with cerebral palsy will take somewhat longer to accomplish a task, such as answering a question or writing down an assignment, than a nondisabled child. Patience and encouragement from the teacher are very important to the adjustment and achievement of these children. Well-informed and caring parents can also make a tremendous difference in the progress of the cerebral palsied child and in the general attitude of the child toward the classroom teacher and others seeking to provide services.

CASE HISTORIES

Darlene

Darlene was a junior in high school when she first came to the speech and hearing clinic. A child with mild cerebral palsy (spasticity), her speech was labored and at times not very intelligible. Speech attempts were accompanied by facial grimaces and stiffened fingers and arms that would point randomly, first one way then another.

Darlene received good stimulation from the teachers and fellow students who had shown a special interest in her for eleven years. Darlene was well adjusted to her disability. There wasn't a play or sports activity that she would miss voluntarily. Teachers' reports indicated that she participated in oral activities in the classroom even though it took her longer to say what she wanted.

Darlene showed excellent progress in speech therapy. Her struggle with sound and word production was greatly reduced. Through specific exercises she was able to maintain far better neuromuscular control of the speech mechanism and the breathing patterns so necessary for rhythmic and sustained speech. Several years later she successfully graduated from high school.

Jim

Jim was first seen as a four-year-old child in a hospital speech and hearing clinic. He had been diagnosed as having spastic cerebral palsy and showed moderate-severe motor involvement with definite impairment in his ability to walk and to use his hands and fingers in activities such as drawing or coloring. His speech and language were quite well developed for his age. He did not, on test, appear to have any loss of hearing. Jim's speech however, was characterized by a slow and labored delivery and by several articulatory problems.

This child was enrolled in the speech-language therapy program with the hospital clinic for two years. During the course of his therapy he was referred to a clinical psychologist who evaluated his social maturity and intellectual status. He was determined to be slightly below the norms in social maturity and within normal range in intelligence.

At age six Jim was enrolled in a special public school program and was given specialized assistance both in speech and language and in physical therapy. The teacher responsible for his classroom was exceptionally sensitive and insightful in working with handicapped children. Not only did she provide basic learning opportunities but also the special nurturing that is demanded with children with motoric and communication handicaps. Fortunately, Jim's mother was as exceptional as his teacher. She stayed in close liaison with the teacher and the speech clinician. She was completely aware of the long range and short range goals that each was trying to accomplish with Jim. She also provided many nurturing activities at home.

Jim was in an excellent position to make progress and did so. He completed his twelve years of schooling successfully. All the while he was seen periodically at the hospital speech and hearing clinic for an evaluation of his progress.

Upon graduation he assumed a job as a maintenance worker in a local industrial firm. Since that time he has been an independent, self-sustaining citizen. He married and is the father of three children. Had it not been for a skillful speech-language pathologist, a caring and determined mother, and a caring and informed classroom teacher, the story of Jim might have been quite different.

DEVELOPMENTAL DELAY

Teachers in special classrooms are faced with problems of delayed development that in turn can have enormous implications for learning and thus for the development of speech and language. With the emphasis on mainstreaming, teachers in regular classrooms may also be faced with similar problems.

Factors that can contribute heavily to delayed development include mental retardation, motor problems due to brain damage, auditory deficits, and environmental causes. Since the matter of normal speech and language development and disorders, as well as auditory deficit have been discussed in earlier chapters, the factors of mental retardation, motor problems and environmental causes will be reviewed. These factors can stand in isolation as causative factors, and on the other hand, these factors, that can impede normal speech and language development, are frequently seen in combination.

The use of drugs and alcohol during pregnancy have been found to be deleterious to the developing fetus. Improper prenatal care can also be significant in the ultimate development of the newborn.

An important responsibility of the classroom teacher is to detect those children who present problems of delay and bring them to the attention of specialized school personnel, such as the speech-language pathologist, audiologist, and psychologist. Only through the coordinated assistance of these specialists can a good description of the child's problems be made. Furthermore, through the help of these specialized personnel and the classroom teacher, parents can be made aware of the status of the child, as viewed by specialists within the educational system, and of the need for further evaluations that seem to be indicated. Frequently, the specialized services of a pediatrician, neurologist, orthopedist, psychiatrist, or perhaps a visual specialist are needed. Thorough diagnoses and descriptions of the child's problems are very necessary. With these a realistic and meaningful program can be designed that will assure the greatest possibility for maximum development of the child. Without this kind of approach, much important time is lost in the child's training and education.

Retarded Intellectual Development

Perhaps the most frequent cause of retarded speech and language development is retarded intellectual development or mental retardation. Because speech and language are so complex, it is not surprising that those who are severely retarded may have great problems communicating. For those not so severely handicapped and only borderline, the speech and language can develop quite well. It is the degree to which the child is retarded that is highly significant, as one anticipates programs of learning that will facilitate the development of speech.

The mildly, mentally retarded child might show good skills motorically and be able to keep up quite well with other children of his or her age. This does not make the task of differentiating him or her from the normally developing child an easy one. Errors can be made in accurate identification also by concluding that the child who is slow in speech and language development is mentally retarded when such might not be the case.

When the mental retardation is severe, the task of identifying it is not difficult, for there are many signs and clues observed by almost everyone. The difficult task is to identify and accurately describe the level at which a child is functioning or capable of functioning when the retardation is only mild. The speech and language problems might not be pronounced but might still be a part of the picture. This calls for the coordinated services of the experienced clinical psychologist and the speech-language pathologist. It is this type of problem that might present itself in the regular classroom. It takes adroit handling by the classroom teacher to make the proper referrals and to elicit the assistance of the parents in obtaining pertinent data.

As with some other problems, the factors that cause mental retardation (Brown, 1956) are many, including injuries to the brain before, during, or after birth—some of which might be caused by certain illnesses of the infant. Intoxication, disorders of metabolism, prematurity, gestational disorders, nutritional deficits, inadequate cultural and social stimulation and cultural deprivation all can play a part in the mental retardation of children (Leonard, 1986).

The real tragedy occurs when in early childhood, due to inadequate diagnosis or perhaps no diagnosis at all, a child suffering from a severe loss of hearing, for example, is mistakenly placed in an institution for the mentally retarded. He or she may spend years there before someone discovers that the child—or perhaps the adolescent or adult—has been erroneously placed. This writer had the experience on a visit to an institution for the mentally handicapped of discovering a young adult placed there as a small child, who was actually suffering from a profound loss of hearing and not mental retardation. The lost years wherein he had not received training and education coupled with his association with mentally retarded patients made it somewhat difficult to discern the difference between the two. Only thorough evaluations of hearing status, mental capacity, and language made it possible to separate this hearing loss patient, who had been wrongly placed, from those about him.

Conventional wisdom suggests that speech and language in the mentally retarded child varies in accordance with the severity of the retardation. Therefore, it behooves the teacher to ascertain, through specialized personnel, the approximate level at which the child is functioning. With this knowledge, the teacher is constrained from becoming unrealistically optimistic with reference to the progress that can be made and conversely from becoming unrealistically pessimistic.

Motor Problems

The production of speech is a tremendously complicated process. It is both intricate and delicate and requires the fine coordination of muscles that eventually result in the production of a sound, a word, or a sentence. Before the muscles receive the necessary messages to move in certain and coordinated ways, there is planning and programming that takes place in the brain. Following this process, the messages are transmitted to the motoric sections of the brain and along the pathways that innervate the muscles and structures responsible for the movements that produce speech. The structures critical in speech production are the lungs, vocal folds, soft palate, tongue, lips, and jaw (La Pointe, 1986). The muscular control of the air flow and pressures necessary for speech and the final shaping of the sounds of speech through the control of the tongue, lips, and jaw finally result in, what we perceive as, the speech output of the child.

When trauma or disease damage the brain, there can be disruption in the motor speech process. If the damage is widespread, then much more than speech can be affected. If, however, the damage is slight and restricted to one area of the brain, the results are relative to that portion of the brain, for example in motor incoordination or paralysis, blindness, hearing loss or deafness.

The child with a slight motor disorder of speech can frequently go along in the classroom and not be observed as having a problem of speech. The child's desire to communicate and relate to his teacher and peers provides the impetus to struggle on to meeting that objective. As a result, the child can often improve his or her status and in doing so avoid being sent to a class for remedial speech. Sometimes the child is observed as one who is a bit clumsy in speech production, and not much more.

If, however, the child is seen as one who has a motor speech problem by specialists who have provided an examination and evaluation, he or she should receive specialized attention. Frequently a physician, particularly a neurologist, is needed to design the most proper and complete plan for remedial efforts. The assistance of the parents, teachers, or other persons not professionally educated and trained, within a program set up for the child and through consultation with a specialist, can be of invaluable help also. Their help lends critical support in the classroom for what the speech clinician is attempting to accomplish in special sessions with the child.

Not only brain trauma and disease processes have significant effects on the motor speech system (La Pointe, 1986). There also functional factors to be considered also. Excessive fatigue and fear can have adverse effects. Lack of desire to speak with precision and over-excitement on the part of the child can also manifest themselves as significant in loss of control of the systems that are responsible for the motor speech act.

Alert, informed, and caring classroom teachers can be of great help in the identification of children with motor speech problems. They also can alert those specialists in the school system of children in need of help. Teachers thereafter function as individuals who bring into the real-life situation of the classroom opportunities for improved communication for these children.

Environmental Causes

Environmental causes for delayed development are many. Several that stand out as being the most important will be discussed briefly.

Motivation and Stimulation

Among the most important environmental causes are the lack of motivation and stimulation. Children learn to talk because they are stimulated to talk by those around them who are talking. A child who is left alone would not develop speech as we know it, for it is through stimulation that the child responds. Rewards for attempted speech are given by parents who have a positive relationship with their child. The rewards given are spontaneous and sometimes probably not all that apparent to the parents themselves. The child feeds on this kind of relationship and continues to respond appropriately and, therefore, continues to develop and refine his or her oral communication skills with parents and others in the immediate environment.

On the other hand, when the child is not provided with positive speech and language stimulation, the child cannot be expected to develop or expand his or her linguistic repertoire. Some parents do not appear to be interested in their children beyond feeding them and providing them with basic care. The disinterest can vary from indifference to outright rejection. The fun of the give and take with the child in terms of speech is simply not there. How then under such a negative reward situation can one expect the child to make good progress in speech? The child finally enters the schoolroom with a dearth of experience in oral communication and may well be viewed by the teacher as deficient in speech and language.

Overprotection

Perhaps the reader is aware of instances where parents anticipate the every wish of the child. Such behavior on the part of parents might be interpreted as overwhelming love for the child. The parents are "so concerned" with the child's welfare that they meet the child's needs without any demands being made of the child. On the other hand, anticipatory behavior might be interpreted as a manifestation of a subconscious compensatory strategy by parents to assuage feelings of guilt associated with basic feelings of rejection toward the child. Of course there could also be other interpretations.

Irrespective of what the causes might be for overprotective behavior, such behavior does not serve to motivate speech and language development. It has been observed that, as a group, mothers of children with delayed speech tend to be more overprotective of their children than do mothers of children with normal speech development.

Siblings

Speech and language development that is below the norms of chronological age might be affected by the delayed development of an older brother or sister or by some other person in the environment with substandard speech/language. One might speculate in the case of siblings as to whether or not it was the poor modeling that caused the delay or some other factor that caused the delay in the development of both children.

The appearance of a new sibling has also been thought to be a possible factor in the delay of speech and language. Prior to the new sibling's birth, the child was the center of attention. Indeed, for all intents and purposes the world revolved about him or her. Suddenly a newcomer, a competitor, a rival has appeared on the scene. Ways to protest the arrival include regression to earlier speech and language patterns, insistence upon being fed, reverting to behavior that denies he or she has ever been toilet-trained, and withdrawal. In one instance, when a new sibling arrived, a three-year-old child appeared to sustain a minor depression and reverted to earlier patterns of behavior. Fortunately, the child's speech and language development proceeded normally. However, the anger associated with giving up "first place" was clearly evident in many ways in the behavior of the displaced child. Quite likely the adverse effects that accompanied the advent of the newborn sibling could have been forestalled had the parents provided the proper preparation and support.

A parent should prepare a child for the arrival of the new brother or sister. With proper preparation by the parent, the child is not only informed of the coming changes in the home but also can be encouraged to be an active, helpful, and happy participant in making those changes. Fortunately, most children work their way through such events and proceed normally in development.

Poverty

Many impoverished situations, including malnutrition, disease, fractionated families, and the lack of hope for a better life, result in inadequate stimulation needed for normal intellectual and speech-language development of the child. Parents in an impoverished environment are often fraught with concerns for survival that overshadow everything else. The child who is a product of this environment is truly disadvantaged. In her discussion of the biological and social aspects of communicative problems, Hardy (1970) stated that "poor children have more problems."

In a paper prepared on the future of impoverished children (Work, 1991) it was noted that in 1989 children accounted for 39½ percent of the poor in the United States. Nearly 12.6 million account for nearly 20 percent of all children under age 18 years. Also approximately 220,000 children of school age in the United States are homeless. Many of these children are at risk for loss of hearing because of infections. The low birth weight babies, born prematurely, with the lack of environmental stimulation are at risk for developmental disabilities. The delays in development of communicative skills evidenced in the preschool children that are not treated prior to entering school greatly reduce their chances of academic achievement. Many drop out when age permits. Public Law 99-457 gives hope of assisting these preschool children with communicative disabilities. The fast growing numbers of poor children and the inadequate numbers of trained professionals to provide services create a dilemma. Work (1991) suggested 1) the importance of training the public concerning the need for prevention of the communicative disorders and 2) the utilization of nontraditional service delivery models to help these children that are caught up in the grip of poverty.

Some thought and discussion have been given to separating out language problems from language differences that are associated with the cultural milieu in which the child is reared. This is extremely important if the teacher and the speech-language pathologist are to deal intelligently with the impoverished child and the cultural diversity that presents itself in the speech and language of some children in the classroom.

Syndromes

Geneticists have contributed substantially to the knowledge of diseases of genetic etiology that are important to the classroom teacher, the speech-language pathologist, and the audiologist. There have been surveys of children at one year of age that show as many as ten percent have genetically caused problems (Jung, 1989). Many of these disorders of genetic origin contribute to speech, language, and hearing problems. Discussion of all of these disorders goes beyond the scope of this text. (For a more complete discussion of genetic disorders and communication, the reader is referred to the references by Jung, and those of Gerber, Stoel-Gammon, Scharfenaker, and Sparks at the end of this chapter.)

Down Syndrome
It is estimated that chromosomal disorders affect about seven in every one thousand births (Gerber, 1990). It is further estimated that approximately one out of every seven hundred live births is suffering the chromosomal abnormality referred to as Down's Syndrome (Stoel-Gammon, 1990). More than 75 percent of Down's Syndrome individuals have a unilateral or bilateral hearing loss. The cognitive development handicap which is a frequent characteristic, is the most significant with which to deal as regards speech and language development. Insofar as voice is concerned, frequent breathiness and huskiness and low pitch are observed. The linguistic and articulatory skills show a lag in development that are related to the cognitive and motor problems. It has been suggested that language production skills lag behind those of comprehension. The child with speech, language, and hearing problems can be expected to improve in all of these areas if he or she has the cognitive capabilities, is identified early, is skillfully evaluated, and is placed within a therapy program that is tailored to meet the communicative needs that have been identified. Since the range of intelligence is from the severely impaired to within normal, there are those children that can be prepared to lead independent productive lives as adults.

Fragile X Syndrome
This is the most common syndrome with respect to mental retardation. There are an estimated one in every one thousand live births according to Scharfenaker (1990), who suggested that the syndrome is characterized by hyperactivity and short attention span in males prior to puberty. Difficulty in integrating sensory stimuli and delay in the development of motor skills present problems in learning and in general management. Speech, language, and cognition deficits vary along a continuum of severity. Speech is often characterized by a rate that is too fast, perseveration on words and phrases and an increase in loudness; as a result, the general intelligibility suffers. Use of the appropriate words, auditory memory, and pragmatic skills are often found to be a problem. Visual memory, however, is a strength and should be taken into account by the teacher and the speech-language pathologist as they seek to provide a program for the child.

Intelligence quotients range along a continuum from mild to severe retardation, and the ability to learn is affected accordingly. Genetic counseling by the appropriate specialist should be given important consideration as a strategy of prevention (Sparks, 1990). The long range success of a child with Fragile X Syndrome is largely dependent upon the degree of mental retardation sustained.

Fetal Alcohol Syndrome

This is an important environmental syndrome that should be noted by the teacher and speech-language pathologist. According to the National Institute on Drug Abuse, three out of every five women of childbearing age currently drink alcoholic beverages (Annonymous, 1991). It has been found that three of every one-thousand babies are born with problems known as Fetal Alcohol Syndrome. Problems that characterize some of the newborns are in the areas of weight, growth and size, central nervous system dysfunction affecting both motor and intellectual development, and learning disabilities. Development of the head and face, malformations of vital organs and, in particular the heart have been identified. Problems associated with Fetal Alcohol Syndrome can affect speech and language development and hearing. Auditory processing can be adversely affected which, in turn, can affect learning. With occurrence of hearing losses, speech and language development as well as academic achievement can suffer.

Alport Syndrome

This syndrome is characterized by renal disease and sensorineural hearing impairment in both ears. The hearing loss found in the Alport Syndrome is responsible for approximately one percent of hearing loss in the general population that originates from genetic causation. The onset of progressive hearing loss starts around age ten and has the same impact on speech as would any other sensorineural loss of hearing following language development, for example, loss of high frequency consonants (f, s, sh, ch, and voiceless th) and difficulty in the monitoring of loudness (Jung, 1989).

This syndrome gives males many more problems than females. The classroom teacher and speech-language pathologist will be concerned with providing auditory rehabilitation and preferential seating in the classroom to facilitate learning possibilities. Periodic hearing testing is highly recommended in order to keep abreast of the progress of the hearing loss.

DRUG ABUSE

A problem of more recent concern is that of drug abuse by pregnant women and its effects on the newborn. It has captured the attention of many in medicine, law, social work, religious organizations, governmental agencies, education and, more recently, those in speech-language pathology and audiology. The effects of the use of drugs during pregnancy can be devastating to the growth and development of the fetus and can have far reaching effects on the child following birth.

The deleterious effects of the use of drugs, both prescription and over-the-counter, during pregnancy have been documented and published in professional literature and in the popular press on numerous occasions. On one occasion, a statement was made to the popular press concerning the use of drugs during pregnancy that lists the extent of the damage that can be done by such drugs as antiacids, laxatives, diuretics, tranquilizers, etc. The extent of the damage can range from minor problems to more majors ones, for example discoloration of the teeth to severe brain damage (MHJF, 1983).

A figure frequently used for drug-exposed babies born in the United States in 1989 is 375,000 with state welfare agencies in eight cities claiming that 9000 babies were born to mothers addicted to crack in the same year in their city hospitals alone (Elshtain, 1990). Some would contend that the 375,000 figure is too high and set the national figure at one or two percent or between 40 to 80 thousand crack babies being born in the United States each year (Besharov, 1990). The gravity of the situation is portrayed by the increase in drug-associated fetal deaths in Los Angeles County alone from nine in 1985 to 56 in 1987 (Besharov, 1990). In 1988 the cost to Los Angeles County for drug-exposed babies was approximately $81 million. The cost estimate by Florida officials to get crack-babies ready for school is $40,000. According to the U.S. Senate Finance Committee Chairman, the cost to the nation for babies who survive and must be prepared to enter school will soon reach $15 billion a year (Yeager, 1991).

Some would argue that prenatal substance abuse is a form of child abuse. To deliver drugs to a child after birth is considered as such. The matter of fetal rights and constitutional rights after a child is born are the areas in which debate and discussion continue. As suggested by the Director of the Center on Children and the Law of the American Bar Association, child protection and child welfare agencies both favor treatment and prevention. This is where a very unique opportunity exists, for both can make a real difference (Horowitz, 1990).

The deleterious effects of drug abuse on the developing fetus are notable in terms of later learning and behavior disorders. Damage to the central nervous system, the vital organs, the brain and ultimately the intelligence of drug damaged children have vast implications for the classroom teacher and for the speech-language pathologist as they attempt to deal with matters of learning and speech and language. Invariably, drug-exposed children score lower in standardized developmental tests (Yeager,

1991). All of this is complicated by a home environment that might not be particularly amenable to suggestions relative to specialized help for the child.

AIDS-HIV POSITIVE

These children present another group with whom classroom teachers may interact. As of late 1990 there were 2734 cases of children known to have AIDS in the United States and an estimated 20,000 to 30,000 children who are HIV positive according to the Centers for Disease Control and Prevention (Pressman, 1992). In her study of 96 children, Pressman determined that 69 percent had deficits in receptive language that were in the range of moderate-profound. Both voice (12½ percent) and articulation (27 percent) problems were seen among this group of children. Those children with HIV infection and/or AIDS who remain stable can attend school. When such children have speech-language problems, the teacher should, in concert with the speech-language pathologist, work out the necessary followup.

The implications for speech-language pathologist and audiologists who provide service to children who are HIV positive or have AIDS are spelled out in detail in a report update by the Committee on Quality Assurance of the American Speech-Language and Hearing Association (Kulpa et al., 1990). This report should be of interest to the classroom teacher as well.

LEAD POISONING

Another group of children that are at risk of brain damage are those exposed to lead. This can have implications for auditory processing, for speech and language development, and for general intellectual development. It appears that children from impoverished areas are particularly vulnerable to this hazard. Teachers and clinicians alike should be alert to the possibility of lead poisoning when gathering background data on children with speech-language-hearing disorders accompanied by neuro-motor and learning problems.

HEAD INJURIES

Only recently has the issue of head injury become visible as a major concern and a primary cause of deaths of children in the United States. Each year there are approximately one million children who suffer head trauma. The incidence is about one out of every five hundred children.

Ten out of every 100,000 children up to age 14 years will die as a result. The incidence of head injury increases greatly throughout adolescence, and escalates to 500 per 100,000 at nineteen years of age (Annegers, 1983; Klauber et al., 1981). The accidents associated with head injuries include falls, child abuse, sports, and automobile accidents. Preschoolers and teenagers seem to be at greatest risk and elementary school-age children at lowest risk (Lehr, 1990).

The question arises as to the sequelae or effects of head trauma and to the relevance these have for the classroom teacher. One can see immediately how behavior in the classroom and achievement can be affected in view of the fact that brain injured children frequently sustain memory deficit, impairment in information processing, difficulty in problem solving, and socially in inappropriate behavior (Levin, 1987). Also, the child who suffers a blow to the head may sustain actual physical problems in addition to cognitive, behavioral, perceptual and social problems (Taylor, 1992). Additionally, speech and language in its various forms can be adversely affected.

Since *closed head injury* (CHI) causes generalized damage, the deficits observed are multiple, reflecting the diffuse nature of the insult. Thus the observable manifestations to the classroom teacher and the speech-language pathologist will be combinations of aberrant behaviors. Impairments in physical strength and coordination as well as problems of communication, memory, motor skills, emotional maturity, and social adjustment all have to be considered when setting up the individual education plan (IEP). The teacher, working with the speech-language pathologist, should develop a systematic profile of the speech, language, social, emotional, and educational behaviors. It should be made with special reference to the severity of the various involvements. With such a diagnostic profile at hand, both the teacher and the clinician are made aware of those areas that are in need of intervention and can plan the sequence of such intervention. A splendid guide for accomplishing this is presented by DePompei and Blosser (1987).

Once again, the classroom teacher, speech-language pathologist and the parents comprise the team that is responsible for making the entry or re-entry of the child with head trauma into the school program a successful one. It is a challenging and in some cases, a formidable task but not an impossible one.

EMOTIONAL DISTURBANCE

The term *emotional disturbance* within the context of school children refers to a condition in which the child displays prolonged problems that interfere with the ability to learn that cannot be identified as stemming from deficits of intellect, sensory deprivation, or health. Psychosocial relationships with the classroom teacher and the other students may suffer, and inappropriate behaviors may be manifested. Mood swings and unwarranted fears may be observed. One or several of these factors may be evident to the classroom teacher and others having responsibility for the child.

There are many causes for emotional disturbance. Anxiety, abuse, rejection, unstable home environments, inability to compete with peers or siblings, and other undetermined factors can contribute to a picture of emotional instability. Autism and schizophrenia, which will be discussed later, are also potential causes of emotional disturbance.

Although there are special programs designed to help children with emotional problems, many mildly-moderately emotionally involved children are now mainstreamed into regular classrooms with a portion of their time in special settings. This placement presents a unique challenge to the classroom teacher. The more severely disturbed are usually assisted in settings beyond the regular classroom.

Some emotionally disturbed children have accompanying speech and language problems. In a study of 38 school children, all mainstreamed in regular classrooms and identified as mildly to moderately affected by behavioral disorders, it was noted that on *all* five subtests of the Test of Language Development-Intermediate (TOLD-I) the performance of these children was below the performance of the normal population (Camarata, Hughes, and Ruhl, 1988). The investigators suggested that all mildly-moderately behaviorally disordered children should be considered at risk with regard to potential language problems.

Emotional disturbances can occur as secondary to speech-language-hearing disorders and, conversely, delayed language development can be a product of emotional disturbance. The interrelationships among speech-language, communicative competence, and emotional health of children are complex (Prizant, et al., 1990). The identification, treatment, and management in the classroom of these children calls for the input of the classroom teacher, the speech-language pathologist, the psychologist and, in some cases, other specialists. Effective intervention demands multidisciplinary efforts.

The classroom teacher might also be involved with unfortunate children who come from homes where they are damaged physically or psychologically either through willful intent or simply disinterest and neglect. These children may display emotional problems with implications for speech and language. One only needs to read the daily paper, listen to radio or television, or work with children in the schools to be aware of these tragic cases. Memories of such are clear to this writer upon recalling vividly those within his public school caseload that showed signs, both physically and psychologically, of outright abuse or neglect. Home visits on several occasions helped to support these impressions. A noteworthy statistic in relation to this is that in excess of 80 percent of all child abuse cases in the District of Columbia in 1989 involved substance abuse (Elshtain, 1990).

Of all children under age five who sustain injuries, approximately 10 percent of them will be caused by circumstances other than accidental. It is estimated that each year 25 out of every 100,000 children still suffer child abuse. Approximately 50 percent of abused children suffering cerebral damage will suffer permanent neurological and intellectual impairment (McClelland et al., 1980; and Helfer and Pollock, 1968—cited in Cooper, 1987). The speech and language of the unfortunate children are not always adversely affected; however, some research has indicated that scores on various tests of language are lower than they are for children who are not abused or neglected. When such children are detected in the classroom, they should be brought to the attention of the relevant personnel within the school system. When speech-language deficits are observed, the teacher will want to make the necessary arrangements with the speech-language pathologist for evaluation.

Autism is a disorder that has serious implications for speech and language. As with most other disorders, it can range from mild to severe. It is a developmental disability involving emotional withdrawal; behavior, speech, and learning disorders; and often a repertoire of repetitive behaviors. It usually is observed during the first three years of life (infantile autism) with a frequency of about five out of every 10,000 births (NINCDS, 1983).

Sometimes infantile autism is confused with peripheral hearing loss because of the symptoms of delayed speech and mutism (Myklebust, 1954). The likelihood that a regular classroom teacher will be called upon to deal with the speech, language or learning of a severely autistic child is quite remote. However, mildly autistic children may be present in the classroom. They may appear to have learning disabilities and aphasic symptoms. In these cases the classroom teacher will want to learn more about the child and to work closely with the speech-language pathologist in order to maximize every opportunity for language learning and for the development of speech skills.

Some important objectives in working with the emotionally disturbed language-impaired child include learning the coping devices that the child uses and having a clear idea as to how the child's behavior is to be managed. Additionally, the expansion of the child's impoverished vocabulary is in order to help him or her describe in more precise ways his or her personal feelings rather than having to rely on acting them out or to continue to use only a few less precise words.

Learning the language of the classroom and learning to listen more carefully are also important objectives for both academic achievement and social adjustment with peers (Diddan, 1991). Other emotional disturbances that are related to speech, language and hearing are severe anxiety states and childhood schizophrenia.

CASE HISTORY

Jeff

Jeff was always a problem in school. Now in the third grade, he was a special challenge to his teacher. He did well in math but did not seem to grasp the content or concepts of other subjects. Frequently he would appear to be deaf, and attempts to communicate with him were unsuccessful. He was clumsy and seemed to be unaware of tripping over other children or spoiling an art display.

One day the school's new speech-language clinician made a call on Jeff's teacher and was told about Jeff. "He uses words in the strangest ways, when he chooses to talk—they don't make sense," the speech-language clinician was told. "I don't know whether he is mentally retarded, half deaf, or just plain ornery," the teacher added.

The speech-language pathologist arranged for a speech-language evaluation of Jeff and she found Jeff showing signs of autism. He was not deaf, not mentally retarded, and not just plain ornery. Neurological and psychological workups confirmed this evaluation. Subsequently, a special program was designed for Jeff by the speech-language pathologist, the psychologist, the classroom teacher, and closely coordinated with the parents. At last report Jeff was beginning to show some signs of progress.

DIALECT DIFFERENCES AND BILINGUALISM

To understand and respond appropriately to the social dialect of a child within a classroom can be a complex and sensitive undertaking. First of all, it must be recognized that a social dialect is *not* a communicative disorder and thus should not be treated as such by a teacher or speech-language pathologist. "It is the position of the American Speech-Language-Hearing Association (ASHA) that no dialectical variety of English is a disorder of a pathological form of speech or language" (ASHA, 1983).

There are several variations of the English language spoken in the United States, and one reasonably asks why these variations occur. They are caused by several influences, the most important of which are 1) the influence of foreign languages brought by settlers from foreign countries such as German, French, Polish, Chinese, etc.; 2) those influences that are due to indigenous languages of the Native Americans; (3) the cultural mix of the groups settling within certain communities and regions; 4) influences of political and economic power of the components of a cultural group with a community; 5) geographical isolation; and 6) self-imposed isolation or legal segregation (Taylor, 1986).

With most cultural groups, there are subgroups that are socially delineated. Thus a particular subgroup can reflect a social class level wherein the language differs somewhat from that of another subgroup within the main cultural group. Taylor (1986) suggested that *Black English* is the most controversial and the most frequently discussed dialect in the literature.

It must be understood, however, that a social dialect and a communicative disorder can be present simultaneously (Freeman, 1977). For example, if a child with a Spanish or Black English dialect has defective articulation or stutters, the classroom teacher should, as with any other child, refer the child to a speech-language pathologist. It may be somewhat more difficult to detect an articulatory problem if a teacher is not thoroughly familiar with the features of the dialect. In other words, it is most important that teachers and clinicians learn to distinguish accurately between linguistic diversity and disorder. Since social dialects provide necessary adjustments to particular social groups to which their users belong, the speech-language clinician should not disrupt the desire or ability of the child to use the original dialect when appropriate.

Social dialects are rule-based and are not to be considered "less than" but only "different from" that which is recognized as standard English. A teacher is in a strategic position, as the authority in the classroom, to promote understanding and acceptance of a child who has a different dialect.

The bilingual child has some facility in two or more distinct languages. There will be times when the syntax or vocabulary of the first language might be used when speaking the second language. As with social dialect, this is not to be considered a disorder of speech/language. Frequently it seems that parents speaking a language other than English at home are eager to have their children speak English. As with the child with a social dialect, the teacher and speech-language pathologist can provide a program for the bilingual child aimed at achieving standard English and thereby work toward the elimination of the effects of the first language on the second. This would be undertaken, however, only at the request of the child and parents, as the influences of bilingualism are not considered to be a speech/language disorder.

ALTERNATIVE-AUGMENTATIVE MODES OF COMMUNICATION

For those children who will never be able to develop speech, there is help through alternative modes of communication. An alternative mode is one that permits messages to be developed and sent without the use of the vocal tract. There may be some children in your classroom at some point who must depend upon augmentative communication devices. Whether or not one has a communication problem, one augments what he/she wishes to communicate by using certain techniques or aids. The person with normal speech/language development uses body language quite naturally. Smiling, pointing, nodding of the head, and other nonverbal techniques are employed. For example, "yes" and "no" are easily understood by the head gestures we use. To bid someone goodbye is easily interpreted from the handwave we make. To encourage someone to come closer is accomplished easily with a beckoning hand gesture. (These gestures work well in our culture but often may not evoke the same kind of responses in other cultures.) Perhaps closest to the simple gestures is pantomime. It is a particularly useful means of communicating when a noisy environment precludes the use of oral speech.

The person who is disabled by a communication deficit utilizes, if possible, certain nonverbal strategies. However, if the communication deficit is great, as we have seen that it can be, in the preceding sections of this chapter, then the augmentation of the attempts at communicating is of great significance. Through the years specialized systems have evolved quite naturally—such as signs, fingerspelling, etc.—particularly for those whose auditory reception is impaired (Vanderheiden and Yoder, 1986). Sign language is perhaps the most sophisticated form of non-oral communication; and it is considered a total language, not a poor alternative to speech. Different cultures develop their own sign languages. For example, American Sign Language (Ameslan or ASL) used by deaf persons in the United States is not the same as American Indian Sign Language (Amerind). Fingerspelling is another nonverbal form of communication, but it takes much longer than signing and calls for knowledge of spelling.

Communication boards vary substantially. Some are set up with letters for spelling words, whereas others have pictures indicating a variety of messages, such as "I want a drink" or "I want to go to the bathroom." Many communication boards have electronic components. Specially designed symbol systems, electronic devices, computer assisted schemes, etc.—when used by speech-language-hearing handicapped individuals who have no oral communication—can literally help to transform their lives.

There have been various estimates of the number of persons in the United States who are unable to communicate orally. These estimates vary from over a million persons (Diggs, 1981) to 1.4 million (Baker, 1983). A later estimate suggests that 200,000 to 2.0 million persons in the United States are not able to speak or that they demonstrate severe communication impairments (Shane, 1986). Given that an estimated 2.5 to 6.0 percent of the children who are enrolled in special education programs cannot be understood because of the severity of their communicative disorders underscores the need for augmentative assistance (Blackstone, 1989). In view of the fact that PL-142 mandates that all students—regardless of the nature of their handicaps—be educated, one quickly sees the importance of augmentative communication.

The whole matter of communication aids for those without speech has received considerably more attention over the past twenty years and is described by various writers. To present the many examples of specialized applications of communicative and facilitative approaches goes beyond the scope of this chapter. For the student who wishes to follow up on this topic, excellent comprehensive discussions of communication aids are presented by Silverman (1980), Fishman (1987), Brandenburg and Vanderheiden (1987), Beukelman et al. (1985), Angelo and Goldstein (1990), Biklen (1992), and Durand and Berotti (1991).

SUMMARY

CEREBRAL PALSY

Causes

- Many causes
- Complications of pregnancy
- Maldevelopment of the fetus
- Problems in the birth process
- Deprivation of oxygen

Some Important Points to Remember

- Cerebral palsy is not contagious
- Cigarette smoking and excessive use of alcohol and drugs during pregnancy can affect development of the fetus
- Different types of cerebral palsy exist. Three principal categories are spasticity, athetosis, and ataxia.
- There are different degrees of involvement: one arm, one leg, both arms, both legs, one arm and leg on one side, both arms and legs, or three limbs.

- Often speech is disordered.
- Hearing and vision may be impaired.
- Multiple disabilities are often present.
- Speech might not be present, might be labored, or only slightly affected.
- Facial, head, and body movements may be affected.
- Low self-esteem often accompanies cerebral palsy.
- Intellectual disability may be present.
- The classroom teacher will not usually have the severely disabled in class.
- Notify a speech-language pathologist of a cerebral palsied child you have in class who needs special assistance in speech, language or hearing and provide needed background data.
- A child without oral speech might have to rely on augmentative devices.
- Speech and language might not be at the level expected for chronological age.

Do's and Don'ts for Teachers

Do's:
- Be patient with the cerebral palsied child.
- Encourage the child to participate in every activity possible.
- Give praise for achievements.
- Elicit the support of other students.
- Build self-esteem.
- Explain to other students the problems of the child with cerebral palsy.

Don'ts:
- Do not demand more than physical abilities will allow.
- Do not be condescending.

Referral Sources
- Speech-language pathologist
- School psychologist
- Learning disorders specialist
- Orthopedist
- Physical therapist
- Occupational therapist

DEVELOPMENTAL DELAY

Causes

- Problems in fetal development
- Deprived environment
- Sensory problems, i.e. hearing and vision
- Genetic anomaly
- Brain damage
- Drug abuse
- AIDS

Some Important Points to Remember

- Activities demanding physical coordination may be below the level expected for chronological age.
- The child will probably need a substantial amount of extra attention.
- There are often several factors responsible for a delay in development.
- When a developmental delay occurs, it usually has great implications for speech and language development.
- If the developmental delay is great, the child might be placed in a special program or school.

Do's and Don'ts for Teachers

Do's:
- Detect these children as early as possible and bring them to the attention of a speech-language pathologist.
- Seek to support the child at all times and create an atmosphere of trust.
- Sensitize parents to the possible need for further referral if such exists.
- Design an IEP with all relevant specialists that is tailored specifically to the child's needs.
- Help other children in the classroom to understand the problem and elicit their support.

Don'ts:
- Do not push a child beyond her/his capabilities.
- Do not permit ridicule by other students.
- Do not demand less than a child is capable of giving.

Referral Sources

- Speech-language pathologist
- Audiologist
- Psychologist
- Neurologist

HEAD INJURIES

Causes

- Accidents
- Abuse

Some Important Points to Remember

- Approximately one million children suffer head trauma each year.
- Preschoolers and teenagers are at greatest risk.
- Behavior and achievement are often affected.
- Memory deficit sometimes occurs.
- Information processing is often impaired.
- Consider total range of involvements when setting up the IEP.

Do's and Don'ts for Teachers

Do's:

- Consult with the speech-language pathologist if speech and/or language are affected.
- Obtain complete history from parents or caregiver.
- Try to help the child to make a good social adjustment to the classroom.

Don'ts:

- Don't overstimulate the child.
- Don't penalize for unusual behaviors.

Referral Sources

- Speech-language pathologist
- Audiologist
- Psychologist
- Learning disabilities specialist

EMOTIONAL DISTURBANCE

Causes

- Anxiety
- Abuse
- Rejection
- Unstable home situation
- Inability to compete with peers
- Schizophrenia
- Neglect
- Autism
- Other undetermined factors

Some Important Points to Remember

- The label emotional disturbance is broad and covers many types of problems.
- Try to understand with the help of specialists the nature of the emotionally disturbed child or children in your classroom.
- Some children are seen in the regular classroom, whereas others are scheduled for special programs.
- Some emotionally disturbed children have speech-language-hearing disorders.
- Some speech-language problems can result from emotional problems.
- Autism is usually observed within the first three years of life and in five out of every 10,000 births.
- It is unlikely that the classroom teacher will deal with a child severely disabled by emotional disturbance.
- Speech-language disorders are varied, depending upon the type of the emotional disorder.

Do's and Don'ts for Teachers

Do's:
- Seek to support the emotionally disturbed child in every way.
- Provide a stable atmosphere in the classroom.
- Promote understanding and acceptance of the child by other children in the classroom.
- Follow the suggestions of the specialists involved in the care of the child.
- Encourage the child to participate in classroom activities.

Don'ts:
- Don't demand more than the child is capable of giving.

Referral Sources

- Speech-language pathologist
- Psychologist
- Psychiatrist

DIALECT DIFFERENCES AND BILINGUALISM

Causes

- Influence of foreign language brought from foreign countries
- Influences indigenous to Native American languages
- Cultural mix of groups within communities
- Influence of political and economic power within a cultural group
- Geographical isolation
- Self-imposed isolation or legal segregation

Some Important Points to Remember

- A child can have a dialect difference and a communicative disorder simultaneously.
- The American Speech-Language-Hearing Association has determined that no dialect difference is to be considered a pathology of speech or language.
- It may be difficult to detect an articulation disorder when a social dialect exists.
- Social dialects provide a means of adjustment to social groups.
- Social dialects are rule based.
- Bilingualism that causes occasional confusion of syntax should not be considered a disorder of language.

Do's and Don'ts for Teachers

Do's:
- Refer a child to the speech-language pathologist if a speech disorder, such as stuttering, voice anomaly, or other pathology exists.
- Learn to distinguish between linguistic diversity and speech-language disorders.
- Promote acceptance of the child with a social dialect.
- Encourage participation in recitation and discussion activities.

Don'ts:
- Do not try to eliminate a dialect unless the child or the parents request it.
- Do not penalize a child with a social dialect or a confusion in speech/language caused by bilingualism.

Referral Sources

- Speech-language clinician

AUGMENTATIVE COMMUNICATION

Some Important Points to Remember

- Some children might never develop speech and might have to rely on alternative ways of communicating.
- Gesturing is a basic alternative mode of communicating.
- Alternative modes of communication may take many forms.
- Hand signs can be helpful to the deaf and to others as well.
- Ameslan (ASL) is the hand sign system used by deaf people in the United States
- Amerind is the hand sign system used by Native Americans
- Picture drawing, symbol systems, fingerspelling, and communication boards, etc., are used.
- Some communication boards are electronic.
- Computer assisted devices are sometimes employed.
- Aids for children without speech are growing in popularity and use.

SELF-TEST

True or False

1. Cerebral palsy is a disease affecting poorly nourished children. ____
2. There are approximately 750,000 people in the United States who ____ have cerebral palsy.
3. Speech of the cerebral palsied child is always disordered. ____
4. The classroom teacher should work with the speech-language clini- ____ cian to aid the transfer of training from the clinical session to the classroom.
5. Neuromuscular incoordination is seen in cases of cerebral palsy. ____
6. The classroom teacher should view most social dialects as minor ____ disorders of speech.
7. Emotional disturbances have little to do with the development of ____ speech and language in children.

8. Bilingual children should always be singled out for special assistance ____ from the speech-language pathologist.
9. A deprived home environment can cause a child to experience a ____ developmental delay.
10. Referrals of children with delayed development are sometimes ____ necessary.
11. Simple gestures constitute a form of alternative communication. ____
12. A communication board is not considered an augmentative device. ____
13. Sign languages are identical the world over irrespective of culture. ____
14. Children who speak and hear normally still use some non-speech ____ modes of communication.
15. Electronics plays a part in some alternative communication aids. ____
16. Preschoolers and early elementary aged children present the greatest ____ risk for head injuries.
17. Memory deficits are sometimes caused by head injuries. ____
18. Deficits resulting from closed head injury (CHI) are multiple. ____
19. AIDS in children has implications for language performance. ____
20. Infantile autism is sometimes confused with peripheral hearing loss. ____
21. Drug usage by expectant women can have profound effects on fetal ____ development.
22. Alport Syndrome is seldom if ever associated with hearing loss. ____
23. The Down Syndrome child never shows "within normal" in- ____ telligence.
24. The advent of a new sibling can have adverse effects on the adjust- ____ ment of another child.
25. Mothers of children with delayed speech are often more over- ____ protective than mothers of children with normal speech.

REFERENCES

Angelo D. H., & Goldstein, H. (1990). Effects of a pragmatic teaching strategy for requesting information by communication board users. *Journal of Speech and Hearing Disorders, 55*, 231–243.

Annegers, J. F. (1983). The epidemiology of head trauma in children. In Shapiro, K. (Ed.), *Pediatric Head Trauma*. Mt. Kisko, New York.

Annonymous (1991). Fetal alcohol syndrome. *ASHA, 33*(8), 53–54.

ASHA Committee on the status of racial minorities. (1983). Social dialects. *ASHA, 25*(9), 23–24.

Baker, B. (1983). Communication—an overview. *Rehabilitation World, 7*, 2, 3–5. Cited in Shewan, C. M. & Blake, A. (1991). Augmentative and alternative communication. *ASHA, 33*(5), 46.

Besharov, D. J. (1990). Crack children in foster care. *Children Today, July-August*, 21.

Beukelman, K. M., Yorkston, M., & Dowden, P. A. (1985). *Communication Augmentation. A Casebook of Clinical Management*. San Diego, CA: College-Hill Press.

Biklen, D. (1992). Typing to talk. *American Journal of Speech-Language Pathology, 1*(2), 15–17.

Blackstone, S. W. (1989). Augmentative services in the schools. *ASHA 31*(1), 61–64.

Brandenburg, S. A., & Vanderheiden, G. C. (1987). *Communication, control and computer access for elderly and disabled individuals. ResourceBook 1: Communication aids; ResourceBook 2: Switches and environmental controls; ResourceBook 3: Software and hardware.* San Diego: College-Hill Press.

Brown, S. F. (1956). Retarded speech development in Johnson, W., Brown, S. F., Curtis, J. F., Edney, C. W., Keaster, K. J. *Speech Handicapped School Children* (revised ed.) (pp. 308–309). New York: Harper and Brothers.

Camarata, S. M., Hughes, C. A. & Ruhl, K. L. (1988). Mild/moderate behaviorally disordered students: a population at risk for language disorders. *Language, Speech, and Hearing Services In Schools, 19*(2), 191–200.

DePompei, R. & Blosser, J. (1987). Strategies for helping head injured children successfully return to school. *Language, Speech, and Hearing Services In Schools, 18,* 292–300.

Diddan, J. J. (1991). School children with emotional problems and communication deficits: implications for speech-language pathologists. *Language, Speech, and Hearing Services In Schools, 22,* 293.

Diggs, C. C. (1981). Action school services. *Language, Speech, and Hearing Services In Schools, 12,* 269.

Durand, M. V. & Berotti, D. (1991). Treating behavior problems with communication. *ASHA, 33*(11), 37–39.

Elshtain J. B. (1990). Pregnancy police. *The Progressive, 54,* 26–28.

Fishman, I. (1987). *Electronic communication aids: selection and use.* San Diego: College-Hill.

Freeman, G. G. (1977). *Speach and Language Services and the Classroom Teacher.* A publication of the National Support Systems Project under a grant from the Division of Personnel Preparation, Bureau of Education of the Handicapped, U.S. Office of Education, Department of Health, Education, and Welfare, 21. Council for Exceptional Children, Reston, Virginia.

Gerber, S. E. (1990). Chromosomes and chromosomal disorders. *ASHA 32*(9), 39.

Hardy, J. D. (1983). *Cerebral Palsy.* Englewood Cliffs: NJ, Prentice-Hall.

Hardy, J. M. B. (1970). Some biologic and social aspects of communicative problems. Ch. 3 in Hardy, W. G. (Ed.) *Communication and the Disadvantaged Child.* Baltimore: Williams and Wilkins.

Horowitz, R. (1990). A coordinated public health and child welfare response to perinatal substance abuse. *Children Today, 19,* 12.

Jung, J. H. (Ed.) (1989). *Genetic Syndromes In Communication.* Boston: College-Hill Press, 3.

Klauber, M. R., Barrett-Conner, E., Marshall, L. F., & Bowers, S. A. (1981). The epidemiology of head injury: a prospective study of an entire community—San Diego County, CA. 1978. *Journal of Epidemiology, 112,* 500–509. Cited in Lehr, E. (1990). *Psychological Management of Traumatic Brain Injuries In Children And Adolescents.* (pp. 2–3). Rockville, MD: Aspen Publications.

Kulpa, J. I. et al (1990). AIDS/HIV: implications for speech-language pathologists and audiologists. *ASHA, 32,* 46–48.

La Pointe, L. (1986). Neurogenic disorders of speech. Ch. 12 in Shames, G. H. & Wiig, E. H. *Human communication disorders.* (2nd ed.) (p. 503). Columbus, OH: Charles H. Merrill.

Lehr, E. (1990). *Psychological Management of Traumatic Brain Injuries In Children And Adolescents* (pp. 6–7). Rockville, MD: Aspen Publications.

Leonard, L. (1986). Early language development and language disorders. In Shames, G. H. & Wiig, E. H. *Human Communication Disorders* (2nd ed.) (p. 301). Columbus, OH: Charles E. Merrill.

Levin, H. S. (1987). Neurobehavioral sequelae of head injury. In Cooper, P. R. (Ed.) *Head Injury* (2nd ed.). Baltimore, MD: William and Wilkins, 461.

MHJF. (1983). Drugs and pregnancy don't mix. *Good Housekeeping, 196,* 184.

Myklebust, H. R. (1954). *Auditory Disorders In Children.* New York: Grune and Stratton.

National Institute of Neurological and Communicative Disorders And Stroke. (1980). *Cerebral Palsy.* Bethesda, MD: National Institutes of Health.

Perkins, W. H. (1971). *Speech Pathology.* St. Louis, MO: C. V. Mosby.

Pressman, H. (1992). Communication disorders and dysphagia in pediatric AIDS. *ASHA 34*(1), 45.

Prizant, B. M., Audet, L. R., Burke, G. M., Hummel, L. J., Maher, S. R., Theodore, G. (1990). Communication disorders and emotional/behavioral disorders in children and adolescents. *Journal of Speech And Hearing Disorders, 55,* 191.

Scharfenaker, S. W. (1990). Fragile X syndrome. *ASHA, 32*(9), 45.

Shane, H. C. (1986). Goals and uses. In Blackstone, C. W. & Bruskin, D. M. *Augmentative Communication.* Rockville, MD: American Speech-Language-Hearing Assocation, pp. 29–48.

Silverman, F. H. (1980). *Communication for the Speechless.* Englewood Cliffs, NJ: Prentice-Hall.

Sparks, S. N. (1990). Prevention of chromosomal disorders: Roles for clinicians. *ASHA, 32*(9), 51–53.

Stoel-Gammon, C. (1990). Down syndrome, effects on language development. *ASHA, 32*(9), 42.

Taylor, J. L. (1992). *Speech-Language Services in the Schools* (2nd ed.). Boston: Allyn & Bacon, 203.

Taylor, O. L. (1986). Language differences. In Shames, G. H. & Wiig, E. H. (Eds.). *Human Communication Disorders* (2nd ed.). Columbus, OH: Charles H. Merrill, 395.

Vanderheiden, G. C. and Yoder, D. E. (1986). Overview. In Blackstone, S. W. and Bruskin, D. M. (Eds.). *Augmentative Communication.* Rockville, MD: The American Speech-Language-Hearing Association.

Van Riper, C. (1972). *Speech Correction Principles and Methods.* Englewood Cliffs, NJ: Prentice-Hall.

Work, R. S. (1991). Children of poverty. What is their future? (This briefing paper was prepared by R. S. Work, a member of the ASHA Longe Range Strategic Planning Board.) *ASHA, 33,* 61.

9

GENERAL RESPONSIBILITIES OF TEACHERS TO STUDENTS WITH COMMUNICATIVE PROBLEMS

It has been emphasized throughout this book that the classroom teacher has a tremendous impact on children in general, and especially on children with problems. It has been suggested by McFarlane, Fujiki, and Brinton (1984, pp. 107–108) that "there is little doubt that the classroom teacher plays a significant role in the lives of most young children. The teacher serves as an important role model and a major force in shaping ideas. In addition, the classroom teacher may also influence the emotional development of children. Considering these factors, it stands to reason that teacher involvement in a child's program of (speech) therapy is highly advantageous." Garbee (1985, p. 75) was even more explicit: "The classroom teacher, of course, greatly influences the development of a child who has a speech or language disorder."

There is no doubt that teachers have busy schedules and little time for extra duties; however, teachers do have a number of general responsibilities in relation to communication. Teachers should find that as they become more involved in and knowledgeable about communication, they will require less time for these responsibilities, and, it is hoped, that as a child learns to communicate better in the classroom, the teacher will feel that the time spent was worthwhile.

GENERAL RESPONSIBILITIES OF A TEACHER

The following general responsibilities will hold true regardless of the communicative situation or disorder.

Be a Good Speech Model

By being a good speech model the teacher subtly tells students that good communication is desirable. If you have any doubts whatsoever about your own communicative status, seek out a speech-language pathologist who can evaluate your speech. If you are a student, determine if there is a speech and hearing science department at your college or university. This specialty may be a separate department or it may be a part of a larger department, such as communications or special education. If you locate one, call and ask how you can obtain an evaluation. If you do have a problem, there probably is a clinic at which you can receive help at no cost or for a nominal fee. If you are reading this book as part of a course, you might also ask your instructor if he or she is qualified to assess your speech skills. It should be noted that some universities and colleges require that students majoring in education pass a speech and hearing screening before beginning student teaching. In other words, if there is a problem, it must be remediated before a student can begin student teaching. If you are already a teacher, you may wish to talk to the speech-language pathologist who serves your school. She or he can assess your speech as well as give you suggestions concerning the remediation of any problems.

Moreover, a teacher or prospective teacher does not want to maintain a correctable behavior that would be a potential source of teasing or name calling by students. Realistically, children may be wonderful to work with, but children do not just tease other children; at times they also tease or find names to call teachers behind their backs. Do not provide them with an easy target. Furthermore, parents may object to obvious communicative problems.

Create a Classroom Atmosphere Conducive to Communication

A relaxed atmosphere in which children are expected to be attentive listeners and respect what others say is conducive to communication. The verbally shy child should be provided an opportunity and encouraged to participate orally. The goal is for children to view communication as fun.

Accept a Child with Communicative Problems

Truly accept a child as he or she is, remembering that there is a difference between acceptance and tolerance. Approval is implicit in acceptance, whereas tolerance may be likened to the capacity to endure (Webster, 1983). Understand that a child may not be able to produce the "correct" speech behavior just because he or she is told or ordered to do so; the child may not even hear the difference between his or her speech and the "correct" speech. Be assured that the speech-language pathologist will inform the teacher when a child can be expected to use his new communicative behaviors outside of therapy.

Encourage Classmates to Accept a Child with Communicative Problems

There is little doubt that a child's ability to communicate may affect how he or she is treated by peers, which may in turn affect the child's communication and willingness to communicate. No teacher can ever prevent or stop all teasing, or make children befriend other children; however, there are some strategies that may be helpful.

Discussions regarding feelings and attitudes are an integral part of some classroom texts and materials. There are commercial materials, such as *Developing Understanding of Self and Others* (DUSO) (Dinkmeyer & Dinkmeyer, 1982), developed solely for this purpose. Mercer and Mercer (1985) include a 13 page list of activities and materials (both teacher made and commercial) that they recommend for developing social-emotional skills. Make use of such resources whenever possible, not only for the benefit of a disabled child but also for other children who may be teased or ridiculed and for children who tease when they need to learn more acceptable adult behaviors. Pointing out to children that they are not the only ones who are teased, and that even friends tease each other may be real eye-openers for them. Appendix A includes an annotated bibliography of children's books, with calculated readability levels, that deal with communicative problems as well as normal communication. The teacher may find some of these books appropriate for either individual readers or for the whole class. Heron and Harris (1982) suggested that small group work can be conducive to social integration as well as academic achievement when a teacher carefully selects the children for each group.

When classmates have questions about a disabled child, it may be appropriate to discuss the child's problems and how the other children can help. Depending on the circumstances, it may be more appropriate to hold this discussion with or without the disabled child being present. However, first the teacher might be wise to discuss this approach and the reasons for it with the child's parents so that the parents will not learn of such a discussion through the "parental grapevine." We were particularly impressed with the mother of a severely physically disabled but completely mainstreamed child who came to class and, with her child, discussed what the child's problems were, how she coped with everyday activities, and how the classroom children could help. They then answered all questions.

At other times, a teacher may need to help a child "fight back." For example, a third grade girl was being mercilessly teased by a pair of sixth grade boys in the hallways and on the playground. After considering the situation in terms of what would be most repugnant to boys of that age, the teacher remarked to the girl that when a boy teases a girl, it often means that he likes her. That afternoon as the boys confronted the girl, the girl yelled, "Boys who like girls tease them," and kept shouting it as she chased them across the playground. From then on, the boys avoided that little girl! Not all of your attempts may turn out as well, but you can at least try. Mercer and Mercer (1985) suggested that a teacher counsel children who are teased to ignore their tormentors, and then reward the teased children when they do ignore the teasing. In this way, the child doing the teasing receives no attention from either the children being teased or the teacher.

Consult and Collaborate with the Speech-Language Pathologist

All school personnel have a responsibility to understand the goals and procedures being used by others who are working with a particular child and to work to integrate those goals and procedures into their own work with the child. This can only be accomplished by taking the time to explain what you are doing, listening to others explain what they are doing, and working out compatible goals, objectives, materials, and procedures. This is a major goal of the IEP committee. However, even once the IEP has been established, the consultation and collaboration must continue for daily and weekly problems to be worked out and goals to be accomplished. For example, with the traditional pull-out service delivery model the classroom teacher can ask the speech-language pathologist to help the child with a particular task that the child is having difficulty with in the classroom, and the speech-language pathologist can ask the teacher to remind a child to use a particular language structure that the child has worked on in therapy. Obviously, with the classroom-based service delivery model consultation and collaboration would be constant.

Furthermore, a teacher's knowledge and understanding of other services that a child receives, such as speech therapy, are also helpful when parents, who typically have more communication with the classroom teacher than the speech-language pathologist, ask the teacher questions about such services. The teacher may be able to answer the questions but, if not, can at least talk knowledgeably about the questions while suggesting that the parents contact the speech-language pathologist, or, better yet, offering to have the speech-language pathologist contact the parents. A teacher should share information that may affect a child's performance or interaction with others. For example, because of more contact with the parents, a teacher may be better able to assess the parents' interest, willingness, or ability to help a child with his or her speech at home.

Detect Possible Communicative Problems and Make Appropriate Referrals to a Speech-Language Pathologist

When teachers detect possible speech or language problems, they should make referrals to a speech-language pathologist. Most speech-language pathologists will agree that they would prefer that teachers overrefer rather than underrefer so that children, especially those with subtle language problems and voice problems, are not missed. Generally, school districts will have referral forms available in the principal's office. On these forms (see Figure 9-1) a teacher may be asked to describe the problem and to state how he or she has attempted to deal with it and with what success. However, this does not preclude a teacher talking directly with the speech-language pathologist about a child.

Contribute to the Motivation of a Child

Motivating a child is always important. Therapy is not something done to a child but instead requires cooperative effort on the child's part. Children need support from parents, teachers, and important others in their environment in order to put forth the effort to be a part of the remediation team. It should be noted that this book has examined the various speech-language-hearing problems in isolation; however, two or more problems can coexist creating a more complex disorder. Motivation is then particularly important, as therapy is not only apt to be long-term, but progress may be slow and "normal" may never be achievable.

Long before teachers can reinforce new communicative behaviors, they can encourage and motivate children through their interest in what the children are doing in therapy. Ask each child what he or she is learning. If the child has a "speech book," ask to see it and have the child tell you about it.

Reinforce the Goals of Speech Therapy

When a speech-language pathologist and teacher have consulted with each other, the teacher is in a position to reinforce the goals and procedures of speech therapy. As children progress and become capable of producing correct speech or language behaviors (whether it is a good "r" sound, a better voice quality, or a complete sentence), they must break old habit patterns and habituate new behaviors. This is the carryover stage during which a teacher can truly reinforce the new behavior. The speech-language pathologist recognizes that the teacher is not trained in speech-language pathology and does not expect the teacher to hear or correct every error. In fact, having every error corrected could quickly discourage and alienate a

XYZ SCHOOL DISTRICT
SPEECH-LANGUAGE-HEARING REFERRAL FORM

Student Name _____   Date _____

Age _____   Grade _____

Gender _____   School Building _____

Current Placement and Services _____

Referring Teacher _____

Check the area(s) that you are concerned about:

☐ Articulation/Production of Speech Sounds   ☐ Voice

☐ Stuttering/Fluency   ☐ Language

☐ Hearing   ☐ Other

Please describe the student's communicative problem. (Include frequency of problem and times/situations when problem is most noticeable.)

Please describe any technique(s) that have been tried in the classroom to address this problem and the success achieved:

Any other pertinent information:

FIGURE 9–1   Sample form for referral to speech-language pathologist

child. However, there will be times when a teacher is aware that a child is using better speech or language. When this happens, the teacher should praise the child by saying, "You remembered to use your good "s" sound," or "Your voice certainly sounds better this morning." Remember, though, that such remarks in front of other children might embarrass a child. If you think this might be so, praise the child in private.

Help the Child Remember Therapy Appointments

This may be as simple as pointing out to a child that every Monday, Tuesday, and Thursday after morning recess, he or she should go to speech therapy. However, a visual reminder may be necessary. For example, a small clock with the hands pointing to the therapy time could be taped to a child's desk or inside the desk if it needs to be inconspicuous. It is suggested that this be a clock face rather than the written time so that a child can match the reminder to the clock on the classroom wall. It seems that with the prevalence of digital clocks and watches, some children today are not learning to tell time easily and quickly using a clock with hands.

Some children, whether due to impaired cognitive functioning or other reasons, will not remember their therapy times regardless of what visual clues a teacher or speech-language pathologist provides. If such children are to get to therapy on time, the teacher must assume responsibility for remembering and reminding. Such help will be a tremendous benefit to the speech-language pathologist and to the children. If a child does not arrive at therapy on time, the speech-language pathologist will need to go personally or to send another child to the classroom to get the tardy child. This shortens the therapy time for all of the children. Similarly, a teacher certainly has the right to expect that children will be dismissed and sent back to the classroom on time.

Help the Child Catch Up On What Is Missed While in Speech Therapy

Whenever possible, a speech-language pathologist will schedule each child for the same time each day that the child attends therapy sessions in order to make it easier for the child (and the teacher) to remember that time. Therefore, it is suggested that teachers consider implementing (if they have not already done so) the currently popular practice of scheduling various subjects at different times each day. In this way a child will not be missing the same subject matter every therapy day.

Scheduling becomes more complicated at the secondary level since class schedules are more inflexible and the length of therapy sessions may not equal the length of class periods (Battle & Van Hattum, 1985). Frequently, attempts are made to schedule students during study halls, but this is impossible for all students. Rotating schedules may be used, but this approach makes it a bit more difficult for a student to remember therapy times. Scheduling speech therapy as part of the regular academic schedule for which students may earn credit has been suggested and tried in some school districts with success (Task Force Report on Traditional Scheduling Procedures in Schools, 1973).

A teacher may want to spend some extra time with a child, reviewing subject matter missed during therapy. An alternative or additional technique would be to use a form of peer tutoring. The teacher would select a peer who would be responsible for explaining and reviewing the lessons and activities that the child missed. This peer might rotate according to the subject matter missed and might also rotate throughout the semester or year. If note taking were involved, the peer could photocopy, carbon copy, or lend his or her notes. This might even be a part of a larger peer tutoring system within the classroom. It is beyond the scope of this book to delve into peer tutoring. However, studies have demonstrated it to be useful with benefits to both the tutors and tutees. Suggested references are included at the end of this chapter regarding peer tutoring in both elementary and secondary classrooms.

SUMMARY

Some Important Points to Remember

- The classroom teacher is an important role model for children and thus is important in shaping their development.
- A teacher should become involved in a child's program of speech therapy.
- Being a good speech-language model tells children that good communication is highly desirable.
- If you, as a future teacher, think you have a speech problem, have your speech checked by a speech-language pathologist.
- An atmosphere conducive to easy communication should be established and maintained in the classroom.
- Show geniune acceptance of the child with a communicative disorder.
- The speech-language pathologist will inform a teacher when a child can be expected to use new communicative behaviors outside of therapy sessions; wait for this notification before demanding corrected speech-language behavior.

- Encourage classmates to accept a child with communicative disorders.
- Consult with the speech-language pathologist concerning each child with a communicative disorder in your classroom.
- Reinforce the goals of speech therapy.
- Reinforce good speech-language performance.
- Help children remember the times that they go to speech therapy.
- Be conscientious about helping children catch up on the classroom information they missed while in therapy.
- Consider peer tutoring to get children caught up on the classroom information they missed while in speech therapy sessions.

Questions to Ask Yourself

1. Name at least four ways that a classroom teacher can be a good speech model.
2. Develop a list that contains ten suggestions for developing an accepting atmosphere in the classroom for the speech, language, or hearing impaired child.
3. What role do parents play in the remediation process for their communicatively disabled child? At home? At school?
4. How might you, as a teacher, reinforce the work of a speech-language pathologist with a speech disabled child in your classroom?
5. How might the speech-language pathologist reinforce the work you are doing in the classroom with a language-disabled child?
6. Elaborate on the concept of peer tutoring in either the elementary or secondary classroom for the child who must miss classroom activities to participate in speech therapy sessions.

Suggested Readings on Peer Tutoring

Allen, V. L. (1976). *Children as teachers: Theory and research on tutoring.* New York: Academic Press.

Candler, A. C., Blackburn, G. M., & Sowell, V. (1981). Peer tutoring as a strategy individualizing instruction. *Education, 101,* 380–383.

Cloward, R. D. (1967). Studies in tutoring. *Journal of Experimental Education, 36,* 14–25.

Cooke, N. L., Heron, T. E., & Heward, W. L. (1985). *Peer tutoring: Implementing classwide programs in the primary grades.* Columbus, OH: Special Press.

Dineen, J. P., Clark, H. B., & Risley, T. R. (1977). Peer tutoring among elementary students: Educational benefits to the tutor. *Journal of Applied Behavior Analysis, 10,* 231–238.

Ehly, S. W., & Larsen, S. C. (1980). *Peer tutoring for individualized instruction.* Boston: Allyn & Bacon.

Harrison, G. V. (1978). *Five steps to successful tutoring*. Blanding, UT: METRA.

Heward, W. L., Heron, T. E., & Cooke, N. L. (1982). Tutor huddle: Key element in a classwide peer tutoring system. *The Elementary School Journal, 83,* 115–123.

Howell, K. W., & Kaplan, J. S. (1978). Monitoring peer tutor behavior. *Exceptional Children, 45,* 135–137.

Jason, L. A., Erone, L., & Soucy, G. (1979). Teaching peer tutoring behaviors in first- and third-grade classrooms. *Psychology in the Schools, 16,* 261–269.

Niedermeyer, F. C. (1970). Effects of training on the instructional behaviors of students tutors. *Journal of Educational Research, 64,* 119–123.

Williams, R. W. (1981). *Developing a peer tutoring program: A self-instructional module* (ERIC No. ED 207–632). Chicago: Chicago City Colleges.

REFERENCES

Battle, D. E., & Van Hattum, R. J. (1985). Scheduling. In R. J. Van Hattum (Ed.), *Organization of speech-language services in schools* (pp. 224–285). San Diego: College-Hill Press.

Dinkmeyer, D., & Dinkmeyer, D., Jr. (1982). *Developing understanding of self and others* (rev. ed.). Circle Pines, MN: American Guidance Service.

Garbee, F. E. (1985). The speech-language pathologist as a member of the educational team. In R. J. Van Hattum (Ed.), *Organization of speech-language services in schools* (pp. 58–129). San Diego: College-Hill Press.

Heron, T. E., & Harris, K. C. (1982). *The educational consultant: Helping professionals, parents, and mainstreamed students*. Boston: Allyn & Bacon.

McFarlane, S. C., Fujiki, M., & Brinton, B. (1984). *Coping with communicative handicaps*. San Diego: College-Hill Press.

Mercer, C. D., & Mercer, A. R. (1985). *Teaching students with learning problems* (2nd ed.). Columbus, OH: Charles E. Merrill.

Task force report on traditional scheduling procedures in schools. (1973). *Language, Speech, and Hearing Services in Schools, 4,* 100–109.

Webster's Ninth New Collegiate Dictionary. (1983). Springfield, MA: Merriam-Webster.

APPENDIX A

Books Useful to Teachers

The books in this section are all suitable for your students. The readability level of each book (when appropriate) is listed just before the description. The readability levels were determined by a formula worked out by Fry (Fry, E. (1968)). A readability formula that saves time. (*Journal of Reading, 11,* 513–516, 575–578.) The books are arranged alphabetically by the last name of the first author.

These books were written for children and deal with the normal processes of speech and hearing and/or with impaired speech and hearing. It is hoped that teachers will be able to use them in some of the following ways: as part of a literature-based reading program, as supplements to science and health curricula, as recommended books for students doing book reports, as books to be read by the teacher to the entire class, as a supplement to discussions concerning feelings, and as suggested reading for individual students to either help them understand others' disabilities or to put their own disabilities into a better and healthier perspective. May your reading be enjoyable and informative!

Adams, B. (1979). *Like it is: Facts and feelings about handicaps from kids who know.* New York: Walker and Co. (96 pages) (approximate **7th grade readability** level)

This book portrays real children who reflect a variety of disabilities. They share with the reader factual information as well as their feelings about their disabilities. The purpose is to help readers become more comfortable and natural in their contacts with disabled peers. Thirteen year old Danny, who is deaf, talks about hearing and speech problems. Other chapters include children with visual impairments, orthopedic handicaps, developmental disabilities, learning disabilities, and behavior disorders. A glossary is included.

Adler, D. A. (1980). *Finger spelling fun.* New York: Franklin Watts. (32 pages) (approximate **4th grade readability** level)

Fingerspelling is defined and explained. The finger positions are depicted for each letter and the author suggests that they can be used as a secret code as well as for talking to deaf people. Riddles with answers given in fingerspelling will attract the young reader. Also included are games that utilize fingerspelling.

Adler, I., & Adler, R. (1963). *Your ears.* New York: John Day. (48 pages) (approximate **4th grade readability** level)

Beginning with a definition of sound, this book explains how we hear, how having two ears helps us localize sound, and how the ear is protected from dirt, unequal air pressure on either side of the eardrum, and very loud noises. Hearing tests, types of hearing loss, and various forms of remediation for the hearing impaired are also discussed.

Aimar, C. (1975). *Waymond the whale.* Englewood Cliffs, NJ: Prentice-Hall. (28 pages) (approximate **2nd grade readability** level)

Raymond and Elizabeth are brother and sister whales. Because of their speech problems they call each other Lithabeth and Waymond. They challenge each other to a contest but wind up helping each other learn to pronounce their sounds correctly.

Arthur, C., & Talbot, N. (1979). *My sister's silent world.* Chicago: Children's Press. (31 pages) (approximate **2nd grade readability** level)

This is a book of short narrative descriptions of a child, Heather, who is hearing impaired and must wear a hearing aid. The setting for the story is Heather's eighth birthday party. The narrative is enhanced by excellent colored photographs of Heather and others. This book could provide a basis for discussion of the effects of hearing loss on children's oral communication and thereby be instructive to all children in a classroom.

Baastad, B. F. (1965). *Kristy's courage.* New York: Harcourt, Brace, and World. (159 pages) (approximate **3rd grade readability** level)

Cheek and tongue injuries from being hit by a car leave Kristy with a scarred cheek and unclear speech. These problems are compounded by the fact that Kristy must start second grade in a new school. The big boys tease her and her classmates shun her. An understanding doctor helps the adults comprehend Kristy's problem and helps Kristy deal with it successfully.

Baldwin, D., & Lister, C. (1984). *You and your body. Your senses.* New York: The Bookwright Press. (32 pages) (approximate **6th grade readability** level)

Chapter 5 deals with the anatomy and function of the various parts of the ear. The text is written in simple language that can be understood by youngsters. Many colorful pictures illustrate points the authors wish to make. Suggestions are made on how to take care of one's ears.

Blatchford, C. (1976). *Yes, I wear a hearing aid.* New York: Lexington Family Series. (43 pages) (approximate **3rd grade readability** level)

Mumps caused the six year old girl in this story to lose her hearing. The reader follows this girl from the time that she learns to cope with her first hearing aid as a twelve year old through school, college, and parenthood.

Bloom, D. (1977). *The boy who couldn't hear.* London: The Bodley Head. (23 pages) (approximate **1st grade readability** level)

While fishing, Mark becomes frightened by some obviously angry boys who shout at him. His mother intervenes, explaining to the boys that Mark does not hear but lip reads instead. Amplification is briefly introduced in this picture book.

Bourke, L. (1981). *Handmade ABC. A manual alphabet.* Reading, MA: Addison-Wesley Publishing Company. (57 pages) (**picture book**)

This is a small book which is easy for little hands to grasp. The handshape for each letter is presented in clear black and white pictures.

Bove, L. (1980). *Sesame Street sign language fun.* New York: Random House. (62 pages) (**picture dictionary**)

Words and the signs for them (as presented by Linda Bove, a deaf actress on "Sesame Street") are arranged in concept families, such as family, morning, school, farm, playground, opposites, seasons, and feelings. Following each page of signs is a picture featuring the "Sesame Street" muppets and a sentence that the reader can practice signing.

Bove, L. (1985). *Sesame Street sign language ABC with Linda Bove.* New York: Random House. (29 pages) (**picture book dictionary**)

Linda Bove, a deaf actress on "Sesame Street," presents signs of words that begin with each letter of the alphabet. Other "Sesame Street" characters also appear in the book.

Broekel, R. (1984). *Your five senses.* Chicago: Children's Press. (48 pages) (approximate **4th grade readability** level)

How we hear is simply and clearly explained in large type in the hearing and sound chapter in this book. A glossary is included.

Brown, T., & Ortiz, F. (1984). *Someone special just like you.* New York: Holt, Rinehart and Winston. (64 pages) (picture book with captions at approximate **2nd grade readability** level)

This is a general book about being a special child. It is illustrated with numerous photographs. It emphasizes the point that children with disabling conditions are highly similar to other children in many respects. This book should be very helpful to the teacher who wants to educate all children regarding attitudes toward the disabled. An additional feature at the end of the book is the annotated bibliography which presents books, some written by disabled persons, that describe various disabling conditions.

Charlip, R., Beth, M., & Ancona, G. (1974). *Handtalk. An ABC of finger spelling and sign language.* New York: Four Winds Press. (40 pages) (**picture book**)

The handshape for each letter is presented along with the fingerspelling and sign for a word that begins with that letter.

Christopher, M. (1975). *Glue fingers.* Boston: Little, Brown and Co. (48 pages) (approximate **2nd grade readability** level)

Billy Joe is embarrassed by his stuttering, fears being laughed at, and feels that his stuttering interferes with his ability to make friends. Although he at first refuses to play football on an organized team because of his stuttering, Billy Joe finally rationalizes that he could join the team since he will not have to talk while playing. Happily, his prowess at football enables him to make friends with his teammates and to put his stuttering into perspective.

Corcoran, B. (1974). *A dance to still music.* New York: Atheneum. (180 pages) (approximate **4th grade readability** level)

Due to ear infections, Margaret becomes deaf while in eighth grade. Refusing to go to a school for the "handicapped," Margaret does not go to school at all. She lives in a silent lonely world, refusing to try to talk for fear she will talk too loudly and harshly as her deaf grandfather had. When her mother plans to remarry, Margaret runs away and finds friendship with Josie and an injured Key deer. Events lead Margaret to talk again and agree to enter a university program designed to help deaf children learn to cope in a regular school.

Curtis, P. (1981). *Cindy: A hearing ear dog.* New York: E. P. Dutton. (55 pages) (approximate **6th grade readability** level)

Cindy, a small gray dog, is chosen from the animal shelter to be trained as a hearing ear dog. Such dogs help their hearing impaired owners respond to various sounds, such as the telephone, door bell, alarm clock, and smoke detector. Lots of pictures explain the training process. At the end of the training period Cindy goes home with Jennifer, a deaf junior high student.

Elgin, K. (1967). *The human body: The ear.* New York: Franklin Watts. (49 pages) (approximate **5th grade readability** level)

Topics in this book include the variety of sounds that we can hear, the anatomy of the ear, how sound travels through the ear to the brain, and balance.

Emert, P. R. (1985). *Hearing ear dogs.* Mankato, MN: Crestwood House. (47 pages) (approximate **5th grade readability** level)

This book is very informative regarding hearing ear dogs. It begins with a story that shows the need for a hearing ear dog. A brief historical account is given of dogs who have helped hearing disabled people in days gone by. A description is given of the breeds of dogs most frequently serving as helpers to deaf people. A most interesting section is the one on how these dogs are trained and then made available to their new masters. This book should be of interest not only to children but to parents as well. Edited by a professor of reading and language arts, it is well organized and interestingly written.

Fryer, J. (1961). *How we hear: The story of hearing.* Minneapolis: Medical Books for Children: Lerner Publications. (30 pages) (approximate **7th grade readability** level)

The relationship of sound waves to pitch is explored. Then the author traces the path of sound from the time it enters the ear until it reaches the brain. Discussions regarding balance, motion sensitivity, and the purpose of the Eustachian tube are included. Possible causes of hearing problems and a brief description of hearing aids, including the first hearing aid used by Beethoven, conclude this book.

Gold, P. (1975). *Please don't say hello.* New York: Human Sciences Press. (47 pages) (approximate **3rd grade readability** level)

The neighborhood children are excited about the new family on their street. However, one of the three new children is a puzzle; Eddie is autistic. The neighborhood children learn that even though Eddie makes strange, eerie sounds and exhibits unusual behaviors, he is neither deaf nor retarded and will occasionally talk. Eddie is often afraid and confused and has difficulty concentrating. His feelings are hurt when he is teased. Additional information regarding autism is revealed through a visit to Eddie's school. Most importantly, the children learn that they can help Eddie by treating him naturally even though he does not respond as other children do.

Greenberg, J. E. (1985). *What is the sign for friend?* New York: Franklin Watts. (28 pages) (approximate **7th grade readability** level)

Lots of pictures are used to show Shane engaged in the ordinary everyday activities that children enjoy. Shane, who was born deaf, has difficulty learning to talk. His voice is sometimes high pitched, he may omit sounds in words, and he is sometimes hard to understand. Shane has hearing friends as well as deaf friends. At school, he spends most of his day in classes with children who can hear. His interpreter signs the lessons for him and helps him keep up in his school work. Signs for words, such as **friend**, **deaf**, and **pizza**, are given.

Greene, L., & Dicker, E. B. (1982). *Sign Language.* New York: Franklin Watts. (66 pages) (approximate **8th grade readability** level)

The relationship between language and speech is briefly explained. Several sign language systems are introduced. The history of sign language includes a history of how hearing impaired people have been viewed and treated through the years. A story (a Greek myth about the origin of the seasons) is told in words and sign. Sign language games can be found at the end of the book.

Hanlon, E. (1979). *The swing.* Scarsdale, NY: Bradbury Press. (209 pages) (approximate **5th grade readability** level)

Beth, who is deaf, is excited over the family's annual visit to the mountains. As Beth shares her many experiences, including coping with having to share her swing with Danny, hiking up the mountain for the first time by herself, and trying to save the bears—the reader learns that deafness has some limitations but certainly does not preclude talking or knowing that promises should be kept.

Haskins, J. S. (1978). *Who are the handicapped?* Garden City, NY: Doubleday and Company. (109 pages) (approximate **9th grade readability** level)

Several of the chapters in this book would be useful to teachers as they attempt to acquaint students with the concept of disability and the problems that are associated with being disabled. A special attempt is made by the author to address the prejudice often shown disabled people. Of particular interest are the sections on "Being Deaf" (pages 39–50) and "Cerebral Palsy" (pages 57–62).

Hirsch, K. (1981). *Becky.* Minneapolis: Carol Rhoda Books. (35 pages) (approximate **2nd grade readability** level)

Becky who is deaf, hears only very loud noises even with her hearing aid. She lives on a farm but stays with another family during the school week in order to go to a school where she can receive special help. The daughter of this family tells how she is surprised to find that Becky in many ways is just like other children. However, Becky is frustrated when she does not know how to communicate her thoughts. At her new school Becky learns how to use sign language and how to read lips, thus reducing that frustration. The two girls become good friends.

Hunter, E. F. (1963). *Child of the silent night.* Cambridge, MA: The Riverside Press. (124 pages) (approximate **7th grade readability** level)

This is a compelling true story of a little girl, Laura, who became deaf and blind at the age of two following an illness. The daughter of farmers, this little girl was one of three children. Only limited time could be given to her as life on the farm in those days (nineteenth century) was very hard and demanding. Her real help came from a kindly neighbor man without a family who literally became her teacher. She was also helped by a student from Dartmouth who worked for Laura's father as a farm hand. It was through the help of this student, his professor, and others that Laura was enrolled in the Perkins Institution in Boston. Her progress was remarkable and she became known over the world. She lived at Perkins for 52 years and died at age 60.

Hyman, J. (1980). *Deafness.* New York: Franklin Watts. (64 pages) (approximate **10th grade readability** level)

Some infants are at high risk for hearing problems. Hyman discusses how it is often the parents who first notice that something seems to be wrong with their infant's hearing. How we hear; types of hearing loss; treatment, including surgery, medication, and hearing aids; ways for the hearing impaired to communicate; mainstreaming; acceptance by peers; and difficulty with school tasks that require language, such as word problems in math, are among the topics explored.

Kamien, J. (1979). *What if you couldn't. . . . ? A book about special needs.* New York: Charles Scribner's Sons. (83 pages) (approximate **7th grade readability** level).

Kamien states that the purpose of this book is to help the reader understand more about various disabilities. One chapter addresses hearing loss. Lipreading, hearing aids, speech therapy, sign language, and total communication are presented as ways of coping with a hearing impairment. Other problems addressed in this book include visual impairments, learning disabilities, physical disabilities, emotional disturbance, and mental retardation.

Keller, H. (1954). *Helen Keller. The story of my life.* Garden City, NY: Doubleday and Company. (382 pages) (approximate **8th grade readability** level)

This is an autobiographical account of the life of Helen Keller. It outlines in detail the tremendous hurdles that Keller had to surmount as she worked with her dedicated and highly capable teacher, Anne Mansfield Sullivan. A supplementary report of her educational experiences is provided by her teacher. It is a splendid example of how a disabled person who is determined to learn can do so under the care of a knowledgeable and devoted teacher.

(NOTE: There are many accounts of Helen Keller's life written for many age levels and reading abilities.)

Kelley, S. (1976). *Trouble with explosives.* Scarsdale, NY: Bradbury Press. (117 pages) (approximate **3rd grade readability** level)

This story is told by a woman who is a stutterer. It exposes the many frustrations, fears, and anxieties caused by stuttering. It describes the reactions of her family and classmates. Written in a highly readable manner, it is laced with good humor and is hard to put down. This book should help students appreciate some of the difficult situations a stutterer must face.

Kettelkamp, L. (1967). *Song, speech, and ventriloquism.* New York: William Morrow and Company. (96 pages) (approximate **6th grade readability** level)

Voice production as a reflex action depends on the complex processes of respiration, phonation, and resonation. Each of these is explained in a straightforward manner. Production of many of the vowels and consonants is reviewed. Singing, breath control, voice ranges, and voice projection are explored, followed by a discussion on ventriloquism which uses the information learned about speech sound production. A glossary is included.

Krasilovsky, J. (1972). *The boy who spoke Chinese.* Garden City, NY: Doubleday and Co. (29 pages) (approximate **3rd grade readability** level)

Amanda explains to everyone that her younger brother, Nicholas, who doesn't speak clearly, is really speaking Chinese. Nicholas is frustrated because no one will listen and talk to him. Then he finds that his new baby brother is a very attentive listener. Some readers will be interested in knowing that this book was written and illustrated by a 15 year old girl.

Lee, M. (1969). *The skating rink.* New York: Seabury Press. (126 pages) (approximate **6th grade readability** level)

Fifteen year old Tuck Faraday reacts to his stuttering problem with embarrassment and then withdraws from communicating. Befriended by Pete, who is building a skating rink in the rural town, Tuck learns to skate well enough to be an exhibition skater at the grand opening of the rink and to get a job giving skating lessons. With his newly found self-respect, Tuck decides that he does have a future after all and changes his mind about quitting school.

Levine, E. S. (1974). *Lisa and her soundless world.* New York: Human Sciences Press. (30 pages) (approximate **2nd grade readability** level)

This story helps the reader understand what it would be like not to be able to hear. Lisa did not learn to talk because she could not hear. When her parents discovered that she was deaf, they were able to get her help, which involved hearing aids and speech therapy, to learn to lip-read, to talk, and to use sign language.

Litchfield, A. B. (1976). *A button in her ear.* Chicago: Albert Whitman and Company. (30 pages) (approximate **3rd grade readability** level)

This is a well-illustrated book for children that tells the story of a little girl, Angela, who has a hearing loss. Angela's hearing loss, identified by her parents, was further confirmed by her pediatrician, who sent her to an audiologist for further examination. The audiologist fitted her with a hearing aid that was of great help. This little book could be ever so helpful to other children who must wear hearing aids, and also to boys and girls in general, by giving them a better understanding and appreciation of children who must rely upon hearing aids.

Litchfield, A. B. (1980). *Words in our hands.* Chicago: Albert Whitman & Co. (29 pages) (approximate **4th grade readability** level)

Nine year old Michael tells this story about his parents, who were born deaf, his two sisters, and their dog Polly. Michael and his sisters, who are not hearing impaired, learned sign language from their parents and speech from their grandparents, friends, and neighbors. Some of the topics worked into the story include fingerspelling, hearing ear dogs, teletypewriters, lipreading, and the National Theatre of the Deaf. Although embarrassment and shame are felt on occasion, the point is that Michael's family can take part in the same activities that other families do.

Litchfield, A. B. (1984). *Making room for Uncle Joe.* Niles, IL: Albert Whitman & Co. (26 pages) (approximate **2nd grade readability** level)

Uncle Joe has Down's syndrome and is coming to live with Danny, his younger sister Amy, his older sister Beth, and their parents. But how will he fit in? Will the children still be able to have their friends over to play? When they find that Uncle Joe listens to Amy read, teaches Dan to bowl, takes piano lessons from Beth, and helps around the house, he is accepted as a "neat guy."

Little, J. (1962). *Mine for keeps.* Boston: Little, Brown and Company. (186 pages) (approximate **4th grade readability** level)

This story is of a girl who returned home after having lived in a school for disabled children for over five years. Her fears at returning to her home are described. As a cerebral palsied child, she knew that there would be many adjustments. Even though she had made two trips home each year for holidays, she sensed that coming home for good meant something different because others would have to adjust to her as well. The many situations described by the writer show the adjustments that can be made by a caring family and friends who understand.

MacIntyre, E. (1975). *The purple mouse.* New York: Thomas Nelson, Inc. (108 pages) (approximate **6th grade readability** level)

Because of four words that Hattie had been unable to hear, she manages to dye a white mouse a permanent purple. She has always believed that most people feel sorry for her because of her hearing impairment and so has just avoided people in general. However, in trying to help the little purple mouse she learns to face her fears of difficult listening situations and to do as the purple mouse does—to never give up but to go forth.

McConnell, N. P. (1982). *Different and alike.* Colorado Springs, Colorado: Current. (28 pages) (approximate **6th grade readability** level)

The concepts of different and alike are used to emphasize the similarities between people who are and are not handicapped. Hearing and visual impairments, learning disabilities, speech disorders, and physical and mental handicaps are described. The book concludes with hints on how to help handicapped individuals.

Martin, P. D. (1984). *Messengers to the brain. Our fantastic five senses.* Washington, D.C.: The National Geographic Society. (103 pages) (approximate **7th grade readability** level)

The chapter on hearing and balance provides a clear explanation of sound, how we hear, and how we maintain balance. The diagrams and pictures are excellent supplements to the text. A glossary is included.

Montgomery, E. R. (1978). *The mystery of the boy next door*. Champaign, IL: Garrard Publishing. (48 pages) (approximate **1st grade readability** level)

The neighborhood children think the new boy is very unfriendly when he ignores them and does not answer the doorbell. However, when they discover that both he and his mother are deaf, they understand how they reached the wrong conclusion and a new friendship looms.

Peter, D. (1976). *Claire and Emma*. New York: John Day. (28 pages) (approximate **4th grade readability** level)

Claire and Emma, both born deaf, are four and two years old respectively. They live with their hearing mother and older brother. They both wear hearing aids and are learning to lipread. Pictures depict the usual childhood activities, such as swimming, climbing trees, and playing games that they enjoy. Some of the inconveniences of being hearing impaired, such as not being able to hear someone knock at the door, not hearing television, and not being able to lip-read unless you are looking at a person are highlighted.

Peterson, J. W. (1977). *I have a sister. My sister is deaf*. New York: Harper and Row. (29 pages) (approximate **4th grade readability** level)

The older sister tells in a gentle, loving manner what it is like to have a sister who is deaf. She tells how her sister is aware of what goes on around her even though she cannot hear. Even though the disadvantages of deafness are many, there are the occasional advantages, such as not being awakened and frightened by a thunderstorm.

Pollock, P. (1982). *Keeping it secret*. New York: G. P. Putnam's Sons. (110 pages) (approximate **2nd grade readability** level)

A sixth grader, Mary Lou, better known as "Wisconsin," has just moved to New Jersey with her parents and brother. Wisconsin is fearful of meeting her new classmates because she wears hearing aids, so she tries to keep her aids a secret. This causes her classmates to misunderstand her actions. Field Day, a developing self-confidence, and Jason, who thinks she is cute, help her develop better social relationships.

Reuben, G. H. (1960). *What is sound*. Chicago: Benefic Press. (48 pages) (approximate **7th grade readability** level)

Sound is discussed in terms of the wide variety of sound sources, sound waves, the medium that carries sound waves, the speed of sound, breaking through the sound barrier, the frequencies and resulting pitches of sound, volume and the perceived loudness of sound, and sound reflections and echoes. The production of voice using expired air from the lungs and a short description of our uses of sound and how we hear complete the book.

Robinson, V. (1965). *David in silence*. Philadelphia: J. B. Lippincott Company. (126 pages) (approximate **6th grade readability** level)

The story is one of a boy, David, who was born deaf. It provides the reader with an excellent account of the many frustrating experiences David has in attempting to work out a place for himself among others as he develops. He is successful in changing the attitudes of classmates and others.

Rosen, L. D. (1981). *Just like everybody else.* New York: Harcourt Brace Jovanovich, Publishers. (155 pages) (approximate **3rd grade readability** level)

This is a story of a young girl, Jenny, who was deafened as a result of a bus accident. The writer describes with candor and clarity the many challenges Jenny has to meet in a silent world. The description of her struggle and eventual success in rehabilitation should deepen the student's understanding of deaf children. Since the author also lost her hearing, she is particularly sensitive to Jenny's problems.

Rosenberg, M. B. (1983). *My friend Leslie: The story of a handicapped child.* New York: Lothrop, Lee, and Shepard Books. (42 pages) (approximate **3rd grade readability** level)

Karin tells this story about her friend Leslie who is disabled. Leslie is visually impaired, has muscle stiffness, and is hearing impaired (she wears two hearing aids). Leslie can do most things for herself. It just takes her longer than it does the other children. At school Leslie is mainstreamed. Lots of pictures show what Leslie's school day is like in activities such as art, music, reading, and recess.

Rounds, G. (1980). *Blind outlaw.* New York: Holiday House. (94 pages) (approximate **7th grade readability** level)

Boy, who can only make a few sounds and cannot talk, has a special way of communicating with animals, including rabbits, coyotes, and a magpie. His challenge is to tame a wild blind horse. Boy seems to communicate with chirping and crooning noises, patience, and understanding. If he succeeds, the horse will be his.

Schneider, L. (1956). *You and your senses.* New York: Harcourt, Brace & World. (137 pages) (approximate **7th grade readability** level)

Experiments are suggested to reinforce the discussions on how sound is created, how sound travels, how the frequency and volume of sounds vary, how we hear, how the Eustachian tube functions, how we hear through bone, and how we maintain our sense of balance.

Schwartz, J. (no date). *A handful of colors.* Northfield, IL: cbh Publishing. (31 pages) (approximate **1st grade readability** level)

The signs for 57 high frequency words are illustrated. Many of these signs are then repeatedly used in sentences that are also signed.

Showers, P. (1966). *How you talk.* New York: Thomas Y. Crowell. (35 pages) (approximate **1st grade readability** level)

In order to talk people must use their lungs for a source of air, their vocal cords as a source of vibration, their teeth, tongue, lips, and so on. Talking is explored through humming with the nostrils opened and closed, changing the sound produced by changing the shape of the mouth, and trying to say words without using the tongue or the lips. The overall tone of the book is one of lighthearted-ness and fun.

Silverstein, A., & Silverstein, V. B. (1971). *The sense organs. Our link with the world.* Englewood Cliffs, NJ: Prentice-Hall. (73 pages) (approximate **7th grade readability** level)

One chapter of this book focuses on how we hear. Through the use of analo-gies, the anatomy and physiology of the ear are explained. How sounds may vary in pitch, loudness, and quality; how animals hear different pitches; and potential dangers to the hearing mechanism are touched upon.

Silverstein, A., & Silverstein, V. B. (1981). *The story of your ear.* New York: Coward, McCann, and Geoghegan. (64 pages) (approximate **7th grade readability** level)

The authors provide a relatively detailed explanation of the anatomy and physiology of the ear in an easy to understand manner. The frequencies and intensities of various sounds as they relate to hearing are explored. Noise as a source of potential damage to the ear and one's health and as an initiator of the flight-or-fight syndrome are discussed. This book is a good nonencyclopedic reference for a health or science report.

Slepian, J. (1980). *The Alfred summer.* New York: Macmillan Publishing. (119 pages) (approximate **3rd grade readability** level)

This is the story of a special friendship between "special" children. Cerebral palsy causes Lester to have problems with his speech and with walking. Alfred is retarded. Along with two other children, Lester and Alfred have their first experiences going places and doing things without a parent tagging along. At the end of one such outing Lester must muster the strength to save his friend.

Smith, L. B. (1979). *A special kind of sister.* New York: Holt, Rinehart and Winston. (23 pages) (approximate **2nd grade readability** level)

Seven year old Sarah finds that it can be hard having a five year old brother who is retarded. She shares with the reader her feelings and emotions regarding Andy, from jealousy over the attention that he requires to the empathy and love she feels.

Stanek, M. (1979). *Growl when you say R.* Chicago: Albert Whitman and Company. (29 pages) (approximate **2nd grade readability** level)

This is a story of an elementary school boy, Robbie, who had a problem articulating his "r" sounds. Because of this, he was teased by the other children. He got into fights and withdrew from play activities and his social development suffered. The teacher contacted the parents concerning Robbie's problem, and it was decided to send him to speech class. With reluctance Robbie went and his efforts were rewarded by learning to say the "r" sound correctly. As a matter of fact, he was the child who was able to keep himself and some other children from becoming hopelessly lost at the zoo by being able to ask aloud over a microphone for his school bus driver to wait for them. The message was "Robert's School Bus Number 9 wait for us!"

Stecher, A., Wentworth, D. F., Couchman, J. K., & MacBean, J. C. (1973). *Your senses.* Toronto: Holt, Rinehart and Winston of Canada. (118 pages) (approx-imate **7th grade readability** level)

A variety of activities is outlined to help students better understand how we hear, how some people do not hear as well as others, how we identify sounds, how we localize sounds, how loud sounds affect our hearing, and so forth. Many of these activities are suitable for small groups.

Sullivan, M. B., & Bourke, L. (1980). *A show of hands—Say it in sign language.* Reading, MA: Addison-Wesley Publishing Company. (96 pages) (approximate **7th grade readability** level)

This book consists of a series of drawings which point out the importance and the use of hands by everyone in communicating ideas. It is a book not particularly to be read to students, but by them. It is suitable for adults as well. Signing and fingerspelling are explained through the narrative and through the drawings. This would be a good book to use in educating students as to how the hearing disabled are helped and would be particularly useful if a child in the classroom had a hearing impairment.

Talbott, M. (1982). *My treasure is my friend.* Northridge, CA: Joyce Media. (27 pages) (approximate **3rd grade readability** level)

David thinks the new boy next door is a snob. Then he learns that Chris ignores him because he is deaf and does not hear David's greetings. Chris and his mother help David learn about signing and lipreading. The two boys become good friends, even confronting a bully together. The next year at school the first words that Chris learns to speak are "My treasure is my friend David."

Wahl, J. (1978). *Jamie's tiger.* New York: Harcourt Brace Jovanovich, Inc. (43 pages) (approximate **3rd grade readability** level)

The author states that this book was written for both hearing impaired and normal hearing youngsters to promote a better understanding between the two. A bout with German measles leaves Jamie hearing impaired and very lonely until, gradually, his friends become intrigued with signing and Jamie's ability to play the drums (he feels the rhythm).

Walker, L. A. (1985). *Amy: The story of a deaf child.* New York: Lodestar Books, E. P. Dutton. (59 pages) (approximate **3rd grade readability** level)

Eleven year old Amy and her parents are deaf. Her older brother is hearing. Pictures are used to show the normal activities, as well as those that are associated with a hearing impairment (e.g., how to use a teletypewriter-telephone, or TTY) that Amy engages in. At school Amy is in a regular classroom but also goes to see a speech-language pathologist and a teacher for the deaf for special help. There are two pages of resources at the end of the book.

Ward, B. R. (1981). *The ear and hearing.* New York: Franklin Watts. (40 pages) (approximate **9th grade readability** level)

With the help of colored diagrams the anatomy of the outer, middle, and inner ears is explained. Then the path of sound is followed from the time that it enters the outer ear until it is interpreted in the brain. How sound travels in waves, the range of sensitivity of the human ear, the ability to ignore unwanted sounds, the use of context to increase understanding, types of hearing loss, and how we maintain our balance are topics that are also included. A glossary is included.

Wolf, B. (1977). *Anna's silent world.* Philadelphia: J. B. Lippincott Company. (48 pages) (approximate **4th grade readability** level)

Illustrated with numerous pictures, this volume explains in a very graphic way all of the steps taken to help Anna, a six year old who was born deaf, to lead a full life. Auditory training, lipreading, speech therapy, and adjustment to a hearing aid are just a few of the aspects of habilitation shown by the pictures. Students would learn a great deal about the problems and steps taken to help a child who is deaf.

Yolen, J. (1978). *The mermaid's three wisdoms.* Cleveland, OH: Collins World. (110 pages) (approximate **5th grade readability** level)

The mermaid Melusina is banned from the sea and given legs because she has allowed herself to be seen. Unable to talk because she has no tongue, Melusina is found by Jess, a hearing impaired girl, and Captain A. Jess is able to communicate with Melusina by teaching her sign language. Through this experience Jess learns to better accept her hearing impairment and for the first time agrees to pull her hair back behnd her ears (allowing her hearing aids to be seen) and proudly wear the earrings that Captain A promises to make from Melusina's crystal tears.

Zelonsky, J. (1980). *I can't always hear you.* Milwaukee: Raintree Children's Books. (31 pages) (approximate **2nd grade readability** level)

This well-illustrated book is narrated by a little girl who wears a hearing aid. She relates the ways in which the hearing aid is helpful to her. Her misunderstanding of words at times is a source of amusement to classmates. An understanding teacher helps her by arranging a visit to the school principal who also wears a hearing aid. As the little girl becomes better adjusted to others and the others to her, they all realize that there is something different about each of them—an allergy to chocolate, braces, no television at home, etc. This is a book that should be helpful to all children in a classroom in which there is a child with a hearing loss.

Zim, H. S. (1956). *Our senses and how they work.* New York: William Morrow & Co. (64 pages) (approximate **6th grade readability** level)

A portion of this book explains the anatomy and physiology of the ear. The frequencies and loudness levels of various sounds are also discussed. Diagrams are used to supplement the text.

APPENDIX B

Answers To Self-Test Questions

CHAPTER 1

1. Individuals with Disabilities Education Act (IDEA)
2. the enactment of PL 94-142
3. identify students who need further testing
4. individualized education program (or plan)
5. least restrictive environment
6. mainstreaming
7. phonology, semantics, morphology, syntax, and pragmatics
8. stimulability
9. self-contained program, resource room program, itinerant program, consultation program, and classroom-based program.
10. consultation

1.	True	6.	False
2.	True	7.	False
3.	False	8.	False
4.	True	9.	True
5.	False	10.	False (a waiting list is illegal)

CHAPTER 2

1.	False	9.	False
2.	True	10.	False
3.	True	11.	True
4.	True	12.	True
5.	False	13.	True
6.	True	14.	False
7.	True	15.	True
8.	True		

CHAPTER 3

1. False	11. False
2. True	12. True
3. True	13. False
4. False	14. False
5. False	15. False
6. True	16. True
7. False	17. True
8. False	18. True
9. True	19. True
10. True	20. True

CHAPTER 4

1. False	14. False
2. True	15. True
3. True	16. False
4. True	17. True
5. False	18. False
6. True	19. True
7. True	20. True
8. True	21. False
9. True	22. True
10. True	23. True
11. True	24. True
12. False	25. True
13. True	26. True

CHAPTER 5

1. True	14. True
2. True	15. False
3. True	16. True
4. False	17. False
5. True	18. True
6. True	19. False
7. True	20. False
8. False	21. True
9. False	22. False
10. True	23. True
11. False	24. True
12. True	25. False
13. False	

CHAPTER 6

1. B
2. C
3. B
4. C
5. A
6. D
7. D
8. A

9. A
10. B
11. C
12. D
13. D
14. C
15. C

CHAPTER 7

1. True
2. True
3. False
4. True
5. False
6. False
7. True
8. False
9. False

10. False
11. True
12. False
13. False
14. False
15. True
16. True
17. True
18. True

CHAPTER 8

1. False
2. True
3. False
4. True
5. True
6. False
7. False
8. False
9. True
10. True
11. True
12. False
13. False

14. True
15. True
16. False
17. True
18. True
19. True
20. True
21. True
22. False
23. False
24. True
25. True

INDEX

A

Academic performance
and language disabilities, 71
and speech sound problems, 46–47
Acoupedics, 134
Age, and stuttering, 88–90
AIDS-HIV positive, implications for
speech-language clinicians, 165
Alport syndrome, 163
hearing loss in, 163
American Sign Language (ASL), 136–137, 171
American Speech-Language-Hearing
Association, 2, 21
Articulation, 31–35
developmental sequence for, 32, 34
requirements for, 31
Articulation errors
assessment of, 38–40
compared to phonological errors, 39
developmental articulation errors,
32
Articulation test, 11
Articulation therapy, 40–43
goal of, 40–41
progression of tasks in, 41–43
Assessment, 38–40
for articulation and phonology, 38–40
differential assessment, 39
for language disabilities, 61–64
process of, 8–9, 38
stuttering, 85–86
of voice disorders, 98–99, 105
Assistive listening devices, 138, 142,
143
types of, 142
Audiogram, 121, 122
Audiometer, 121
Auditory discrimination test, 11
Auditory-global method, 134
Auditory-visual-oral method, 134

Augmentive communication, 171–172
body language, 171
nonverbal communication strategies,
171
Autism, 168
case history, 169

B

Bilingualism, 170
characteristics of speech, 170
Black English, 170
characteristics of, 47
Body language, 171

C

Case history, 11
Cerebral palsy, 153–156
case histories, 154–156
effects on speech, 153–154
speech-language therapy, 154
types of, 153
Certificate of clinical competence, 3
Classroom based programs, 13–14
Classroom teacher
acceptance of child with communication problems, 183–184
aid with work missed during therapy, 188–189
collaboration with speech-language
pathologist, 185
consultation with speech-language
pathologist, 19–20
and hearing impaired children, 144–146
interpersonal classroom atmosphere,
management of, 184–185
motivation of child, 186
referral, role in, 186
as speech model, 183
and stuttering child, 82–83, 89–90
support of child's therapy, 45–46,
186, 188

211

Cleft palate, 104, 107–109
  cause of, 107
  correction of, 108
  speech of, 108
Cochlear implant, 139, 143
Cognates, 29, 41
Communication, use of term, 6, 21
Communication boards, 171
Communication competence, 61
Communication disorders
  fluency disorders, 7–8
  speech sound disorders, 7
  voice disorders, 8
Community resources, use by speech-
    language pathologist, 20–21
Computer-assisted treatment, 14
Consonants, 27, 29
  cognates, 29
  consonant acquisition chart, 33, 34
  voiced and voiceless, 27
Consultation
  community resources, 20–21
  interactions with classroom teacher,
    19–20
  interactions with parents, 18
  interaction with school personnel,
    20
Consultation programs, 13
Cued speech, 135

D

Deafness
  definition of, 125
  and language learning, 135–137
Development
  delayed. *See* Developmental delay
  outgrowing speech sound errors,
    39–40
  of phonology, 35
  of speech sound acquisition, 32, 34
Developmental articulation errors, 32
Developmental delay, 156–161
  and birth of sibling, 160–161
  and lack of stimulation, 159–160
  and overprotection, 160
  and poverty, 161

retarded mental development, 156–
    158
Diagnosis
  procedures in, 11
  See also Assessment
Dialects, 169–170
  Black English, 47, 170
  influences in, 170
Diphthongs, 26
Down syndrome, 162
  treatment of speech-language prob-
    lems, 162
Drug abuse, effects on children, 164–
    165

E

Emotional disturbance, 166–169
  autism, 168, 169
  causes of, 167
  characteristics of, 166–167
  speech-language problems in, 167
  speech-language remediation, 168–
    169
Expressive language test, 11

F

Fetal alcohol syndrome, 163
  speech-language problems of, 163
Fingerspelling, 171
Fluency
  characteristics of, 83
  evaluation of, 11
Fluency disorders, characteristics of,
    7–8
Fragile X syndrome, 162–163
  speech-language problems in, 162–
    163
Frontal lisp, 34
Fronting, 36

G

Genetic syndromes
  Alport syndrome, 163
  Down syndrome, 162
  fragile X syndrome, 162–163

H

Hard glottal attack, 101, 106
Hard of hearing
  definition of, 125–126
  and language learning, 133–135
Head injuries, 165–166
  deficits related to, 166
  incidence of, 165–166
Hearing
  measurement of, 121–122
  mechanisms of, 119–120
  and sound, 118–119
Hearing aids, 137–138
  behind-the-ear aid, 138–139
  body hearing aid, 138
  cochlear implant, 139, 143
  improvements in, 138
  in-the-ear aid, 139
Hearing impaired, definition of, 125
Hearing loss
  in Alport syndrome, 163
  case histories, 126–127
  causes of, 123–125
  classification of, 122, 125–126
    deafness, 125
    hard of hearing, 125–126
    hearing impaired, 125
  detection of, 131–132
  functional and central, 124
  prevalence of, 126
  speech and language problems of, 133
Hearing loss and speech/language
    learning, 133–146
  assistive listening devices, 138, 142, 143
  case histories, 146–148
  classroom teacher, role of, 144–146
  for deaf children, 135–137
  for hard of hearing child, 133–135
  hearing aids, 137–141
  special school programs, 144
Hearing test, 11
Hypernasality, 104–105
Hyponasality, 104

I

Individualized educational program
    (IEP), 4, 21
  goals in, 72
Individualized family service plan
    (IFSP), 5–6, 21
Inflectional forms, 60
Intelligibility, and speech sound prob-
    lems, 30–31
International Phonetic Alphabet, 26
Itinerant programs, 13

L

Language
  definition of, 57–58
  morphology, 59–60
  pragmatics, 60–61
  semantics, 58–59
  syntax, 59
  use of term, 6
Language disabilities
  and academic performance, 71
  assessment for, 61–64
  case history, 75
  causes of, 57
  future view for, 74–75
  incidence of, 56–57
  morphology problems, 69
  pragmatics problems, 69–71
  and psychological adjustment, 72
  semantic problems, 65–68
  syntax problems, 68–69
  terms related to, 54
  therapy for, 72–74
Lateral lisp, 34
Lead poisoning, and development, 165
Learning disabilities, 54–55
  clusters/syndromes of, 56
  definition of, 55
Least restrictive environment, 4
Legislation, related to speech-language
    students, 3–6
Lipreading, 134, 137

Lisp
  frontal lisp, 34
  lateral lisp, 34
Loudness, disorders of, 99

M

Mainstreaming, 5
Maintenance, 41
Metalinguistic ability, 61
Minimal contrasts, 44
Morphology, 59–60
  morphology problems, 69
Motor problems, and motor speech
    disruption, 158–159
Multicultural children
  bilingualism, 170
  dialects compared to Standard Eng-
    lish, 47–48
  stuttering, 86–87
Mutational falsetto, and phonation
    disorders, 103

N

Nasal grimace, 104
Nasality, hypernasality/hyponasality,
    104–105
Nodules, vocal, and phonation dis-
    orders, 102

O

Oral peripheral examination, 11
Organic problems, 34
  AIDS-HIV positive, 165
  Alport syndrome, 163
  cerebral palsy, 153–156
  developmental delay, 156–161
  Down syndrome, 162
  fetal alcohol syndrome, 163
  fragile X syndrome, 162–163
  head injuries, 165–166
  lead poisoning, 165
Otitis media, 123

P

Papillomata, and phonation disorders,
    102–103

Parents, consultation with speech-
    language pathologist, 19–20
Phonation, nature of, 100
Phonation disorders, 100–103
  causes of, 101
    mutational falsetto, 103
    papillomata, 102–103
    polyps, 102
    puberphonia, 103
    vocal abuse and misuse, 101–102
    vocal nodules, 102
Phonemes, 25–26
Phonology, 35–38
  development of, 35
  problems related to, 36
Phonology disorders
  assessment for, 38–40
  compared to articulatory disorders,
    39
  functional problems, 36–37
Phonology therapy, 43–44
  goal of, 43
  progression of tasks in, 43–44
Pidgin, 137
Pitch, disorders of, 99
PL 94–142, 3–5, 17, 21, 54
PL 99–457, 3–5
Polyps, and phonation disorders, 102
Poverty, and delayed development,
    161
Pragmatics, 60–61
  pragmatics problems, 69–71
Prosody, 48
Psychological factors
  and language disabilities, 72
  and learning disabilities, 55
  See also Emotional disturbance
Puberphonia, and phonation dis-
    orders, 103

R

Receptive language test, 11
Referral
  and classroom teacher, 186
  form for, 187
Resonance
  definition of, 103
  disorders of, 100

Resonance disorders, 103–105
  hypernasality, 104–105
  hyponasality, 104
Resource room programs, 12
Retarded mental development, 156–158
  causes of, 157
  confusion with hearing loss, 157
Rochester method, 135

S

Screening, process of, 9–11
Seeing Essential English, 137
Self-contained programs, 12
Semantics, 58–59
  semantic problems, 65–68
Sensorineural hearing loss, 123
Siblings, effects of birth of new sibling, 160–161
Signing Exact English, 137
Sign language
  American Sign Language (ASL), 136–137, 171
  sign codes, 136
Singer's nodules, 102
Sound, nature of, 116–117
Spanish speakers, characteristics of, 48
Speech, use of term, 6–7
Speech-language pathologist
  collaboration with classroom teacher, 185
  qualifications for, 3
  role of, 2–3
    assessment, 8–9
    consultation, 18–21
    diagnosis, 11–12
    screening, 9–11
    service of many schools, 16–18
    therapy, 12–16
Speech-language pathology aids, 3
Speech sound problems
  and academic subjects, 46–47
  additions, 29
  case histories, 48–49
  characteristics of, 7
  distortions, 29

  factors related to, 37–38
  incidence of, 29
  and intelligibility, 30–31
  most frequently misarticulated sounds, 34–35
  omissions, 29
  outgrowing problem, 39–40
  substitutions, 29
Speech sounds
  consonants, 27, 29
  diphthongs, 26
  phonemes, 25–26
  vowels, 26
Stimulability test, 11
Stimulation, lack of, 159–160
Stuttering
  and age, 88–90
  assessment of, 85–86
  case histories, 90–92
  causes of, 84–86
  definitions of, 84
  multicultural factors, 86–87
  treatment of, 87–90
Submucous cleft, 104
Syntax, 59
  syntax problems, 69

T

Teacher. *See* Classroom teacher
Therapy
  articulation therapy, 40–43
  classroom based programs, 13–14
  computer-assisted treatment, 14
  consultation programs, 13
  dismissal from, 15, 45
  itinerant programs, 13
  for language disabilities, 72–74
  philosophy of therapy, 15–16
  phonology therapy, 43–44
  resource room programs, 12
  selection of children for, 14
  self-contained programs, 12
  teacher support in, 45–46
  time span for session, 14
Total communication method, 137
Tracking, 40

V

Viral infection, and hearing loss, 123–124
Vocal folds, 100
  vocal fold action, disorders of, 99–100
Vocal hygiene, 103–104
Voice disorders
  assessment of, 98–99, 105
  characteristics of, 8
  incidence of, 97
  phonation disorders, 100–103
  referral, criteria for, 107
  resonance disorders, 103–105
  treatment of, 105–106
  types of
    loudness, 99
    pitch, 99
    quality related to resonance, 100
    quality related to vocal fold action, 99–100
Voiced sounds, 27
Voice evaluation, 11
Voiceless sounds, 27
Vowels, 26